MANCHESTER
1824
Manchester University Press

Neither left nor right?

The Liberal Democrats and the electorate

ANDREW RUSSELL AND EDWARD FIELDHOUSE

Manchester University Press

Manchester and New York ▪ distributed exclusively in the USA by Palgrave

Published by Manchester University Press
Oxford Road, Manchester M13 9NR, UK
and Room 400, 175 Fifth Avenue, New York, NY 10010, USA
www.manchesteruniversitypress.co.uk

Distributed exclusively in the USA by
Palgrave, 175 Fifth Avenue, New York, NY 10010, USA

Distributed exclusively in Canada by
UBC Press, University of British Columbia, 2029 West Mall, Vancouver, BC, Canada V6T 1Z2

British Library Cataloguing-in-Publication Data
A catalogue record for this book is available from the British Library

Library of Congress Cataloging-in-Publication Data applied for

ISBN 0 7190 6600 X *hardback*
EAN 978 0 7190 6600 9
ISBN 0 7190 6601 8 *paperback*
EAN 978 0 7190 6601 6

First published 2005

14 13 12 11 10 09 08 07 06 05 10 9 8 7 6 5 4 3 2 1

Typeset in ITC Charter with Eras display
by Servis Filmsetting Ltd, Manchester
Printed in Great Britain
by Bell & Bain Limited, Glasgow

Contents

Tables

Figures

Acknowledgements

We are grateful to the ESRC for supporting the research reported in this book (grant no R000238204). This project employed Iain MacAllister for the duration of the research. Iain was the research associate on the project and kept the project moving on a day-to-day basis. Iain, who now works for the Scottish Executive, was co-author on articles which have previously appeared in journals and which were important in the evolution of this book. In particular Chapter 7 is based on research that appeared in *Political Geography* (volume 21) and Chapter 5 is a development of a paper that appeared in the *British Journal of Politics and International Relations* (volume 4, no. 1) both of which were co-authored by Iain. We are grateful to the editors of both these journals and of *party politics* for giving permission to reproduce parts of these articles in Chapters 5, 7 and 6 respectively, which are developed from these articles.

We are especially grateful to all our (anonymous) interviewees from the Liberal Democrats who gave up valuable time to be involved in this project, and everyone else in the party around the country and at Cowley Street who assisted us in our research. In particular we would like to thank Chris Rennard for facilitating meetings, introductions to constituency parties, and not least for contributing his own ideas to the project from the outset. Needless to say we have attempted to interpret and report the words of our interviewees with great care, but any errors contained in the book are our own. We would also like to thank the anonymous referee for comments on the draft of this text.

The data used to produce the maps in Chapter 7 are provided with the support of the ESRC and JISC and use boundary material which is copyright of the Crown, the Post Office and the ED-LINE consortium. Data from the British Election Surveys were supplied by the UK Data Archive at the University of Essex.

Finally we would like to thank our families who have supported us throughout the writing of this book. Andrew is indebted to Jackie, Huw, Rhydian and Beth (who wasn't even born when the project began) for their love and patience, allowing him the time and space to keep working. Ed would like to thank Liz who has made his contribution possible by caring for Joe and Louis both of who were born during the course of this research. Joe (now three) was born in November 2000 with a serious heart condition and spent much time in Alder Hey Children's Hospital when this book was being written. Ed and his family are especially grateful to all the staff on ward K2 who helped Joe recover to good health.

Introduction

The Liberal Democrats are the third biggest party in British politics and yet remain under-researched. This account attempts to analyse the party's formal and informal structure and its electoral strategy and support, at a key point in its development. We set about this task in three ways. First, we analyse the party's electoral performance and the nature of its support using election and survey data. Second, we use interviews with MPs, party officials and party activists, carried out in the period 1999–2002, to understand the strategy of the party. Third, we investigate eight case studies in an attempt to see how the party's tactics altered according to context.

In this book, we regard the Liberal Democrats as a multi-layered, multi-faceted party, a modern party with a traditional heritage, a party striving for its own identity and yet continually portrayed in relation to the Labour and Conservative parties. The book is split into three sections: first, the history and organisation of the party; second, the nature of Liberal Democrat support; and, third, Liberal Democrat electoral strategy.

The decade from 1992 was notable for a comprehensive power-shift in British politics. The 1992 General Election saw the return of the Conservative Party for a fourth successive term of office. The Labour Party under Neil Kinnock had failed to overcome the Conservatives, despite an apparently promising position in the opinion polls. The third party, the Liberal Democrats, had consolidated their position as the natural successors to the Alliance of the 1980s but failed to alter the real dynamics of British politics. In particular, the party had to reflect on their inability to capitalise on the widespread public goodwill towards them and transform that goodwill into votes and seats in parliament. According to some commentators, the essential problem for the party was that it was vulnerable to attack from both sides. The Conservative and Labour parties were able to portray a Liberal Democrat vote as a potential opening for the other side. Moreover, the Liberal Democrats encouraged this vulnerability with their official policy stance of equidistance between the other parties.

As the 1992 parliament wore on, British politics changed dramatically. The September 1992 ERM debacle stripped the Conservatives of their mantle of economic competence, and undermined the basis of their eight election victories since World War II (see Wickham-Jones, 1997). John Major found this disadvantage impossible to overcome in 1997, despite a relatively promising set of objective economic conditions. Mired by allegations of sleaze and mismanagement, the Major government suffered 'death by a thousand cuts', finally falling from office in May 1997 (see Cowley, 1997; Denver, 1997). Moreover, subsequent Conservative leaders – William Hague, Iain Duncan Smith and Michael Howard – have similarly struggled to cast off the stigma of the 1992 ERM crisis. On the other hand, the Labour Party, led from 1994 by Tony Blair, had emerged as the dominant electoral force in contemporary British politics. New Labour was able to sweep into power in the 1997 General Election – assisted by the significant haemorrhage of Conservative support and was permitted (by a more sceptical electorate) a second electoral landslide in the 2001 General Election.

The Liberal Democrats had by 1994 come to accept that they could no longer sustain the notion that they were prepared to work with the Conservative administration in any post-election coalition. Equidistance was abandoned, and – at a stroke – Labour's hostility to their own supporters voting tactically for Liberal Democrat candidates was undermined.

As Table 0.1 reveals, the Liberal Democrats secured 46 seats in the 1997 General Election. This was the best performance by a third party in British politics since 1929 (Fisher, 1997), although their share of the vote actually fell slightly. Their sustained hostility to the Conservatives under William Hague continued to bear fruit and a close relationship between the leadership of the Liberal Democrats and the New Labour government continued to offer hope that some sort of anti-Conservative alliance could be forged on a more permanent basis.

As the new institutions of government were founded in Scotland and Wales, Liberal Democrats were delighted to find themselves involved in the governing administrations – forming a coalition with Labour in the Scottish Executive after the 1999 Scottish parliamentary election, to be followed by a partnership agreement between Labour and the Liberal Democrats in the Welsh Assembly government.

In the run-up to the 2001 General Election, the Liberal Democrats faced two challenges, firstly, to increase their share of the vote and, secondly, to increase their number of seats in parliament. In the event they managed to do both – although it is possible that these advances were not so great as they may have realistically hoped for.

In 1999, Paddy Ashdown, the man who had led the Liberal Democrats since their inception, announced his desire to step down. Despite being in charge of the party for 11 years, the shock with which this news was greeted

Table 0.1 **The British General Elections of 1992, 1997 and 2001**

	1992		1997		2001	
	Vote (%)	Seats	Vote (%)	Seats	Vote (%)	Seats
Conservative	41.9	336	30.7	165	31.7	166
Labour[a]	34.4	271	43.2	419	40.7	413
Lib-Dem	17.8	20	16.8	46	18.3	52
SNP	1.9	3	2.0	6	1.8	5
Plaid Cymru	0.5	4	0.5	4	0.7	4
Others	3.5	17	6.8	19	3.9	19
Majority		C 21		L 179		L 167
Turnout		77.7%		71.4%		59.4%

Source: Rallings and Thrasher, 1993, 1998; Electoral Commission, 2001.
Note: [a] The speakers from both parliaments are included in the Labour totals since both seats were contested. In 1997, Betty Boothroyd was opposed, in West Bromwich West, by two Independents. In 2001, the Scottish Nationalist and Scottish Socialist parties contested Michael Martin's seat of Glasgow Springburn.

demonstrated the grip that Ashdown had come to have on the party. Indeed for many, Ashdown had come to personify the party. Although Charles Kennedy was quickly installed as the bookmakers' favourite to replace Ashdown as leader, the leadership race was genuinely open. In the end, Kennedy saw off the challenge of five other candidates and was officially installed as the second leader of the Liberal Democrats in August 1999.

Kennedy inherited a party with 17 seats in the new Scottish parliament, 6 seats in the National Assembly for Wales and the party won 10 seats in the European Parliament elections in June 1999. The Liberal Democrats were about to embark upon a period of coalition in Scotland and Wales with Labour, and the party continued to play a pivotal role in the local governance of Britain, running many councils and holding the balance of power in many more. Membership figures (circa 83,000) suggest that the party was steady if not booming.

Despite this, remarkably little attention has been paid to the third party in contemporary British politics[1]. Many aspects of the Liberal Democrat political and electoral strategy and the nature of their support are greatly under-researched. This account aims to improve the knowledge and understanding of the Liberal Democrats, their changing role in British party politics, their strategic decision-making process and the nature and distinctiveness of their support.

This book has the following objectives:

1 to provide a comprehensive and considered account of the nature of Liberal Democrat politics in contemporary Britain;

2 to explore the specific challenges facing the Liberal Democrats in their struggle for identity, distinctiveness and votes;
3 to examine the different layers of the party, in terms of organisational structure, strategy and representation.

In achieving these objectives this book explores five key themes:

The alternative opposition hypothesis

Strategically, the Liberal Democrats have chosen to align themselves as an anti-Conservative party in recent years. In Westminster, the party finds itself competing with the Conservatives for the majority of its existing and target seats, while coalitions in Scotland and Wales, and constitutional agreements with Labour have made the party less hostile politically to New Labour. As a consequence, and regional variation in local government notwithstanding, it might be feasible that the long-term strategy of the party would represent an attempt to replace the Conservatives as the main opposition to Labour. However, this presents a paradox. During the period of the study, the Liberal Democrats presented themselves as an anti-Conservative party and were therefore best placed to do well where Labour is weakest. This is grounded in historical patterns of support, with Liberal Democrats doing better where the Labour Party never really replaced the Liberals as the main opposition to Conservatism (see Chapter 7). The obvious exception is the expanding urban heartlands where Liberal Democrats have built on the unpopularity of Labour in local government (e.g. Sheffield and Liverpool). However, Liberal Democrat voters are more similar to Labour voters in their political outlook, but are more similar to Tory voters in their social and geographical background (Chapter 5). The paradox is, therefore, that the party must fight Labour in Labour-held seats, but still win Labour sympathisers in Conservative–Liberal areas. We see how the party attempts to resolve this by adopting different strategies in different areas (Chapters 8 and 10).

The alternative opposition hypothesis was given credence by the Liberal Democrats in the aftermath of the 2001 election. In the triumphant atmosphere of becoming the first Liberal Democrat leader to see both the share of the vote and the number of seats in Westminster rise, Charles Kennedy claimed in the *Observer* that: ‘Elections are usually about forming the Government. But this election, uniquely, has been just as much about forming the Opposition.’

Effective opposition was a theme that the Liberal Democrats returned to perennially. After the declaration of the war on terrorism following September 11, 2001, and Conservative party support for the Labour’s policy on Afghanistan, Kennedy released a dossier of Liberal Democrat achievements. In contrast he claimed: 'There is a need for a considered voice in opposition. What we don't need and what the country doesn't want is little more than Little Sir Echo. The Liberal Democrats are now that considered voice, the effective voice of opposition' (*Guardian*, 29 November 2001).

In the aftermath of their second disastrous General Election, even some senior Conservatives were willing to voice their concern that the Liberal Democrats could become the alternative Opposition. In the aftermath of the 2001 defeat, Ian Taylor MP, from the dwindling Europhile wing of the party, claimed: 'If we don't get this rethink of strategy right then it's possible that we'll drift further away from the mainstream of British politics and the Liberal Democrats would love to take our place.'

A word of caution should be struck here. In the 1980s it seemed possible that the Liberal Democrats' predecessor, the Liberal–SDP Alliance, could have forged for itself a future as the new opposition to the Conservatives at the expense of the Labour Party. In the 1983 General Election, the Alliance came within two percentage points of Labour in terms of the popular vote (25 per cent compared to Labour's 27 per cent) but failed to convert this promise into reality. In the 1980s, the Alliance had underestimated the resilience of the Labour Party, and their own cohesiveness. Ultimately, the Alliance was unable to overcome the structural obstacles of a comparatively weak national organisation and entrenched voting patterns of their opponents. By 1987 the Alliance was in retreat from its 1983 heyday. The point to be reinforced here is that those who see the rise of the Liberal Democrats at the expense of the Conservative Party need to acknowledge the same structural obstacles in a different context. Conservative support at General Elections has indeed haemorrhaged to less than one-third of those voting, but Liberal Democrat support has still some way to go before they could claim to have replaced the Conservatives in terms of either votes or seats.

In particular, the legacy of the Ashdown–Blair project – of greater co-operation between the two parties – which died a natural death due to Labour's inability (or unwillingness) to deliver anything of meaningful substance to the Liberal Democrats, may have been to push the notion of alternative opposition further down the agenda. After all, it relies on the relative popularity of the Labour government and the continued unpopularity of the Conservative opposition. Ashdown himself seemed to realise this, when he wrote in the *Independent*:

> We will not always be able to rely on the extremely unusual combination of a growingly unpopular Labour government and a remainingly unpopular Tory opposition. Sooner or later, the Tory party will return from their journey to nowhere . . . Then they will reoccupy the only place from which they can win

> elections again – the centre-right. And then, all those decent moderate Tories who voted Lib Dem as a refuge from the awfulness of their own party will go home again.

The credibility gap hypothesis

The single biggest obstacle to Liberal Democrat progress is electoral credibility. Indeed, perhaps the main problem any third parties faces is to convince voters that they can win, either nationally or locally. As Duverger (1954) argued, majoritarian electoral systems tend to precipitate two-party systems, as voters, fearful of wasting their vote, are forced to make a choice between the two most likely winners (see also Rae, 1971; Lijphart, 1994). However, because each constituency contest in a simple plurality system is independent, minor parties with geographically concentrated support might be able to overcome this disadvantage (Gudgin and Taylor, 1978; Cox, 1997). The problem for the Liberal Democrats (and their predecessors) in recent years has been the relatively even geographical spread of their support. The 1983 election is the prime example; the Liberal–SDP Alliance polled 25.4 percent of the vote – only 2.2 percent less than Labour – but won just 23 seats (compared to Labour's 209). Although the party have also traditionally had popular leaders and popular policies and have been the second choice party of a large section of the electorate (Chapter 5), the wasted vote syndrome has seriously harmed the party's electoral credibility. In the eyes of many voters, the Liberals remained very much a third party in a two-party system. The Liberal Democrats thus endeavour to breach the 'credibility gap' at a number of levels. By building on local traditions of Liberal voting in their heartland areas, and on rigorous local activity and local election success outside these areas.

Credibility is therefore the key to third and minor party success in a majoritarian electoral system. A key tactic employed by third parties in such a system is the targeting of campaign efforts in winnable seats. This is explored in Chapter 9. Another opportunity for building credibility arises through by-elections. We argue that for the Liberal Democrats, by-elections are a vital tool in the battle to establish their credibility. From time to time, resignations or deaths can give the opposition parties the chance to oust the sitting party from a parliamentary seat. Often, by-election results can be spectacular – as short-term protest politics can serve to give the incumbent party a kick in the pants. In 2003, the Brent East by-election victory gave the Liberal Democrats a foothold in Labour's heartland despite starting from third place. Moreover, for the Liberal Democrats (and their predecessors), by-election victories have a habit of becoming the vital breakthrough in terms of credibility and the building block necessary to mount a sustained challenge.

Of course, resources can be cascaded into specific areas at by-election contests that are unavailable to the local party at a General Election. For a resources-poor party like the Liberal Democrats one might expect this to result in the occasional spectacular victory followed by a retreat to defeat at the next General Election. What is remarkable about the Liberal Democrats is that their record of defending by-election victories can sometimes also defy all logic. Simon Hughes won Bermondsey for the Liberals in an acrimonious by-election that seemed to be more about the state of the local Labour party than the Liberals. Examining the demographic profile of the seat, it is hard to see how any party other than Labour could hope to win. And yet, despite a change in Labour personnel, Hughes retained the seat in the 1983 election. Moreover, a further five General Elections, and only slight boundary changes, have left Hughes as the sitting MP for Bermondsey and North Southwark for over twenty years, and an overspill effect has benefited the Liberal Democrats in their annual battles with Labour at the local level. In 2000, the Liberal Democrats were able to win Romsey, the Conservatives' 51st safest seat. The victor, Sandra Gidley, undoubtedly benefited from the descent of the professional Liberal Democrat machinery into their headquarters on an industrial estate in Romsey, in order to facilitate her remarkable by-election win. Moreover, Gidley was in no small measure assisted by the local knowledge that the Liberal Democrats had won a by-election in 1994 in the neighbouring constituency of Eastleigh. Nevertheless, the most remarkable achievement of Gidley and the Romsey Liberal Democrats is that she managed to retain the seat at the 2001 General Election at a time when the Conservatives really ought to have been mounting a challenge to the Labour government rather than losing safe seats to the Liberal Democrats.

In Chapter 7 we show that success in local government elections can play a crucial role in demonstrating electoral credibility, especially outside heartland areas, and in Chapter 10 we demonstrate how the efforts of local activists and candidates can also contribute to the parties credibility locally. Winning locally can instil in the minds of voters, the idea that the Liberal Democrats could also win the parliamentary constituency. Many candidates and parties can benefit from an incumbency effect but for the Liberal Democrats, the rewards of incumbency are multiplied if a decent record of achievement can be added to the knowledge that voting Liberal Democrat is not necessarily a waste of time.

Time and time again, party canvassers told us that the most crucial step in the conversion of new Liberal voters was the one they took in deciding to vote Liberal Democrat for the very first time. Thus Liberal Democrat canvassers put effort into converting tactical switchers at the local, European, national (in Scotland and Wales) and Westminster level, reasoning that a vote – at any order of election – for the Liberal Democrats increases the likelihood of a vote for the Liberal Democrats at the next General Election.

Since the days of the Alliance, third party activists have felt personally slighted by the refusal of the British electorate to think the third party could win. The comedian – and Liberal Democrat supporter – John Cleese made a party election broadcast in which he 'pointed out' that if all those people who reported that they would vote Liberal if the Liberals had a chance of winning, managed to suspend their disbelief for long enough to actually vote Liberal, the party would romp home with a landslide majority – a tactic re-employed by the party in 2001 with their election poster (see Figure 0.1). The secret of converting latent support into actual votes is in convincing the electorate that the party is a credible electoral force – and this remains the stiffest challenge facing the Liberal Democrats in contemporary Britain.

Of course, credibility is frequently an evolving process, and often the best tactic for increasing credibility is to point potential voters to Liberal Democrat success nearby. 'If it can happen in the neighbouring seat, why can't it happen here?' is a question that Liberal Democrats are keen to ask voters. It directly taps into the next theme of the book: that Liberal Democrat success can spread from seat to seat, region to region, in almost the same way that a virus can spread from individuals in one geographic location to another. This is the creeping Liberalism hypothesis.

Figure 0.1 **Liberal Democrat campaign poster, 2001**

The creeping Liberalism hypothesis

Local elections and by-elections can be the route to achieving credibility, by demonstrating a capacity to win. Similarly, success in contiguous seats can help the Liberal Democrats to bridge the credibility gap. This is reinforced by an enhanced ability to campaign in areas where there are strong grass roots locally. Together, these factors contribute to apparent creeping Liberalism as observed in south west England and in areas where an initial breakthrough has been achieved at by-election. A simple glance at a map of Liberal Democrat first and second place finishes in the 2001 General Election reinforces this point (see Figure 7.5).

It is easy to forget, but important to remember, that Paddy Ashdown's victory in Yeovil in 1983 ended 73 years of continuous Conservative rule in that part of Somerset. Ashdown's breakthrough allowed the party to consolidate its support there and to emerge as a potential electoral force in the broader region over the coming years. Yeovil and Somerset are key examples of the creeping Liberalism hypothesis. A single but significant victory can provide the foundation for the construction of an apparent 'heartland' of electoral support, as the new seat becomes the reference point to which other successful challenges in nearby seats are anchored.

Woods (1996) has noted the 'orange wave' of Liberal Democrat success at the local level in Somerset, Dorling *et al.* (1998) mapped the pattern of Liberal Democrat success in a similar 'contagion' model, while Tregidga, (2000) plotted the spread of Liberal success in south west England.

The creeping Liberalism hypothesis is premised on the proximity of a thriving set of local activists. This leads us to a related theme of this book – the dual identity of the Liberal Democrats, as an increasingly centralised party with a powerful leadership, and the party of local communities and 'pavement politics' at the same time.

The dual identity hypothesis

As a party of both local and national focus, the Liberal Democrats face a potential conflict between grassroots and leadership. New institutional arrangements in Scotland and Wales have introduced another potential arena for conflict between the different facets of the party. The ability to bring cohesion and peaceful coexistence (although not necessarily uniformity) to the different foci of the party is a key test for the Liberal Democrats.

Chapters 3 and 4 of this book deal with the dual identities of the Liberal Democrats in contemporary British politics. Structurally the party is proud of its federal organisation, which cedes power from the core executive to the regional level and the grassroots of the party. However, we also highlight that the growth of the parliamentary party since 1997 has transformed the unofficial power dynamic of the party, and has amounted to what one MP called a '*de facto*, right of veto' for the parliamentarians over policy matters that bypasses the formal structure of the party. We argue that the Liberal Democrats are by their very nature a party that believes in the ideological principle of subsidiarity, and that this is reflected not just in their political standpoint, but is also ingrained in the psyche of the individual members and in the organisational structure of the party. However, in an era of increasingly professionalised political parties, a potential tension arises between a relatively influential leadership and the grassroots.

Certainly, the electoral success of the Liberal Democrats in recent years has been accompanied by an increased power of the electoral machinery in the party's London headquarters in Cowley Street. There is no New Labour style concentration of power at the centre of the party. For sure, the resources available to Cowley Street pale into insignificance compared to those in the hands of Labour's HQ at Millbank Tower, and in Smith Square for the Conservatives. Furthermore, the party would not be comfortable ideologically with an over-powerful centre controlling the ranks of the party, but within the party there is a feeling that the power of those in Cowley Street has increased significantly in recent years. Indeed many see the party's campaign and elections director as the single most powerful person in the party. Yet at the same time, local parties seem keen to stress their independence from Cowley Street as an article of faith, and moves to centralise the party – membership drives and election campaigns being obvious examples – are likely to be viewed in a hostile manner by the local parties.

In Chapter 4 we illustrate the tension between the leadership and the grassroots, with reference to three examples. First, Ashdown's desire to give the new party the name 'Democrats' rode roughshod over the desire of the vast majority of the membership to retain the word Liberal in the new party's nomenclature. Second, we suggest that Ashdown's project – of a closer relationship with Labour – created a similar tension and had reached the stage where any further accommodation between Ashdown and New Labour was unlikely to be accepted by the party at large. This impasse may have even played a role in Ashdown's decision to stand down as leader of the party, it certainly provided the backdrop for the leadership election, as all candidates had to express their views on closer collaboration with the Labour government. Third, we highlight the inconsistency in the party's pro-European outlook and the dilution of this stance in some of the party's most resilient electoral heartlands. We use the European policy of the party to show that although often highlighted as one of the unique selling points of the party in contemporary politics, the commitment to further integration is weaker than might be imagined.

The issue based mobilisation hypothesis

This hypothesis states that a third party must pursue popular policies in order to maximise its votes, but also that it must work hard to convert sympathy for its policy positions into votes and seats. Without the traditional links to trade unions and business communities associated with their main competitors, the Liberal Democrats have to fight for every vote, convincing electors to vote for them on the basis of their policies. As the traditional link between Liberalism and nonconformism has diluted with the passage of time, the party has embarked on a course of programmatic renewal that sits ill at ease with orthodox models of party behaviour (see Downs, 1957; Panebianco, 1988; Katz and Mair, 1994, for example). The party has chosen to 'brand itself' using issues, such as education and taxation, which resulted in the party's image becoming increasingly radical and distinctive rather than centrist and non-controversial.

In Chapter 5 we analyse the basis of the Liberal Democrat vote. We suggest although the third party in Britain is prone to a certain dislocation due to the vagaries of the electoral system – and that traditionally the Liberal (in all its guises) vote is what Curtice termed 'fickle and inconsistent' (1996), in recent times the Liberal Democrats have fashioned an identifiable collection of voters.

In Chapter 6 we show how the Liberal Democrat policy in recent years has built up a potential reservoir of support. However, whilst occupying the median position on issues might seem a recipe for success this is true only if the distribution of voters along those policy positions is normally distributed. Should the opinions of the public be skewed there might be no rational reason for appealing to the median voter – since he or she may not represent the most 'popular' position. We show that there are, nevertheless, a number of policy areas where the Liberal Democrats occupy an identifiable set of principled policies and which might provide the platform for electoral success.

The party has traditionally struggled to overcome the problem of being locked out of two-party competitions. The realistic concentration of the media on the politics and policies of the two main parties has meant that the Liberal Democrats (and their predecessors) have struggled to overcome the syndrome that 'no one knows what they stand for'. As a consequence the party has endeavoured to brand its image onto a number of policy arenas in the hope that, firstly, it would improve public awareness of what the party was about, and, secondly, that the adoption of popular policies might be translated into popular support (Chapter 8).

The policies that the party has chosen to attach itself to are interesting since they do not conform to the everyday notion of rational choice policy making. In short, while the Labour party was busy trying to distance itself from an image of tax and spend, the Liberal Democrats were constructing a set of policies that revolved around an increase in income tax in order to fund improvements to education. Received wisdom was that political parties needed to eschew any tax increasing policies in order to be popular, but the Liberal Democrats designed a method of tax increases as one of their unique selling points. This is just one example of how the Liberal Democrats were willing to reject the left–right axis of politics in favour of a more radical campaigning edge.

In Chapter 6 we demonstrate the partial success of these policies. In the 1997 election, the vast majority of British voters were closer to the Liberal Democrat position than that of the other two main parties. In 2001, the *Guardian* newspaper recognised the radical nature of the Liberal Democrat manifesto and labelled them 'the leaders of the left'. This illustrated, if nothing else, a degree of goodwill towards the Liberal Democrats that ought to have been encouraging to the party strategists. In 1997, nearly 70 per cent of Conservatives favoured the Liberal Democrat policy on education. Unfortunately for the Liberal Democrats, they did not favour this policy enough to vote for the party committed to its implementation. This is the continuing challenge for the Liberal Democrats in contemporary politics. To be effective, the Liberal Democrats' issue based mobilisation has to be combined with electoral credibility.

This book is split into three sections since it is our contention that the modern Liberal Democrats cannot be understood by analysis at a single level. We can analyse the relationship between the party and the electorate but we would need to appreciate how the party's decision- and policy-making strategy was determined. We can provide evidence from the political elite to show how the party thinks of itself from the top down, but we would need to appreciate how the party operated in different regions of Britain and under different political circumstances. Hence we investigate how the different levels of the party relate to each other (Part I); who votes for the Liberal Democrats and why (Part II) and how the party projects itself to the voters locally and nationally (Part III).

Methods

The research reported in this book was conducted between 1999 and 2002 and combined quantitative and qualitative methods.

Quantitative analysis

The following data sources were employed:

- British Election Study survey series (1974–2001);
- the British Election Panel Study, 1997–2001;
- General Election results, contemporary and historical;
- local elections data;
- census data and other constituency level data, such as levels of religious non-conformity.

Data were analysed at the individual and constituency levels, including individual and aggregate levels of Liberal Democrat voting.

Qualitative methods

Interviews were conducted in eight case study areas and amongst key players at the national level, mainly in the year preceding the General Election of 2001. Overall, 67 interviews were conducted, including 36 in constituency case studies and 31 amongst carefully selected personnel nationally (Table 0.2). Contact was made through local constituency addresses (for the case studies), through Party HQ or the Houses of Parliament (for the party elite). SAOs and other interviewees were approached at the Liberal Democrat conference in September 2000 or through contacts in the party.

The interviews were semi-structured discussions normally lasting 45–60 minutes. They covered a wide range of areas including personal political experiences, issues and ideology, the relationship with other political parties, electoral strategy and party organisation and control. All interviews were fully transcribed, coded and analysed using the qualitative software *Atlas-ti*.

Case studies

A key methodological tool in our research was the use of eight constituency case studies enabling an analysis of party life in different locations and under

Table 0.2 **Number of interviews conducted**

Target group[a]	*No.*
Case studies (including MPs)	36
Additional MPs	12
Strategists/party officers	7
Other (including SAOs)	5
Scottish and Welsh Parties	7
Total	67

Note: [a] In several cases interviewees held a number of different positions within the party and were therefore interviewed accordingly.

different electoral circumstances. These are reported in Chapter 10, but are drawn on throughout the book. The case studies comprised traditional heartland seats (Devon North and Montgomeryshire); expanding heartland seats (Colchester and Sheffield Hallam); Conservative held marginals (Bridgwater and Cheadle); and Labour held marginals (Aberdeen South and Oldham East & Saddleworth). In each constituency, interviews were conducted with the Liberal Democrat candidate in the 1997 election (and the 2001 parliamentary candidate if different), the 1997 election agent, local party organisers (usually the constituency chair or similar) and a local councillor (usually the leader of the Liberal Democrat group on the relevant council).

Note

1 MacIver's *The Liberal Democrats* anthology (1996) is a notable exception containing some excellent chapters although some have now been overtaken by events. Crewe and King (1995) provided the definitive account of the Social Democratic Party, but there remains a significant gap in the literature concerning the Alliance's successor party. Seyd and Whiteley's forthcoming book on the Liberal Democrat membership could be seen as a useful complementary study to this book, but is really a companion piece to their membership studies of Labour (*Labour's Grass Roots*) and the Conservative party (*True Blues*). More recently Walter (2003) has provided a fascinating insider account of contemporary party strategy.

Part I

The party history and organisation

In this part we provide a detailed account of the history and structure of the party and look at how this impacts on its operation. In Chapters 1 and 2 we chart the development of the party from its zenith in the late nineteenth century through its nadir in the mid-twentieth century and its rejuvenation and reformation at the end of that century. This is more than background context since the development of the party shapes its current nature and its position in our electoral system. In Chapters 3 and 4 we examine the organisational structure of the party and the decision-making processes. We argue that the Liberal Democrats are by their very nature a party which believes in the ideological principle of subsidiarity (the devolvement of power to the lowest possible level, ultimately the individual) and that this is reflected not just in their political standpoint, but is also ingrained in the psyche of the individual members and in the organisational structure of the party. However, at the same time, because the party is essentially a minor party, in a predominantly two party system, the parliamentary party is relatively small. In an era of increasingly professionalised political parties this means that a small number of individuals are especially influential, and a potential tension arises between the leadership and the grassroots. We conclude by suggesting that any differences between the federal party and grassroots around the country are pragmatically and ideologically resolved. The party does not have the resources to control all of the local branches from the centre, and the party's ethos of federalism and community politics mean there is little desire to 'control' the localities. This also means that local parties are able to campaign effectively on local issues.

1

Liberal history: from Whigs to Liberal Democrats

This chapter offers a brief history of Liberal Britain from the birth of a recognisable party under Gladstone through to the organisational and limited electoral revival of the party in the 1970s. Relations with other parties are explored with analysis of the Lib–Lab pact, the Alliance with the SDP and the formal merger of the two parties and the formation of the Liberal Democrats.

The birth and growth of the Liberal Party

In 1859 a loose coalition of Radical, Peelite and Whig parliamentarians came together to overthrow the minority regime of Disraeli and Lord Derby. In effect this was the birth of the Liberal Party in Britain, although as Cook points out the new administration that survived until 1865 was 'less a Liberal ministry than a reconstituted Whig government' (Cook, 1998, 1). Furthermore he argues that the Liberal party 'came of age' with their General Election victory of 1868 and the formation of the first Gladstone government finally putting to rest the cleavage in liberal politics between the Whig family dynasties and the Radicals with strong links to newly industrialised areas and religious non-conformity.

The epitome of politics in Victorian Britain was the parliamentary duel between William Gladstone and his Conservative opponent Benjamin Disraeli. Gladstone's towering achievements are well documented (see Jenkins, 1995; or Matthews, 1997, for example) but from our point of view he can be viewed as the father of the Liberal Party. Gladstone, with his upbringing in Liverpool and undoubted charisma, was able to embrace the Radical agenda but as Searle (1992) notes his educational background (Eton and Oxford) allowed him to also appeal to more traditional elements of British society.

Nevertheless, the radicalism of the Gladstone governments was often tempered by the reality of party management and factionalism. A comfortable 100 seat majority in 1868 was insufficient to make real reform possible; the 1880–85 government became gridlocked over land reform in Ireland and tensions between the Radical and Whig tendencies; and in 1886 Home Rule for Ireland split the party irrecoverably, when nearly one-third of Gladstone's own party voted against the Home Rule bill. Dissident Liberal MPs recast themselves as 'Liberal Unionists' and entered a series of electoral pacts with the Conservatives.

Gladstone's final administration of 1892–95 (he was succeeded by Roseberry in 1894) again failed to pass Home Rule – the bill being blocked by the House of Lords – and the 1895 General Election saw the Liberals eclipsed by the Conservatives.

At the turn of the twentieth century, the Liberals benefited from Conservative division over economic protectionism. With the government in obvious difficulties, Prime Minister Balfour resigned in late 1905 and the Liberals – under Henry Campbell-Bannerman – accepted the invitation to form a government. The subsequent General Election in January 1906 was to prove to be the zenith of the Liberal's electoral fortunes, with the party securing 400 seats (including huge gains in London).

On the face of it, the huge majority in the Commons and the talent of the Liberal Cabinet (which included Churchill, Asquith and Lloyd George) presented an outstanding opportunity for radical reform. However, as Cook (1989) states, an analysis of the parliamentary Liberal Party shows that the party remained one of the middle classes, rather than the radical left. With little hope of defeating government bills in the Commons, the Conservative majority in the Lords continually blocked key Liberal measures. The Lords' refusal to pass Lloyd George's 'People's Budget' of 1909 directly led to the election of 1910 but provided the Liberal Party with a sense of purpose not seen since the days of Gladstone. Nevertheless, the Liberals lost over a hundred seats in the January 1910 election, and although Asquith – who had succeed Campbell-Bannerman as Prime Minister in 1908 – was returned to power, a further defeat by the Lords later in the same year led to a second General Election in December, where the Liberals returned as a minority government.

Furthermore, the government had to deal with the international crises that led to the outbreak of World War I, but was also troubled domestically by industrial militancy, continued opposition from the Lords, ongoing problems of Ireland and relations with the increasingly prominent Labour Party. Under these circumstances the Liberal Government took Britain to war in 1914.

Decline and disintegration

The onset of war in 1914 was disastrous for the Liberal Party, although signs of the party's decline were already evident (Dangerfield, 1966). For a party with a strong non-conformist and pacifist element, war presented obvious difficulties. The emergency war economy led the party to compromise many of its liberal values – freedom of trade, individual rights, and freedom of the press. For many, this was too great a sacrifice. In May 1915, with discontent over the handling of the war effort growing, and after the resignation of two Cabinet members, Asquith agreed to an all-party coalition and terminated the last Liberal government.

The introduction of conscription further highlighted divisions in the party, and the final split came in December 1916 as Lloyd George and Asquith became embroiled in a power struggle that eventually led to Asquith's resignation as Prime Minister. Lloyd George became premier, but Asquith remained the leader of the party. Showing their loyalty to Asquith, almost all senior Liberal ministers refused to serve in Lloyd George's first cabinet, which was, consequently, dominated by Conservatives. As the war progressed the divisions between the Lloyd George and Asquithian wings of the party became yet more defined and bitter.

The General Election of 1918 saw the Conservatives, in tandem with the Lloyd George wing of the Liberal Party, achieve a comprehensive victory. Asquith's Liberals were humiliated, winning just 28 seats and 12 per cent of the vote, compared to 133 seats for the Coalition Liberals. Asquith himself was defeated, as were almost all of the most prominent former Liberal ministers. Ominously for the Liberals, the Labour Party polled well over two million votes and secured 57 seats. With hindsight we can regard this as part of the process of Labour's triumph over Liberalism. Industrialisation saw the party squeezed out by the rise of class politics (Lipset and Rokkan, 1967), while the weakening of regional identity further hampered the Liberal attempt to mobilise support.

Although Lloyd George continued to lead the coalition government both factions of the party suffered from the upturn in Labour's support. The Coalition Liberals suffered from electoral and organisational decay, losing by-election after by-election, and had little or no grassroots organisation remaining in many constituencies. Asquith had returned to parliament following the 1920 Paisley by-election but his wing of the party fared little better, losing many of their activists and supporters to Labour. The coalition eventually broke down in 1922, and the subsequent election proved a humiliation for Lloyd George. With opposition from the Conservatives in many seats, he was left with a rump of just 54 MPs. Asquith's Liberals fared little better, winning just 62 constituencies and finishing a distant third. The Conservatives easily became the largest party but, perhaps more importantly, the Labour advance was clearly evident: the party winning 142 seats and securing almost 30 per cent of the popular vote.

Lloyd George and Asquith eventually re-united the Liberal Party for the November 1923 General Election after the Baldwin government's plans to introduce import tariffs allowed a re-engagement of the party around the theme of free trade and the results suggested a Liberal revival had begun. The re-united party polled almost 30 per cent and substantially closed the gap on the Labour Party (winning 159 seats to Labour's 191 and the Conservatives' 258). However, this was just a temporary reprieve, the vast majority of Liberal gains coming a the expense of the Conservatives – reflecting the strength of the free trade protest vote rather than an arrest in Labour's march on Liberal heartlands. Moreover, although the party did well in the old nonconformist areas, such as the West Country, crucially they made little impression on the urban Labour vote – actually losing further ground in many industrial areas.

The real effect of the minority Labour government of 1924 was to show that Labour was now firmly established as the party of the left (see Table 1.1). Although Labour relied on Liberal support to keep them in office, the Liberals were powerless to stop the government from pursuing its own agenda, even though it was clear that their policies would almost certainly lead to electoral defeat for both parties. With the relationship between the two parties fast deteriorating, the government's proposed treaty with Soviet Russia proved to be the final straw for the Liberals who effectively withdrew their support. The country was faced with its second General Election within a year and Labour was now poised to establish itself as the leading party to the left of the Conservatives (Wilson, 1966, 292–3).

The Liberals found themselves insufficiently different from the twin philosophies of socialism and conservatism to make headway and the election of 1924 saw the squeeze that the British electoral system applies to third parties. The Conservatives won an overwhelming victory with 419 seats, Labour fell to 151, but the Liberals were all but obliterated, with only 40. It was a blow from which the Liberals were not to fully recover.

Throughout the 1920s and 1930s the Liberals lost parliamentary seats and share of the vote. The 1931 election saw the party lose almost half of its seats, while in 1935 the Liberals were reduced to 20 MPs and 6.4 per cent of the national share of the vote.

After World War II the Liberals looked like an anachronism of British politics. The party won just 12 seats in the 1945 General Election as Clement Davies emerged as the new party leader. Davies refused calls from the Conservatives to join them (he was offered a cabinet post – Education – by Churchill in 1951) although he was unopposed by the Conservatives at the 1951 and 1955 General Elections. In fact Davies' major achievement may have been to keep the Liberal party together at all as an independent voice in British politics when the forces of decline seemed also irreversible.

Table 1.1 **'Liberal' performance in British General Elections, 1900–87**

Election	*Share (%)*	*MPs*	*State of parties*	*Notes*
1900	44.6	184	Con 402, Lib 184	
1906	49.0	400	Lib 400, Con 157	
1910 Jan.	43.2	275	Lib 275, Con 273	
1910 Dec.	43.9	272	Lib 272, Con 272	
1918	26.6	161	Coalition	133 Coalition Lib, 28 Lib
1922	29.1	116	Con 345, Lab 142	62 Nat Libs, 54 Lib
1923	29.6	159	Con 258, Lab 191	Eclipsed by Labour
1924	17.6	40	Con 419, Lab 151	
1929	23.4	59	Con 260, Lab 288	
1931	12.3	72	Nat Govt 554 (Inc. 13 Lib Nat, 33 Libs)	4 Indep. Libs (outside Nat Govt)
1935	6.4	20	Con 432, Lab 154	
1945	9.0	12	Lab 393, Con 213	
1950	9.1	9	Lab 315, Con 298	
1951	2.5	6	Lab 295, Con 321	
1955	2.7	6	Con 344, Lab 277	
1959	5.9	6	Con 365, Lab 258	
1964	11.2	9	Lab 317, Con 304	
1966	8.5	12	Lab 363, Con 253	
1970	7.5	6	Con 330, Lab 287	
1974 Feb.	19.3	14	Con 297, Lab 301	517 Lib cands
1974 Oct.	18.3	13	Lab 319, Con 277	619 Lib cands
1979	13.8	11	Con 339, Lab 269	
1983	25.4	23	Con 397, Lab 209	17 Lib, 6 SDP
1987	22.5	22	Con 376, Lab 229	17 Lib 5 SDP

Source: Butler and Butler, 2000.

The Liberal revival and community politics

Community politics is a dominant theme in the study of the Liberal Democrats and their predecessors. It is crucial to the Liberal Democrat perspective since it plugs in directly to two of the core themes of this book – credibility and duality. As Meadowcroft (2001) pointed out, community politics has become one of the sacred tenets of Liberal Democrat activity since their inception.

At the 1970 conference, the Liberal party adopted a Young Liberal amendment to party tactics that committed the party to 'primary strategic emphasis on Community Politics'. The amendment stressed that the secret of credibility for the Liberals was 'local roots and local successes', and defined Community politics as:- 'A dual approach to politics, both inside and outside the institutions of the political establishment' (cited in Meadowcroft, 2001, 25). In a seminal piece, one of the leading Young Liberals at the time, Bernard Greaves, neatly defined his (Liberal) vision of community action and more directly focused politics thus:

> A political realignment forged in the grass-roots struggle for human dignity rather than in the reshuffling of MPs on the floor of the House of Commons. (Greaves, 1976, 50)

> Because it is a movement that is (by its nature) diffuse and diverse, it cannot be subject to central direction and it is resistant to the emergence of rigid dogmatism. Its total impact on society is likely to be more comprehensive and more deeply radical than that of any conventional political revolution, an impact that derives not from a rigid political programme nor a disciplined party but from a new style of community politics. (Greaves, 1976, 51)

Such a vision would, naturally, seem attractive to a political party that due to its lack of numbers in the Commons might look at other methods of making a mark on British politics, and which a cruel observer might conclude was far from being ‘a disciplined party’. By throwing in their lot with the advocates of community politics, the Liberals might hope to piggyback on local success without being seen to hijack the entire project from narrow sectional advantage.

In the same anthology of community politics, Gordon Lishman (the author of the 1970 Community Politics Amendment) outlined the benefits to community action groups of throwing in their lot with the Liberals:

> Local Liberal groups have the advantages of a real relationship with power structures, albeit usually hostile, a generally recognized basis of legitimacy with people, a long-term support structure for activists and a more or less clear perspective for their activities. Liberals suffer the disadvantages that go with a concern for votes (occasionally and fatuously argued by community action purists to be the party’s only concern). (Lishman, 1976, 88)

Indeed the Liberals did have the potential to be the small group organisation capable of ‘making a difference’ at the local level if not at the national level. Thus it is important to note a crucial tension between the vision of community politics, as envisaged by its advocates at the time, and the narrower sectional interest of a political party based at Westminster. Moreover, the Liberals would have to be careful not to be seen to hijack the community politics movement for their own partisan aims.

Of course one of the crucial legacies of this reliance on community politics in the 1960s and 1970s is the dual identity of the modern Liberal Democrats. In this way the independence of parties at the local level, the ‘federal’ (in a British sense at least) structure of the party, and the almost pathological lack of deference shown by the membership to the leadership at conference from time to time, can be seen as a logical corollary of the rejuvenation of Liberal politics through community action in the 1960s and 1970s.

Lishman also noted that community politics might focus the activists on more mundane politics, and argued that a broader view should be retained:

> The [elitist] argument runs that we should talk only of drains, houses and roads, because other issues – race, hanging, gypsies, nationalisation, the EEC – may alienate activists . . . The attraction of this argument is that it stresses areas of consensus instead of straying into disagreements. But it is completely contrary to our principles: we should not brush aside basic moral values or ultimate objectives for short-term expediency. (Lishman, 1976, 92)

It is interesting that one issue identified by Lishman in 1976 as potentially troublesome concerned the European question. Chapter 4, and the case study of Devon North in Chapter 10, make clear that the European issue is still problematic for the party – and continues to be a source of dual identity at the local and national level.

Grimond's biographer, Michael McManus, argued that Grimond's version of community politics has been subverted by his successors in the Liberal and Liberal Democrat leadership, arguing that Grimond offered ideological subsidiarity rather than a narrow vision of political advantage. McManus argues that Grimond's 'philosophy' of community politics differed significantly from that utilised nowadays by the modern Liberal Democrats.

> [It] was not merely about cracked pavements, but also about an entirely new, preventative, approach to social and community services, requiring a new attitude towards politics itself. In recent years, the Liberals and their successor party, the Liberal Democrats, have made considerable strides thanks to what has become known as 'grassroots' or 'community' campaigning . . . The approach may have delivered votes and seats but it is nonetheless easily and widely criticised . . . (It) debauches and cheapens politics. With its reliance upon negative and oppositional campaigning, 'grumble sheets' and the exploitation of local grievances, it tends to weaken any conception of the 'general good' and reduces politics to a series of unilateral appeals to separate interest groups. (McManus, 2001, 397)

Notwithstanding the purity of the Liberals' interest in community politics, the importance of local government and of community issues in the revival of the Liberal Party is hard to underestimate.

The traits of individualism, decentralisation and localism remained central to the party in the 1960s. It is perhaps for this reason that more emphasis was placed on local elections; it was rightly assumed that local government was more open than parliamentary constituencies to third party candidates. Leading Liberal politicians sought to appeal to the rhetoric of community politics via local elections; in 1959 Jeremy Thorpe urged Liberals to focus on the kind of small-scale local problems that affected 'ordinary' people; in 1960 Grimond told a Liberal rally in Southport: 'The Liberal Party should be the party to which people look to for reforms which affect their daily lives . . . Let us get things done and let us start in local government.' To the third party in British politics, local elections had a dual appeal. Firstly, they could fit neatly with the growing vision of a new kind of structure to the way that politics ought to be done. Secondly, the national identity of the party might be helped if local election success could act as the building blocks towards increased Westminster representation (we explore this theme in some detail in Chapter 7).

Grimond's rallying call seemed to have an almost immediate effect: the Liberals performed well in the municipal elections of 1962, capturing numerous seats from the Conservatives in the south of England. Within a decade or so, the party were beginning to challenge some of Labour's northern heartlands. In Liverpool, the party increased their representation from one in 1968 to become the largest single group on the council by 1973. By the mid-1970s the Liberals had established themselves as a force in local politics, in power in Eastbourne and the largest party in five other local authorities and the second largest party in another 20 or so councils. As we show in Chapter 7, the importance of local elections to the Liberals has not diminished; much of the party's success in the 1997 General Election can be traced to strong local performances in the preceding decade.

The Liberal revival and by-elections

To a minor party, by-elections represent an unparalleled opportunity to grab the nation's attention. The power of protest and novelty voting can be utilised to persuade the disaffected and the hopelessly optimistic to come on board in apparently inauspicious circumstances. It is unlikely that the Liberal revival of the 1960s and 1970s would have had quite the momentum it did without the seemingly fortuitous happenstance of by-election victories. All of the by-election victories for the Liberals, Alliance and Liberal Democrats, shown in Table 1.2, were important in raising party morale and offered the party the chance of bridging the credibility gap. Of course some of the party's most spectacular successes have been short lived; Elizabeth Shields' dramatic victory in Ryedale in 1986 was followed by a Conservative return in the 1987 General Election, and Mike Carr's poll tax inspired victory over the Conservatives in Ribble Valley in 1991 was wiped out the following year. On the other hand, Graham Tope's short-lived success in Sutton and Cheam, might still be seen as the building block that precipitated a more sustained Liberal challenge culminating in the seat's capture by Paul Burstow in 1997, and Liberal by-election successes for Simon Hughes in Bermondsey, and for Alan Beith in Berwick, have resulted in the establishment of Liberal strongholds.

In March 1958 Mark Bonham-Carter, of the famous Liberal dynasty, won the Torrington by-election (and became the first Liberal by-election victor since 1929). Coupled with a series of promising second place finishes in the following years, this provided a timely morale boost for the party. However, it was the Orpington by-election victory for Eric Lubbock in March 1962 that really signalled the start of the party's revival. The mainly middle-class Kent constituency seemed outside the traditional Liberal strongholds, and so to convert a Conservative majority of 14,760 into a Liberal victory of nearly 8,000 was dramatic to say the least. The seeds for the Orpington by-election success had been planted much earlier, however. In 1955 Liberal activists began to form local ward committees to fight local elections. Through steadfast, even mundane, local campaigning the party was able to increase their council representation to twelve in 1961, providing a solid grassroots platform from which to fight and win the by-election the following year.

Cyr (1977) also points out that the focus on local issues and community politics was the basis of the Liberal by-election successes of the early 1970s. He notes Cyril Smith's victory in Rochdale in October 1972 as the most striking example of this. Smith was elected to the borough council as early as 1952, serving as mayor during 1966–67, and was able to build a powerful local reputation as a result. Moreover, the party machinery in Rochdale was strong enough to survive Smith's retirement before the 1992 General Election, and his successor Liz Lynne was able to retain the seat for the Liberal Democrats until finally being swept aside in Labour's landslide of 1997.

Although a strong local base is usually a necessary condition for Liberal success, this is not always the case. For example, the 1973 Isle of Ely by-election victory was achieved with none of these local factors being in place, and yet Clement Freud was able to stay in the Commons as MP for a redistricted constituency – North East Cambridgeshire – until 1987.

Liberal leaders 1956–88

Jo Grimond: 1956–67

It might be reasonable to claim that the major achievement of Davies' leadership had been to hold together the Liberals as a viable and coherent political party and to expand slightly but significantly the party's organisational reach (notably in some key universities). As the historian and Liberal candidate Roger Fulford stated, 'In politics in recent times there has only been one

Table 1.2 **Third party by-election success, 1945–2003**

Date	*Constituency*	*Held by*	*Winner*	*Notes*
27 Mar. 1958	Torrington	Con	Liberal – Mark Bonham-Carter	Reverted to Conservatives at next election
14 Mar. 1962	Orpington	Con	Liberal – Eric Lubbock	
24 Mar. 1965	Roxburgh, Selkirk & Peebles	Con	Liberal – David Steel	
26 June 1969	Birmingham Ladywood	Lab	Liberal – Wallace Lawler	Reverted to Labour at next election
26 Oct. 1972	Rochdale	Lab	Liberal – Cyril Smith	Held until 1997
7 Dec. 1972	Sutton & Cheam	Con	Liberal – Graham Tope	Reverted to Conservatives at next election Recaptured by Liberal Democrats in 1997
26 July 1973	Isle of Ely	Con	Liberal – Clement Freud	Held redistricted seat until 1987
26 July 1973	Ripon	Con	Liberal – David Austick	Reverted to Conservatives at next election
8 Nov. 1973	Berwick-on-Tweed	Con	Liberal – Alan Beith	Still held by Beith
29 Mar. 1979	Liverpool Edge Hill	Lab	Liberal – David Alton	
22 Oct. 1981	Croydon NW	Con	Liberal – Bill Pitt	Reverted to Conservatives at next election
26 Nov. 1981	Crosby	Con	SDP – Shirley Willaims	Reverted to Conservatives at next election
25 Mar. 1982	Glasgow Hillhead	Con	SDP – Roy Jenkins	
24 Feb. 1983	Bermondsey	Lab	Liberal – Simon Hughes	Still held by Hughes
14 June 1984	Portsmouth South	Con	SDP – Michael Hancock	Reverted to Conservatives at next election
4 July 1985	Brecon & Radnor	Con	Liberal – Richard Livesy	Lost in 1992 Recaptured in 1997
8 May 1986	Ryedale	Con	Liberal – Elizabeth Shields	Reverted to Conservatives at next election
26 Feb. 1987	Greenwich	Lab	SDP – Rosie Barnes	
8 Oct. 1990	Eastbourne	Con	Lib-Dem – David Bellotti	Reverted to Conservatives at next election
7 Mar. 1991	Ribble Valley	Con	Lib-Dem – Mike Carr	Reverted to Conservatives at next election
7 Nov. 1991	Kincardine & Deeside	Con	Lib-Dem – Nicol Stephen	Reverted to Conservatives at next election
6 May 1993	Newbury	Con	Lib-Dem – David Rendel	
29 July 1993	Christchurch	Con	Lib-Dem – Diane Maddock	Reverted to Conservatives at next election
9 June 1994	Eastleigh	Con	Lib-Dem – David Chidgey	
27 July 1995	Littleborough & Saddleworth	Con	Lib-Dem – Chris Davies	Redistricted seat lost to Labour in 1997
4 May 2000	Romsey	Con	Lib-Dem – Sandra Gidley	
18 Sept. 2003	Brent East	Lab	Lib-Dem – Sarah Teather	Third place in 2001 election

Source: Butler and Butler, 2000.

great miracle – that is the survival of the Liberal Party' (Fulford, 1959, 1). The MP for Orkney and Shetland, Jo Grimond, succeeded Davies as party leader in 1956. Grimond took it upon himself to rejuvenate the party and revive their fortunes. Simultaneously the party was to benefit from a new phase of political campaigning and organisation, which came to be known as Community politics.

Grimond's leadership style was epitomised by himself at the 1963 Brighton assembly: 'In bygone days, commanders were taught that, when in doubt, they should march their troops towards the sound of gunfire. I intend to march my troops towards the sound of gunfire.' The strategic doubt explicit in this statement may have been overlooked by subsequent analysts, and Grimond is generally credited with the revitalisation of the party from the grass roots. Indeed, Grimond's legacy has been noted by many of the party's activist core and organisational elite. One leading activist who first joined the party through the Young Liberals in the 1960s paid tribute to Grimond's inspirational qualities:

> Jo rescued the Liberal party single-handedly . . . it was the fact that we had somebody who was incredibly charismatic, who was an intellectual . . . Jo was full of ideas and he was able to communicate those ideas to other people . . . He combined this with great appeal in the country; he was one of the first people who really used television to promote himself.

Certainly Grimond oversaw the revival of the party's potential as much as their fortunes. He undoubtedly made the party feel good about itself at a time when natural optimism was in short supply. He assumed the reins of leadership of a party that was struggling to forge its identity on the minds of the British public. He handed over to Jeremy Thorpe in 1967, a party that seemed comfortable as the third force in British politics and with the potential of a more dramatic breakthrough to come.

Jeremy Thorpe: 1967–76

Grimond's leadership had given the Liberals a glimpse of breakthrough for which they were eternally grateful, but in truth the promise was unfulfilled. In the 1966 General Election, the party fielded only 311 candidates – 54 fewer than they had managed two years previously. Moreover, the election of 12 Liberal MPs in 1966 – to be followed by Wallace Lawler at the Birmingham Ladywood by-election in 1969 – seemed like some sort of success but in too many seats the Liberals were crushed by the classic third-party squeeze and the party were in danger of being marginalised as a result. For the first time, Grimond's leadership seemed problematic. The party had been rebuilding to take on the Conservatives and possibly replace Labour, but were now faced with the prospect of a second Labour victory under Harold Wilson. Grimond signalled his willingness to search for common purpose with Labour, to instant disapproval from the party at large, and criticism of the leadership style grew steadily from this period.

In the aftermath of the 1966 election, Grimond resigned as Liberal leader. As his successor, the party turned to the erudite (Eton and Oxford educated) and ambitious Jeremy Thorpe. As leader, Thorpe combined a reputation for internationalist concerns (hostility to apartheid in South Africa, the rule of Idi Amin in Uganda and the white minority government of Rhodesia for example) and an openness to 'gimmicky' campaign styles (grandiose campaign launches, acerbic performances in the Commons, and an open feud with the foot-soldiers of community politics, the Young Liberals).

Although Thorpe inherited a party with 12 MPs and the ability to win by-elections, the revival in Liberal fortunes was far from smooth. Cook (1998) pointed out that Thorpe was seldom without enemies in the party, while Glover (1998), when writing Thorpe's entry for *The Dictionary of Liberal Biography*, claimed that the first serious attempt to oust him as party leader came as early as June 1968 (when Thorpe was actually on honeymoon).

Despite increasing their number of MPs from 9 to 12 between the elections of 1964 and 1966, the party's share of the vote fell by almost 3 per cent, while in Scotland and Wales the Liberals were increasingly coming under pressure from the nationalist parties. Throughout the country, Liberal organisation was again in danger of withering away disastrously. Cook (1998, 147) notes that by April 1970 the party had full-time agents in just 17 constituencies, while the numbers of delegates to their party assembly fell by 500 between 1966 and 1969.

Despite fielding more candidates than in 1966, the 1970 General Election was a disaster for the Liberals. The party lost seven sitting MPs (including Wallace Lawler) and the party's share of the vote fell further. Thorpe himself, and rising star David Steel only held their seats in Devon North and Roxburgh, Selkirk and Peebles by less than a thousand votes in each case.

After the 1970 General Election, the party was boosted by by-election victories in Rochdale, and Sutton and Cheam, in 1972, as well as success in local elections in 1973 most notably in Liverpool. These events did after all convince many Liberal loyalists that with a higher media profile, increasing dissatisfaction with the two established parties, and a much improved organisational core, a real breakthrough was finally within the grasp of the party.

In the 'Who Governs?' Election of February 1974 the Liberals fielded 517 candidates (their largest slate since 1906) and in percentage terms, the party secured their highest share of the vote since 1929 (19.3 per cent). However, despite polling over six million votes the Liberals won just 14 seats and many in the party considered the election somewhat of a disappointment, especially given that the polls had predicted that the party would win around 22–3 per cent of the vote. The failure to overcome the inequity of the electoral system demoralised the party, and made it more difficult to persuade voters to choose the Liberals at the next General Election in six months time.

The February 1974 election was the most equivocal of recent times. The Conservatives won the popular vote but gained fewer seats than Labour. Moreover, Labour failed to gain enough seats to establish a majority in the Commons. While Labour leader Harold Wilson anticipated a call from the Queen to form the next administration, Conservative leader Edward Heath was not yet ready to relinquish the premiership.

In the aftermath of this inconclusive result, Thorpe was invited by Heath to talk about the formation of a Conservative–Liberal coalition (perhaps along with the Ulster Unionists) to keep out a minority Labour administration. According to Thorpe himself the Liberals were to be offered a seat in the cabinet but this was not as Home Secretary as reported at the time. Indeed Thorpe claims that the discussions never got around to this level of detail but he now understands that he was to be offered a Foreign Office post with responsibility for Europe (Thorpe, 1999). In any event the talks reached a predictable impasse over electoral reform.

To the outside world, Thorpe had got closer to power than any Liberal since Lloyd George. He entered Number 10 through the front door in the full glare of the media and was quick to spot that 'we're all minorities now'. Yet even this moment of glory was illusory. Senior Labour politicians infuriated by the possibility of a Conservative–Liberal coalition apparently considered leaking details of Thorpe's private life to discredit him (Whitehead, 1985, 114) and many Liberal activists were unhappy at the prospect of upholding the Heath regime (a problem exacerbated by the lack of dialogue between Thorpe and the party before his arrival at Downing Street).

Wilson finally formed a minority Labour administration and went to the country again six months later with the intention of securing a proper mandate. Despite fielding candidates in virtually every seat, the Liberal's vote slipped slightly in the October 1974 election and the party also lost two of the seats won in February (Bodmin and Hazel Grove), offset slightly by the gaining of Truro.

By 1975, Thorpe's leadership was in crisis. Accusations, made by Norman Scott, of a love affair between himself and Thorpe were growing more sensational with each passing month. Despite consistent denials from Thorpe, Scott ensured that the Liberal leader was embroiled in scandal. In March

1976, a man was gaoled for apparently trying to assassinate Scott, and by March 1976 Thorpe was forced to publish his version of events in the *Sunday Times*. Aware that this was not going to be end of the matter (he was charged – and acquitted – of conspiracy to murder in 1979) he resigned the leadership of the Liberal party on 9 May 1976, the day after his account was published in the press. Jo Grimond made a temporary return to the Liberal leadership in a caretaker capacity as a leadership election was set up.

Jeremy Thorpe continued to serve as MP for Devon North until the General Election of 1979 when the Conservative Tony Spellar defeated him. His trial for conspiracy took place within weeks of the election. After his acquittal, Thorpe retreated from the limelight of politics, but despite the onset of Parkinson's disease he continued to play an active role in his local party.

David Steel: 1976–88

After the scandal-induced resignation by Thorpe, the Liberals turned to David Steel who defeated John Pardoe in the leadership election in July 1976. Steel came from the Grimondite left of the party and had earned a reputation for a willingness to co-operate with others inside and outside of the party.

On entering the Commons at the 1965 Roxburgh, Selkirk and Peebles by-election, Steel was quick to make his mark. As the youngest member of the House he was the sponsor of the private member's bill – given parliamentary time by the Wilson government to pass into law – that legalised abortion in 1967.

Within a year of assuming the leadership of the Liberals, Steel found himself in demand with the Labour government. By-election defeats had stripped the Labour government (since 1976 led by James Callaghan) of its majority, and thus his administration needed the support of others in order to stay in power. In their active search for semi-permanent friendships with others the government naturally looked to Steel and the Liberals. For his part, Steel recognised an opportunity to practise his vision of multi-party government. The Lib–Lab pact was born.

Whitehead (1985) reported that many in the Labour party could not believe their luck and were astonished by how little the Liberals asked for in return for saving the government's neck. Direct elections (although not by proportional representation) for the European Parliament were the most tangible pro-Liberal result of the arrangement between the two parties, but Steel emphasised the benefits for the Liberals of being involved with government.

In truth having saved the Labour administration, the Liberals might have expected more from the pact. In fact association with an unpopular government blighted them and the party suffered substantial losses in local elections and some disastrous by-election results during the lifetime of the pact (Bogdanor, 1983, 94).

The Lib–Lab pact formally came to a close in July 1978 – although Steel continued to stress that the Liberals had bridged the credibility gap by being involved in government for the first time in fifty years. The failure of the Scottish and Welsh devolution referendums, and most notably the excessive industrial action during the winter of discontent of 1978–79, sealed the fate of the Callaghan government, which lost a vote of no confidence and went to the country in May 1979.

At the 1979 General Election Labour were heavily defeated by the Conservatives led by Margaret Thatcher, the Liberals lost more than a million votes from their October 1974 total and a further three MPs (including Thorpe in North Devon). Furthermore the Liberal share of the vote (13.8 per cent) did not bode well for the immediate future. The Conservative victory would, of course, mark a new era in British politics, but a more immediate result was the opening of a new phase of third party politics in Britain, as Labour defectors were to set up their own new centre party – the SDP – with whom Steel and the Liberals would have to forge a working relationship if they were not to be completely marginalised.

From Liberal to Alliance to Liberal Democrats

Parties that suffer traumatic defeat in elections often resort to prolonged periods of soul searching and internecine warfare in opposition. The reaction of the Conservatives to defeat in 1997 (and to a lesser extent in 1906), and of Labour to defeat in 1951 seems to bear out this adage. However, the classic case of defeat leading to further inelectability concerns the behaviour of the Labour party after their routing by the Conservatives in 1979. Immediately after their defeat, Labour embarked on a long and bitter battle for policy direction and the heart and soul of the party. The victors in this civil war were the left and the far left. New leader Michael Foot (who had been elected as the unity candidate) found it impossible to hold the various factions of the party together and the centre and right of the Labour party found themselves marginalised.

When the left's grip on Labour was strengthened through constitutional reorganisation in the early 1980s, Labour was powerless to avoid the defection of many of its leading – and most experienced MPs – to a new political party, the Social Democratic Party (SDP). This new party represented both an opportunity and a threat to the Liberals; an opportunity since the resurgence of centre party politics might afford precisely the opportunity for realignment that Liberal leaders since Grimond had forecast, a threat since the realignment might well happen without the Liberals themselves. The relationship between the Liberals and SDP was to dominate third party politics for the next two elections. (See Crewe and King, 1995, for the definitive account of the SDP.)

Led by the 'Gang of Four' – Roy Jenkins, David Owen, Bill Rodgers and Shirley Williams – the SDP was officially launched on 26 March 1981 and initially consisted of 14 MPs (13 former Labour MPs and a lone Conservative). A further 13 ex-Labour members defected to the SDP in the second half of 1981, while another two joined in 1982. Jenkins, the ex-Labour Chancellor of the Exchequer, who had returned to British politics fresh from his stint as European Commissioner, was elected leader of the SDP after his return to parliament and he was quick to establish a rapport with Steel.

Following negotiations between the leaders of the Liberals and SDP in the early months of 1981, the two parties issued a joint statement – *A Fresh Start for Britain* – in which they outlined agreed principles and policies. The document also expressed the parties' wish to 'avoid fighting each other in elections' and set out arrangements to fight alternate by-elections.

The electoral impact of the Alliance was immediate: opinion polls suggested strong support but it was the Warrington by-election in July that really provided the springboard. With the Liberals standing aside, Roy Jenkins polled 42 per cent of the vote and came within 1,800 votes of defeating Labour in what was a Labour stronghold. The result provided the party with the sort of credibility that opinion poll ratings could not. Bill Pitt's victory for the Liberals in Croydon North West in October 1981, and the return to parliament of both Williams (Crosby, November 1981) and Jenkins (Glasgow Hillhead, March 1982) gave the impression that the Alliance was virtually unstoppable.

However, events began to conspire against the Alliance. The economy started to improve in early 1982 (inflation first stabilising and then falling), while the Falklands War provided the Conservatives, and Thatcher in particular, with a clear boost in popularity. The sensational victory of Simon Hughes in the Bermondsey by-election of February 1983 illustrated the state of the local Labour party rather than the health of the Liberals (although for the Liberals to hold the seat ever since has been a monumental achievement). As Crewe and King (1995) note, in the four months before Argentina invaded the Falklands in April 1982 the Conservatives average standing in the Gallup opinion polls was 30 per cent; in the four months following it, it was 45 per cent.

With short-term factors appearing to be in their favour, the Conservatives went to the country in June 1983. For the Alliance the results came as a bitter disappointment. Despite securing almost eight million votes (25.4 per cent of the vote) and finishing only 2.2 per cent behind Labour, the Alliance won just 23 seats. The result may have represented the best performance by a 'third' party since 1923 (in terms of share of the vote), but the discriminatory nature of the first-past-the-post system on third parties with an evenly distributed vote could not have been clearer. Labour with 2 per cent more of the national vote, but regionally skewed towards their industrial heartlands, were rewarded with 186 more seats in the 1983 parliament than the Alliance. The SDP were particularly badly hit, losing 23 of the 28 MPs who had defected to the party and seeking re-election (including two of the Gang of Four – Williams and Rodgers). The party's only gain came in Ross, Cromarty and Skye, where 23-year-old Charles Kennedy captured the seat from the Conservatives. The Liberals performance was slightly more encouraging, gaining five additional seats to the loss of only one (the by-election win of Croydon North West).

The immediate consequence of the election disappointment was the resignation of Jenkins as SDP leader, and the unopposed selection of David Owen as his successor. Owen was to go on to dominate the SDP over the following years and Owen's views towards the Liberals were far less friendly than those of his predecessor. Owen was fiercely opposed to a full merger with the Liberals or indeed any further integration that would blur the identity of his own party. Steel, on the other hand, was generally in favour of merger but agreed not to publicly campaign for it. The two men were never to develop the close relationship that was evident between Steel and Jenkins.

In electoral terms, the 1983–87 period was frustrating for the Alliance. Their opinion poll ratings in the year or so following the 1983 election lagged some way behind that of Labour and the Conservatives. They retained the ability to pull off astounding by-election victories and four (Portsmouth South, 1984; Brecon & Radnor, 1985; Ryedale, 1986; and Greenwich, 1987) were added to their impressive canon during the life of the parliament. As we discussed above and in Chapter 7, by-elections are crucially important to the Liberals in building up momentum and visibility. Nevertheless by-election wins may not be sufficient in themselves to bridge the credibility gap and the Alliance was never able to build up the same sort of momentum that was evident during the 1981–82 period.

Despite this, the Alliance entered the 1987 election campaign with some confidence. Opinion polls suggested that by the spring of 1987 they had closed the gap on Labour. However, the election campaign highlighted the differences between the parties and their leaders. It became clear that, given the choice, Owen would support the Conservatives in the event of a hung parliament, while Steel would side with Labour. Thus the dual leadership of the Alliance was an easy target for political opponents to attack and the media to exploit. With Labour concentrating on confirming themselves as the second party in British politics, the 1987 General Election proved too much of a strain for the unnatural bedfellows in the Alliance.

As in 1983, the 1987 election results were a blow to the Alliance as their vote fell by nearly 3 per cent to 22.6 per cent (over 8 percentage points behind Labour), while their number of MPs fell to 22. Again the SDP's performance was particularly disappointing, winning no additional seats and losing three (including Jenkins in Glasgow Hillhead). The Liberals fared only slightly better, gaining 3 seats and losing 5.

Many senior politicians in both parties blamed the Alliance's poor performance on the dual leadership sending contradictory messages to the electorate. Within 48 hours of the election Jenkins and Williams, along with Paddy Ashdown and Alan Beith from the Liberals, publicly called for a merger between the two parties, while David Steel appealed for a 'democratic fusion' of the Alliance partners. Owen remained vehemently opposed (although the first SDP MP to back merger was Charles Kennedy).

Eventually those in favour of merger in the SDP won the day and Owen resigned as leader in August 1987. He was replaced by Robert Maclennan but continued to lead his own faction – as the SDP. Meanwhile, the two negotiating teams began what were to prove long and difficult discussions at the end of September 1987 and ran into serious problems with the new party's constitution and name almost immediately.

Given the real obstacles to a peaceful merger, as Cook (1989) notes, it is almost unbelievable that Steel pressed ahead with the process. Nevertheless, the merger deal was eventually agreed but with the consequence that the leadership potential of Steel and Maclennan had been fatally compromised. The mini-manifesto between the two leaders contained many policies that the Liberal membership was unlikely to support (commitment to NATO, VAT on fuel and children's clothes, and the cutting of benefits). Most amazingly of all the membership of the new party could not agree on a name for the party either; even though the Social and Liberal Democratic (SLD) party had been officially launched with Steel and Maclennan as interim leaders.

In July 1988 Paddy Ashdown – MP for Yeovil – defeated Alan Beith to become the first leader of the new party (Steel and Maclennan declined to stand). Ashdown had only been an MP for five years but was seen as dynamic and likely to appeal to voters. The early days of the new party were difficult. Membership was low, the party was in severe financial trouble, and the arguments over the party's name failed to abate. Electorally, the party fared little better. The 1988 and 1989 local election results were a big disappointment for the party, while they fared terribly in a series of by-elections (losing their deposit in four of the seven by-elections in 1988–89 and finishing behind the continuing SDP in Richmond), and the SLD failing to make any impact in opinion polls. The European elections in June 1989 added to the sense of crisis, with the SLD being pushed down to fourth place (with just 6.4 per cent of the vote) by the Greens who achieved nearly 16 per cent of the vote. In his diary entry for 15 June 1989 (the day of the Euro elections) a despondent Ashdown articulated an extraordinary fear: 'I am plagued by the nightmare that the party that began with Gladstone will end with Ashdown' (Ashdown, 2000, 50). Under these circumstances the Liberals Democrats – a name finally chosen following a long and bitter dispute within the party – came into existence on the 26 October 1989.

2

The Liberal Democrats and contemporary politics

Merger and acquisition

Chapter 1 demonstrated the difficult transition from the Alliance to the Liberal Democrats. In fact, the merger process was problematic for a number of reasons not least because the anti-merger faction within the SDP included David Owen and two of the party's most media-conscious MPs – John Cartwright and Rosie Barnes. Moreover, as Cook (1989) points out, this small but immobile group had the ear of many of the SDP's financial backers, and the continued opposition of Owen to the merger managed to give the impression that the new party was not really the result of a merger between two equal partners but the aggressive takeover of the SDP by the Liberals.

The rump SDP may have been facing an impossible task, trying to hold back the tide of merger, like some latter day King Canute, but they did manage to inflict some serious damage to the fledgeling merged party. In the Richmond by-election of 1989 – won by a whisker by the Conservatives' William Hague – the SDP managed to come second and beat the Democrats' Barbara Pearce into third place by around 5,000 votes. This was however, the apex of the continuing SDP's fortunes and was shortly followed by the nadir. The Vale of Glamorgan by-election in 1989 saw them a poor fourth and all three SDP MPs quarrelled in public about the future direction of the party; in the Bootle by-election of 1990 they were beaten by the Monster Raving Loony Party, and the continuing SDP gave up the ghost shortly afterwards. By 1992 some of the key SDP personnel had joined the Liberal Democrats (including National Organiser, Ian Wright who went on to become Ashdown's Press Officer). Others went in the opposite direction and joined the Conservatives (Danny Finkelstein – director of the Social Market Foundation – went on to William Hague's Policy Unit and stood unsuccessfully for his new party in Harrow West in 2001).

The rather shambolic end to the SDP coincided with an upturn in fortunes for the merged party. Once the disasters of the 1989 Euro elections and the year long battle to rename the party were behind them, the Liberal Democrats were able to embark on a political odyssey which was relatively free from factional in-fighting. That said, the original divisions between the two parties are occasionally mentioned as being pertinent to the way the party is run today.

One MP, reliant on Labour defectors to keep the Conservatives out of his seat in 2001 confided to us: 'I think defending the seat would be a lot easier if I hadn't left the Labour party to join the SDP. [They have] long memories in the [local] Labour party, and they'd rather the Tory won than me. Anyone but me!' Other party members who backed Hughes rather than Kennedy in the leadership election in 1999, hinted that Kennedy was less trusted by some activists because 'he's not really a Liberal' and 'still a Social Democrat'.

As indicated in Chapter 1, the newly merged party found it surprisingly difficult to brand itself with a suitable name. The process that led to the party emerging as the Liberal Democrats is looked at in more detail in Chapter 4 – where we illustrate the tension between the leadership elite and the activist base.

Ashdown had more luck however with his plans to change the party's corporate logo. The Liberal Democrats went on to accept their new logo – the *bird of freedom* – in May 1990. In fact the Ashdown *Diaries* report a lukewarm reception from a smattering of insiders and a couple of gripes that too much money had been spent on the process (2000, 86). Thereafter there seems to have been little criticism of Ashdown himself. At the Conservative conference in 1990, Prime Minister Margaret Thatcher notoriously invoked the Monty Python sketch – 'it is an ex-parrot, it has ceased to be!' – in order to ridicule the Liberal Democrats' new logo. Yet a week later the Liberal Democrats demonstrated their ability to take seats off the Conservatives with a victory at the Eastbourne by-election and the newly branded party firmly established their credibility.

Liberal Democrat consolidation: 1992–97

As we have seen from the introduction, the Liberal Democrats have increased their representation in the House of Commons dramatically since 1992. In the 1997 General Election this was achieved through the ruthless targeting of winnable seats rather than by increasing national vote share (see Chapter 9). In 2001, for the first time in four General Elections, the Liberal Democrats increased both their seats and their vote share. As Figure 2.1 demonstrates, despite being committed to the overthrow of the electoral system – and of course the party still receives a smaller proportion of seats than votes – the Liberal Democrats do seem to have finally begun to learn how to win contests under the Single Member Simple Plurality (SMSP) electoral system.

A critical part of the branding of the Liberal Democrats had to high-

Figure 2.1 **Liberal electoral performance: % share of the vote and share of seats, 1974–2001**

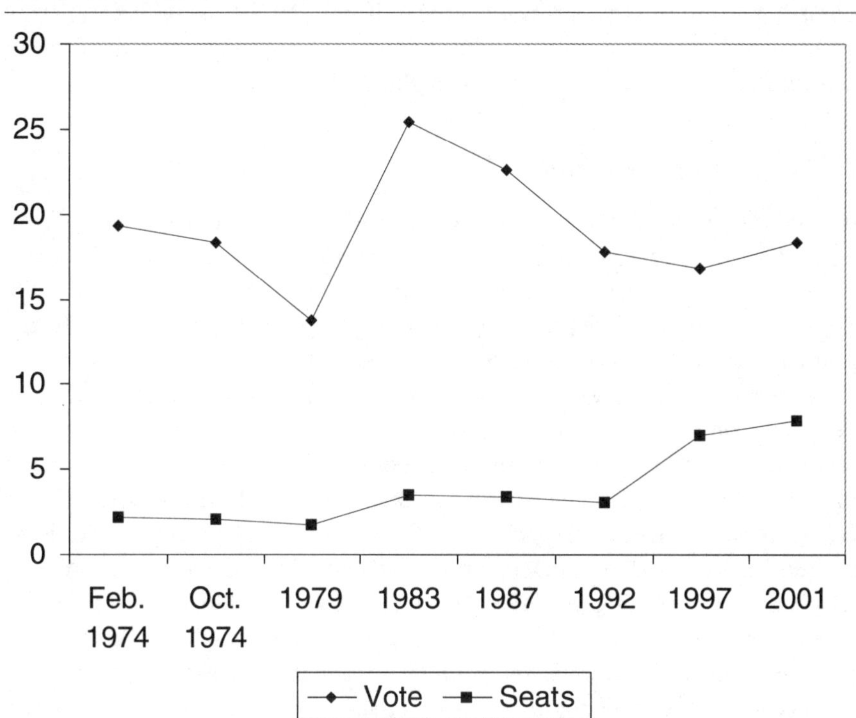

light distinctive policies in order for the party to stamp their mark on British public opinion. In 1992 the Liberal Democrats decided to elide two issues, taxation and education, into their hypothecated taxation pledge. As part of this pledge, the Liberal Democrats advocated raising the level of income tax in order to divert the ringfenced proceeds into improving education. This was a critical part of the branding process for the party. As one of the authors of the policy informed us it became resonant with the public:

> [The party leadership] saw it as a 'make your mind up' item. As it turned out in 1992 it was extremely popular and again in 1997. But that's where it came from and it spoke about being more honest, it spoke about being different, it spoke about being more direct, it spoke about making an issue ours, so that when people talked about education a chunk of people would say 'Yes, the Liberal Democrats are the best on that', which people tend not to say. We could have done the environment and that was the other option – those were the two we could make ours.

By 1997 hypothecated taxation and education had become a flagship Liberal Democrat policy – in marketing terms it was part of the party's unique selling point. The Liberal Democrat policy agenda has evolved significantly since 1992. As we demonstrate in Chapter 6, there is now a clearly defined set of Liberal Democrat policies that the British public can readily identify.

Local government base

As we will see in Chapter 7, local election success is often the bedrock on which Liberal Democrat parliamentary success is built. In the classic study of the 1955 General Election in Bristol North East, Milne and Mackenzie, (1958, 18) dismiss the local Liberals as 'a third party living on its tradition, with virtually no organization whatever'.

Nowadays, the Liberal Democrats seem to believe that local credibility begets national credibility, and strong local election performances in the early 1990s were deemed critical to the successful establishment of the new party. In fact Rallings and Thrasher point out that the local elections of 1988 were crucial to the future health of the party. It was, they claim, the superior local politics base of the Liberal Democrats that helped them overcome the challenge of the continuing SDP (Rallings and Thrasher, 1996, 210). Moreover, as we demonstrate in Chapter 7, the Liberal Democrats have bridged the credibility gap since the 1990s, primarily from the local level: In terms of local government, the Liberal Democrats have proved they have the capacity to win' (Rallings and Thrasher, 1996, 222). The Liberal Democrats performance in the 1990 local elections saw the party claim considerable support across the country (18 per cent of the national vote) but the real breakthrough came in the 1991 elections, as the party gained 531 council seats in England while the number of Liberal Democrat controlled councils in Britain increased from 11 to 28 (Table 2.1).

The Liberal Democrats consolidated their position in local government throughout the 1990s using their local success as a springboard for national advances. For example, the capture of Cheltenham in the 1991 local elections may have precipitated the Liberal Democrat success in the General Election the following year. By 1995 the Liberal Democrats had more elected councillors in Britain than the Conservatives. As a result, the party were thus forging a reputation for success in local government (Stevenson, 1996).

Even the slight decline in Liberal Democrat fortunes in the late 1990s and at the turn of the century was offset by the morale boosting capture of target councils – such as Liverpool in 1998, Sheffield in 1999 and Oldham in 2000.

With the rotation system of local elections meaning that most councillors have to defend their seats four years on, success for any party in one year is

Table 2.1 **Liberal Democrat local election performance, 1990–2002**

	Lib-Dem councillors (England) net gains/losses	*GB councils controlled*
1990	−63	11
1991	+531	28
1992	+57	27
1993	+371	29
1994	+383	37
1995	+483	50
1996	+150	55
1997	−177	50
1998	−114	42
1999	−119	27
2000	−21	27
2001	−92	25
2002	+44	27

often followed by a struggle to retain seats in less favourable circumstances. The Liberal Democrats have done well to ride this wave of public opinion, and despite the slight retreat from the heyday of 1995 the Liberal Democrats increased their number of councillors in 2002 and 2003. While no longer in charge of Liverpool, Sheffield or Oldham, and no longer the second party of local government, they remain competitive at the local level – and local credibility remains the vital springboard for national breakthroughs.

The Project

As Fielding has pointed out, in the 1990s Ashdown embarked on a similar journey to that proposed by Grimond thirty years earlier. While Grimond's Liberals sought to appeal to 'liberally minded socialists' and enjoyed a cordial relationship with the Labour government of 1964–66 (Joyce, 1999, Fielding, 2003, 45; 129–31, 139–40), Ashdown's Liberal Democrats entered the formal structures of government as Ashdown and Tony Blair sought to 'heal the schism' in the politics of the left and centre left.

The Liberal Democrats emerged from an Alliance whose stated ambition was to replace Labour as the main opposition to the Conservatives. Their performance in the 1992 General Election was widely criticised for an unwillingness to nail their colours to the mast and maintaining the pretence that they could work with either Labour or Conservative parties in the event of a hung parliament (see Dunleavy, 1993, for a particularly virulent attack on Ashdown's tactical acumen).

However, by the mid-1990s in the midst of the unprecedented unpopularity of the incumbent Conservative regime, and the boost to Labour popularity that coincided with the leadership of Tony Blair, the Liberal Democrats had become part of an unofficial anti-Conservative alliance. In the run-up to the 2001 election, and with the continued unpopularity of the Conservatives in opposition, it even looked possible that their long-term strategy might be to replace the Conservatives. This constituted a remarkably rapid turnaround from their previous stance (see Leaman, 1998 for an officially sanctioned account of the abandonment of equidistance).

The groundwork for the abandonment of the Liberal Democrats' equidistance was already evident in Ashdown's Chard speech of 9 May 1992 where he talked of the need to: 'work with others to assemble the ideas around which a non-socialist alternative to the Conservatives can be constructed'. We return to the implications of the Chard Speech in Chapter 8.

By June 1992, within months of the resignation of Neil Kinnock and the succession of John Smith as Labour leader, meetings between leading Liberal Democrats and Labour politicians were already occurring with the approval of Ashdown. Leading Liberal Democrat Roger Liddle's contact with Peter Mandelson may have played a role in Liddle's subsequent defection to Labour but at the time it played an important role in convincing the Liberal Democrat leadership that scope for co-operation with the revisionist wing of Labour existed.

Upon assuming control of the Labour party in 1994, Tony Blair was quick to send conciliatory messages to the Liberal Democrats. He had stated an admiration for Roy Jenkins, who as an original member of the Gang of Four was anathema to many in the mainstream Labour party. Personnel from the two parties were working together as part of the Scottish Constitutional Convention, which set the tone for the pattern of devolution in Scotland even in the dog days of the Major government, and the frequent dialogue between Liberal Democrats and Labour personnel, such as the ongoing series of meetings between Archy Kirkwood and Donald Dewar, and Robert Maclennan and Robin Cook now had the official sanction of both party leaders.

By May 1995, Ashdown had announced the end of equidistance.

> [I]t should surprise no one when we say that if the Conservatives lose their majority in Parliament and seek our support to continue in office, they will not receive it. People must know that if they kick the Tories out through the front door, we Liberal Democrats will not allow them to sneak in through the back.

According to the Ashdown *Diaries*, Blair's willingness to accommodate the Liberal Democrats was breathtaking in its scope. In September 1994 Blair confided to Ashdown that he believed both parties 'should change the culture of politics so we can work together' (Ashdown, 2000, 276).

By now Ashdown had come to refer to the plans to increase co-operation with Labour as 'the Project'. A group of trusted insiders (the 'Jo Group') was constituted to facilitate the Project and in the long run-up to the 1997 election, there was some talk of potential coalition, whether through necessity or by inclination. Indeed one of the most interesting features of the progress of the Project is that Blair – through Jenkins – signalled his determination to have Liberal Democrats in his cabinet regardless of the size of his victory.

The received wisdom now is that the magnitude of Labour's victory in 1997 dealt the fatal (but not final) blow to the Project. However, it is worth noting that Ashdown's *Diaries* make it clear that Blair still seemed inclined towards co-operation rather than confrontation despite his parliamentary hegemony. On the day of the election Blair apparently told Ashdown: 'I am absolutely determined to mend the schism that occurred in the progressive forces in British politics at the start of this century. It is just a question of finding a workable framework. But we are now in a position of strength and I intend to use that' (Ashdown, 2000, 555).

Blair brought up the subject of Liberal Democrat representation inside the New Labour government – and in particular of a Liberal Democrat presence in Cabinet Committees: 'I need you to know that I see this as a means of transition to an end position where you come into the show. Who knows what the ultimate destination for all this might be? It could be merger some way down the track. Or maybe not' (Ashdown, 2000, 560).

Despite the equivocation at the end of this statement the depth of the ambition of the Project was simply stunning. The day after securing the biggest ever Labour majority (179 seats) in the House of Commons, the party's leader – and new Prime Minister – had seriously discussed formal co-operation with, constitutional consultation with, and the possibility of cabinet seats for the Liberal Democrats. Moreover he even offered possible merger between the two parties as a final terminus for the journey of the parties of 'progress'. This was a staggering position to take for a Prime Minster in no need of bargaining and had to represent the apex of the Project's potential. With the benefit of hindsight it is tempting to say that the path of the Project was on a downward trajectory thereafter.

The Joint Cabinet Committee (JCC)

The form of co-operation taken by the Blair–Ashdown axis after the election was more modest than either party leader might have hoped for, but probably more radical than either might have expected. In the end, the Cook–MacLennan talks – which had seen both parties reach agreement on the implementation of devolution, the European Human Rights Convention and reform of the House of Lords – was used as a blueprint for shared work between the two parties. The Joint Consultative Committee quickly became the Joint Cabinet Committee (JCC) to discuss constitutional affairs. In particular the Liberal Democrats welcomed the opportunity to discuss the possibility of reforming the electoral system (although the difficulty in persuading Labour to reform a system that had just delivered its largest ever majority was not lost on them).

Labour had inserted in their 1997 manifesto a commitment to review and hold a referendum on the voting process. Blair declared early in his meetings with Ashdown that he was 'not persuaded' by the need for reform (Ashdown, 2000, 276) but did later give Ashdown the impression that he was more receptive to some forms of electoral reform, but was less optimistic about the prospects of pushing it through the Labour party. Whatever the reality of Blair's personal position, Ashdown did get the impression that it was malleable and that he could be converted to the benefits of PR as a means of securing a second and third term for an anti-Conservative coalition.

This impression was in no small measure reinforced by Blair's appointment of Lord Jenkins of Hillhead to the chair of the independent commission to investigate the potential reform of the electoral system in 1998. After a long period of consultation, the Jenkins Commission officially recommended 'AV plus' – with its retention of constituencies and a top-up party list – to replace SMSP in Westminster elections. As Fielding (2003) states AV plus was probably too radical for Labour and too conservative for the Liberal Democrats. Nevertheless, having set up the Jenkins Commission, and with a commitment to hold a referendum in the 1997 manifesto, Labour and Blair continued to prevaricate on the issue of electoral reform. The lack of progress on this issue effectively killed the Project, and through the second volumes of Ashdown's *Diaries* it is possible to trace the downward spiral of the Liberal Democrat leader's optimism that Blair could deliver on his promise to 'heal the schism in progressive politics' and precipitated the slow withdrawal from the politics of co-operation between the two parties.

The joint statement

Nevertheless, on 11 November 1998 the work of the JCC was officially extended. In a joint statement issued by both leaders the parties declared the next phase of co-operation between them. Critically, Blair and Ashdown announced that they were committed to working together on a much wider brief than merely constitutional matters: 'We are confident this step forward can deepen co-operation and result in widening support for the kind of progressive change which we wish to see and to which we believe the British people are strongly committed.'

Some Liberal Democrats saw this as a signal that co-operation with Labour had ceased to be a means to an end, but had become an end in itself, and this they took to be a bridge too far. It might also be the case that Ashdown realised that this was to mark the beginning of the end for the Project. One election agent from a key target seat in 2001 (where the opposition to the Liberal Democrats were the Conservatives not Labour) told us that: 'Paddy very much controlled the party; very often dragged the party where it didn't necessarily want to go, which I think was his downfall in the end. The joint statement with Tony Blair produced such a reaction in various quarters of the party [that] I think that's when he decided he'd had enough.'

Although the JCC did survive for a further two years under Charles Kennedy's leadership, it had met only infrequently before the parties bowed to the inevitable. Formally the JCC was disbanded in September 2001 with few tears being shed from either side, but there can be little doubt that the Liberal Democrats were the most disillusioned with the Committee's inability to make a significant mark on contemporary British politics.

Ashdown stands down!

In January 1999 Paddy Ashdown announced his intention to retire as Liberal Democrat leader after the European parliament elections of June that same year. Both volumes of Ashdown's *Diaries* make it clear that his resignation was always part of his long-term plan and that the timing was nothing more than the realisation that, with the party on a decent footing and with sufficient time for the next leader to make an impact on the British public before the next General Election, June was as good a time to resign as any.

However, it was tempting to see Ashdown's resignation as the public acknowledgment that the Project has run its course. One MP attributed the failure of the Project to basic human failings:

> I think Paddy was seduced by Blair, he genuinely believed that Blair would deliver on PR and he liked Blair as an individual. He trusted him and I think Blair stuffed him. I think Charles Kennedy doesn't have the same close personal relationship [with Blair] and with the benefit of hindsight can see that Blair was leading Paddy along and so we are not as close.

The end of Ashdown's leadership did signal a change of mood in the party and a reduction in the commitment to co-operate with Labour. All five of the leadership contenders were less keen on the Project than Ashdown. According to the Ashdown *Diaries*, Jackie Ballard and David Rendel who had been openly hostile to the JCC, and Simon Hughes, who tried to stop the joint statement, were highly sceptical of, any working relationship with Labour (2001, 338, 151, 336). Malcolm Bruce's shadowing of Gordon Brown had led to a mutual 'animosity over tax and spending', and even Kennedy had been 'equivocal' over the abandonment of equidistance (Ashdown, 2000, 413, 319).

Indeed Kennedy had already outlined the limits of his support for the Project when in 1998 he spoke out against the extension of formal links with Labour:

> The members . . . favour, as I do, co-operation with the Labour party and the Labour government over constitutional reform, [but] they don't want the process to blunt our distinctive identity. We are an independent political party out to win votes and secure influence and power . . . We have to be extremely careful about using words like coalition. It seems to me, in the present Parliament, with a vast Labour majority, that is, frankly, a non-starter. (Cited in Peter Lynch's entry for Kennedy in *Dictionary of Liberal Biography*)

Kennedy as leader

On 9 August 1999 Charles Kennedy became the second elected leader of the British Liberal Democrats. Although installed as the ante-post favourite for the leadership as soon as Ashdown resigned, Kennedy was far from a racing certainty for the job. A number of those tipped as 'future leaders' of the party failed to throw their hats into the ring. Menzies Campbell, Don Foster, Matthew Taylor and Nick Harvey – all of whom had been mentioned as potential successors by various 'people in the know' (according to his *Diaries*, Campbell and Harvey were among those in Ashdown's mind whenever he turned his attention to his likely successor) – declined to enter the fray. Taylor went on to be Kennedy's campaign manager in the leadership election, while Campbell and Harvey threw their weight behind Kennedy's candidature.

Of the five candidates who did stand for election, Jackie Ballard appeared to be the biggest surprise. However, she had a clear power base from her time as leader of the Association of Liberal Democrat Councillors and her candidature sent a strong signal that the activist and councillor base of the party would be an important factor in determining the next leader. Simon Hughes proved to be the most serious of Kennedy's opponents. Of the five candidates, Hughes and Kennedy were alone in fighting Labour rather than the Conservatives in their constituencies (although the Labour candidate in Ross, Skye and Inverness West gained no more than 17 per cent of the vote). Hughes made a direct appeal to the grassroots of the party with his sceptical approach to Ashdown's project, and his more cynical attitude to co-operation with Labour may have emerged from his history of fighting Labour rather than the Conservatives at the local level. It is interesting to note from Table 2.2 that Hughes was the biggest beneficiary of the transferred preferences of supporters of both Rendel and Ballard.

Table 2.2 **The Liberal Democrat leadership election contest, 1999**

	First Preference	*Second Round Rendel's votes transferred*		*Third Round Ballard's votes transferred*		*Fourth Round Bruce's votes transferred*	
Jackie Ballard	3978	+627	4605	(eliminated)			
Malcolm Bruce	4643	+598	5241	+827	6068	(eliminated)	
Simon Hughes	16233	+1145	17378	+1982	19360	+2473	21833
Charles Kennedy	22724	+895	23619	+1545	25164	+3261	28425
David Rendel	3428	(eliminated)					
Non-transfers			163		251		334

Source: *British Elections & Parties Review*, 10 (2000).

It is often said that the real difference between the former partners is that while the Liberals are dyed-in-the-wool federalists, seeking the devolution of power to the regions and the grassroots of the party, the Social Democrats can be more centralist by inclination. As generalisations go this may have an element of analytical power. Upon taking control of the party, Kennedy's leadership style has been different to Ashdown's in that he seems to have put in less energy in appealing to local activists and the core of the party, he has also cut a fairly confident figure in that he has been less concerned with creating news on a daily basis. One senior strategist told us:

> Curiously although he's been a politician nearly all his adult life, [Kennedy] comes across as somebody who's a little bit detached from politics, a bit more relaxed than the average politician, doesn't speak in politician speak. He looks like a human being. I think Neil Kinnock had a lot of those qualities, but they blew it. Once he became leader, the Labour party started saying you have to look like a leader, and Kinnock became very defensive, very stiff and pompous and it didn't suit his personality. I think with Charles we have to run with Charles as he is. Maybe for some he doesn't look quite as presidential or statesman-like [as Ashdown], but, I think for a lot of people because he looks like an ordinary guy and he's relaxed and speaks your normal language. I think that's actually very strong. In an era of anti-politics, I think he's somebody with a lot of appeal. Clearly you can't make him do the same kind of things as Paddy, because he's a very different sort of guy from Paddy. He's not going to be running up mountains and abseiling down things. That's not his style. But, he's

> very good with people and he comes across as a friendly warm person, which is quite important.

This may be implying that the Liberal Democrats in the Kennedy era are less easily characterised as a party of dual identity since the centralised decision-making process have circumvented some of the ritualised federalism characterised in the Ashdown era (a question we return to below).

One election agent admitted that he had wanted a new style of leadership, but did not have an adequate sense of what constituted the new leadership's style.

> I think Kennedy is being very careful. I don't really know what his agenda is yet. I was very pleased with Kennedy in the Romsey by-election when Hague started with his anti-foreigners thing. Kennedy actually came out and said, 'we're Liberals, we don't agree with this'. And we got a thumping majority against the Tories. And I'm hoping he's going to carry on. However, I have to admit, I didn't vote for Kennedy. I voted for Simon Hughes because I was worried that Kennedy would carry on the Ashdown project.

The devolution revolution

As British politics entered a new phase in the twenty-first century, so did the Liberal Democrats. While attention at Westminster was focused upon limited and potential co-operation with Labour, devolution gave the party an opportunity to practise co-operation with Labour, and participate in coalition government, in both Scotland and Wales.

In May 1999 the Liberal Democrats gained 17 seats in the Scottish parliament, which gave them coalition potential with the largest party in Scotland – Labour. So it came to pass that within weeks of the election, the Liberal Democrats entered the government of the Scottish Executive. With the Scottish parliament already elected by PR, the Liberal Democrats' price for entering the coalition with the minority Labour regime was a compromise over the introduction of undergraduate tuition fees for Scottish Universities. Having been committed to their introduction this was not an easy deal to broker for the Scottish Labour Party, but eventually a system of deferred payment for Scottish students was agreed.

Although the passage to the coalition agreement was far from easy, those who favoured co-operation with the Labour Party in Scotland won the day. A senior Scottish strategist revealed his justification for the coalition:

> I'm not one of those who was in the party because I like it to be a nice pressure group. I was in the party to get things done . . . So I'm quite pleased we're in power in Scotland. Some of my colleagues, one of the senior researchers is totally opposed to the agreement – he's doing his best for it but he'd rather we weren't

> involved . . . There's more happened in Scotland because you've got coalition government. And if you're in favour of proportional representation, you've got to be in favour of coalition governments. You can't keep your hands clean if you believe in that sort of system.

The Liberal Democrats were given three positions in the Scottish Executive cabinet. Jim Wallace was made Deputy First Minister, Nicol Stephen, the Minister for Enterprise and Lifelong Learning, and Ross Finnie, the Minister for Environment and Rural Development.

Serious illness to inaugural First Minister for Scotland, Donald Dewar, in May 2000 meant that Jim Wallace was made Acting First Minister until Dewar was fit to return. Dewar's death in October saw Wallace act up again until Labour could elect a replacement. When Dewar's successor, Henry McLeish, was forced out following an expenses foul-up in November 2001, Wallace filled the breach for a third time as acting First Minister – while the Labour party in Scotland chose Jack McConnell as the new First Minister.

A party official from Scotland confided that Wallace's first stint as acting First Minister solidified the coalition:

> I think a lot of people in the Labour party just couldn't see how the government of Scotland could continue with Wallace in charge, but in fact Jim has done a very good job and he has got a very good press out of it and I think that has to some extent solidified the relationship between at least the Labour members and the Lib–Dem members of the executive – I think a lot of people in the Labour Party thought 'Right, we can let Jim Wallace get ahead with it, while we try and sort out who's going to succeed Donald Dewar.'

The point here is that the Liberal Democrats quickly became synonymous with the governance of Scotland. Wallace's three separate stints as acting First Minister gave him an individual degree of kudos but also gave his party a significant credibility boost.

The 2003 Scottish parliament elections again saw the return of 17 Liberal Democrat MSPs. Another partnership agreement was brokered – this time for the four years of the parliament's lifetime, and Wallace, Finnie and Stephen appointed as ministers in the Scottish Executive. In electoral terms, the Liberal Democrats remain Scotland's fourth party but their continued role in the coalition has endorsed their credibility as a party of government.

In 1999 the Labour party suffered in the devolved assembly elections in Wales at the hands of Plaid Cymru (and to a lesser extent Liberal Democrat) advances into their heartlands. As a consequence Labour was denied the Assembly majority that was expected – the Liberal Democrats had 6 AMs elected. At first the Welsh Assembly government comprised of only the Labour minority but the downfall of First Minister Alun Michael, and his succession by Rhodri Morgan precipitated a 'partnership agreement' between

Labour and the Liberal Democrats signed in October 2000. Mike German, Liberal Democrat leader in the Assembly was made Deputy First Minister and Jenny Randerson became Minister for Culture and Sports.

It is hard to see what the Liberal Democrats in Wales received in return for governing with Labour – since the Welsh Assembly government has significantly less power than the Scottish Executive – apart from the thrill and credibility boost from being involved with sharing power. The pathway to Partnership in Wales was cleared by the events in Scotland. One insider told us: 'Plaid Cymru made the accusation that 'this is a deal made in London' . . . The irony being that the deal was very definitely born in Scotland'.

The Partnership agreement in Wales did cause some problems for the party. The obvious advantages of sharing power with Labour in the National Assembly being somewhat negated by the political reality in many areas of Wales where Liberal Democrat advances might best come at Labour's expense. For example, the Liberal Democrats are the opposition to Labour on Cardiff County council but partners in the Assembly building in the same city.

A leading member of the Assembly government coalition reflected on the changing dynamics in Welsh politics (and its likely impact on Westminster and Assembly elections) as a result of the agreement:

> Well we clearly say that we are an independent party, we work together where we can agree together and where we disagree we fight separately. At the moment we have this partnership that applies only in terms of Wales, it does not apply in terms of the Westminster election. Also we have a very powerful line against the Conservatives. The Conservatives say that they will not share power in Wales so the only time that they would ever be able to influence health, education or whatever, all these key services in Wales – is if they won 50% of the vote and so they have written themselves out of the key areas which are in people's mind at election time.

In 2003, the second Assembly elections saw Labour's fortunes improve. With 30 AMs, they now had sufficient representation to rule on their own, and announced their desire to do so. Nevertheless, future co-operation between Labour and the Liberal Democrats in Wales looks the most likely of all potential coalitions in the foreseeable future.

Co-operation with Labour in Scotland and Wales might have rebounded on the Liberal Democrats. In Scotland in particular, the secret of success was to allow the Liberal Democrats to claim the credit for popular policies (student fees, and pensions for example) and avoid the blame for policy disasters (for example the 2000 Scottish Qualifications Authority scandal). To this extent the coalition in Scotland has worked better for the Liberal Democrats than the party could have dreamed.

Liberal Democrats and the world after September 11

The terrorist attack on the twin towers of the World Trade Center in New York on September 11, 2001 changed the world of politics. One of its slight but definite effects was to alter the dynamics of British politics, as Labour and Conservative front benches found a common voice with the Republican government of President George W. Bush. The Liberal Democrats, on the other hand allowed themselves to be portrayed as sceptical – and sometimes horrified – onlookers on the war on terror.

The Liberal Democrat conference at Bournemouth in September 2001 was severely disrupted by the terror attacks in the USA. Many felt it was wrong for the party conference season to go ahead at all, and few would deny that the atmosphere of the Conference was eerie to say the least. The ambivalence surrounding the 2001 Conference and the Liberal Democrats' preoccupation with local politics, was brilliantly captured by the *Guardian* cartoonist Steve Bell – a sparsely attended debate complete with activists reading *Focus* newsletters with the parallel headlines 'World Ends Tomorrow' and 'Lib-Dems poised to take Norwich – can you help?'

Charles Kennedy, in his first post-election challenge, responded to the events of September 11 by reiterating the limits of the Liberal Democrat support for the Bush regime: 'We do a disservice to democracy itself if our only response is to simply meet terror with terror. We do nothing to protect all that we hold dear if we abandon, in the name of security, the very principles which the terrorists seek to destroy – liberty, democracy, diversity.'

Moreover, he claimed Britain's role in the deepening international crisis should be that of the USA's 'candid friend': 'standing shoulder to shoulder, but always there for the occasional cautionary tap on the shoulder'.

This unease with a perceived rush to judgement was to remain a feature of Liberal Democrat pronouncements on the war in Afghanistan the following winter. Moreover, when the attention of the US President and British Prime Minster turned to Saddam Hussein and Iraq, the Liberal Democrats under Kennedy defined themselves as the anti-war party. Against the advice of some in the party, Kennedy spoke to the anti-war protesters in their public rally at Hyde Park in February 2003. He claimed: 'There can be, as we stand, no just or moral case for war against Iraq.'

With public opinion in Britain undoubtedly anti-war at this stage, it seems odd then that the Liberal Democrats did not pick up more support in the opinion polls for their apparently populist stance. Furthermore, although their success in the 2003 local elections may have been given a fillip by widespread anti-war sentiment, there is little or no evidence that the national standing of the party or the leader has been improved dramatically. In fact this supports our analysis in Chapter 6, which suggests that having popular policies and leadership are a necessary but insufficient condition for success for the third party.

The Liberal Democrats in parliament

The electoral success of 1997 and 2001 had one slightly embarrassing consequence for the Liberal Democrats. They succeeded in making the Liberal Democrats look more like a middle-aged, middle-class, male party.

Of the 46 Liberal Democrat MPs elected in 1997, only 3, Jackie Ballard, Ray Michie and Jenny Tonge were women. In terms of candidates the Liberal Democrats had fielded a slate of 139 women candidates but clearly they had a problem with getting women adopted as prospective parliamentary candidates in winnable seats. Sandra Gidley's victory in the Romsey by-election of 2000, added to the cannon of female Liberal Democrats in parliament, but the 2001 General Election still saw only 5 women among the 52 elected Liberal Democrats. For the record, Ballard was defeated in Taunton and Michie retired from Westminster before the election, leaving Tonge as the sole female survivor from the 1997 General Election. Joining Tonge and Gidley were, Annette Brooke (Dorset Mid and Poole North), Patsy Calton (Cheadle), and Sue Doughty (Guildford).

A senior party officer highlighted a problem with the type of candidate that is selected in winnable seats for the Liberal Democrats. The search for credibility leads to 'local' candidates who have 'served their time' on various party bodies for a number of years.

> I would like to see us put less emphasis in selection of candidates on 'the local man'. It's quite understandable – it's the way we won in the past and it's very difficult to break the habit of a whole generation, but if we're going to get some bright big-hitters in parliament, we're going to have to look a bit wider than that. Without imposing candidates on local parties, [we have to] somehow educate them that just being the local man isn't the be-all and end-all. We've got lots of able people in parliament, but in some of our seats less able people have been selected on the grounds that they are local.

It seems quite illustrative that the term this office holder used was 'local man' since the career paths of men and women make it much more likely that the time-servers with adequate resources to devote to long careers in municipal politics are male rather than female.

The 2002 Sex Discrimination (Election Candidates) Act aimed to increase the number of women in parliament and other elected bodies in Britain. Critically it legalised all-women shortlists as a short-cut to expedite the process. This had, of course been the tactic employed by Labour prior to

1997 to increase their total of female MPs, before being declared unlawful after a challenge in the courts. Despite the possibility of all-women shortlists, the Liberal Democrats seem set not to use them. The autumn Conference of 2001 witnessed a famous battle over the issue of women's representation, when a move to utilise all women lists was beaten via an alliance of old-fashioned libertarianism and the organised opposition of the Liberal Democrat Youth and Students. Struggling to strike the right note in the middle of an international crisis, the 2001 Conference had already created some confusing imagery for the media to digest. Now the prospect of the old guard of Liberal Democrat women on the one hand, and young female activists on the other at loggerheads over the 'illiberal' measures favoured by the old guard to increase women's representation in parliament, plunged the conference into the realms of the bizarre.

The party has used 'zipping' (matching the number of male and female candidates in adjacent constituencies) in European and devolved elections, to ensure more women become Liberal Democrat candidates, and set up the Gender Balance Task Force (GBTF) to address the issue of improving female representation among Liberal Democrats. However, given the intensity of the 2001 Conference debate, the whole issue remains a running sore in the party.

Anti-Conservative future?

Once of the critical decisions that the Liberal Democrats have to make in the near future, is a modern variant of the old realignment question. Having rejected equidistance and allied themselves to an anti-Conservative axis, the party may need to decide if these moves are irreversible. One MP told us that the ending of equidistance had made the relationship between the parties more 'honest' and that there ought to be no real prospect of propping up a future Conservative regime, whereas co-operation with Labour 'might always be an option':

A PPC for a target seat asserted: 'In some ways it was the Conservatives that got me into politics. So if it ever got to the point where I felt I no longer needed to fight that, maybe the need to be in politics would go.'

Yet on the whole, a Conservative recovery of some kind is more likely than unlikely and the party needs a plan for reacting to a Conservative comeback. As Don Macintyre wrote in 2001: 'Waiting for a hung parliament is about as sensible for opponents of the Tories as waiting for an asteroid to fall on Conservative Central Office. In every circumstance that a hung parliament is likely, a Conservative majority is likelier.'

The direction of the party forms a crucial element in Part III of the book, and will be looked at in closer detail in Chapter 8 where the role of equidistance and the definition of the Liberal Democrats as an anti-Conservative party – or otherwise – are dealt with explicitly.

Conclusion

Since 1992 the Liberal Democrats have enjoyed a prolonged period of growth and improved credibility. They have increased their representation in the 1997 and 2001 General Elections, (and saw their share of the vote increase at the 2001 election as well) so that it is the most successful third party in electoral terms since the 1920s, despite the squeeze from the main parties' drive towards the centre ground. The party has consolidated its position in local governance, has joined in coalition government in Wales and Scotland, been involved with serious talk of a realignment of British politics, survived the loss of a popular leader and the safe installation of a successor, and has carved out a set of popular policies as their own. These achievements are considerable, especially since the pressure from the electoral system, and from the media's obsession with the two main parties, seems to work against the Liberal Democrats. Moreover the party has profited from adopting a political strategy that might seem counterintuitive from the perspective of the mainstream political science literature that tends to stress a political party's natural tendency to centralise.

3

The party machine: the organisational structure of the Liberal Democrats

> The Liberal Democrats exist to build and safeguard a fair, free and open society, in which we seek to balance the fundamental values of liberty, equality and community, and in which no-one shall be enslaved by poverty, ignorance or conformity. We champion the freedom, dignity and well-being of individuals, we acknowledge and respect their right to freedom of conscience and their right to develop their talents to the full. We aim to disperse power, to foster diversity and to nurture creativity. We believe that the role of the state is to enable all citizens to attain these ideals, to contribute fully to their communities and to take part in the decisions which affect their lives. (Preamble to the Liberal Democrats' Constitution (abridged))

This chapter examines the organisational structure of the Liberal Democrats exploring the party constitution, the nature of the federal party and the formal policy-making processes. The implications of devolution (and coalition) in Scotland and Wales, with the new levels of responsibility and resources they have brought to the organisational structure of the party, are addressed.

The aim of this chapter is to investigate the formal and informal structures of the party in order to assess their importance in the way the party functions. This chapter will pave the way for the next chapter, which analyses the dual identities of the Liberal Democrats – the grassroots and the leadership elite.

In this chapter we look as the 'federal' nature of the party – arguing that this is the result of an ideological commitment to community politics. Looking at the various tiers of the Liberal Democrats – the federal, the state, the regional and the local – it is possible to see the dispersal of power that is *designed* into the structure of the party. On the other hand the influence of the leadership and bureaucratic elite is evident in many of the federal institutions of the party. Managing the tension between the influence of the base and the apex of the party is an everyday challenge for the Liberal Democrats. The preamble of the constitution champions two strands of liberalism – individuality and community – that impact upon the organisational structure of the party.

Federalism and the Liberal Democrats

With the merger of the Liberal and Social Democratic Parties in 1988, the managerial structure of the SDP was synthesised with the Liberal ethos of independence from the leadership. This synthesis was the basis of the constitution drawn up for the new party, the party that came to be called the Liberal Democrats.

The most obvious feature of the organisational structure of the Liberal Democrats is the self-avowed federalism of the party. Ingle argued that the key feature of the organisation was its 'distinctive federal structure and its absolute commitment to participative politics' (1996, 114). Federalism is not a term that is widely understood in Britain. During the Thatcher years in particular, it almost came to represent almost the opposite of its meaning in Europe, as the Conservatives managed to get the word associated in the public's mind with 'big' government and the dominance of the interest of bigger countries over others. On the other hand, the Liberal Democrats do not shy away from using the term federalism, and are happy to describe themselves as a federal party from the outset.

In simple terms, federalism for the Liberal Democrats represents a kind of subsidiarity, a passing down of power to the smallest possible organisational unit, and a pyramidal power structure that sees the 'Federal party' as the apex of the party's organisation and a decision-making structure that sees conference as the sovereign policy-making body. Below the Federal party, are the party in the nations of the Britain, the regions of England, Scotland and Wales and the local constituency parties.

In formal terms there are four tiers of organisational structure that determine the way that the Liberal Democrats function as a party. Working from the base to the apex of the party, these tiers are the constituency based (local level), the sub-national (regional level), the national parties in Scotland, Wales and England (state level), and the British party (the federal level).

Local parties

Local parties are the smallest organisation unit of the Liberal Democrats. Members are normally mandated to join the party at the local level ('in the area of which the member lives, works or studies' as the constitution has it). They are usually constituency-based units – although constituencies may combine if there are fewer than 30 members per local party. The larger the local party the more power it can exert. The larger the membership figures, the more delegates to party conference the local unit is entitled to. There are around 600 local parties.

Officially the objective of a local party is to secure election for Liberal Democrat candidates to Westminster, the Scottish parliament, the National Assembly for Wales, the European parliament, and local councils. Local parties are responsible for contacting, recruiting and renewing members. They take part in the policy formation process of the party, and in line with the ethos of the party to campaign and work with local people.

Regional parties

The next level of the formal structure of the party comprises the regional parties. In England there are 11 regions – Devon and Cornwall, Western Counties, London, Eastern England, Southern Central, and South East England, East Midlands, West Midlands, the North West, Northern England and Yorkshire and Humberside.

Scotland is divided into eight regions – Central Scotland, Mid Scotland and Fife, City of Glasgow, North East Scotland, Highlands and Islands, Lothian, South of Scotland, and West of Scotland.

There are four regional administration units in the party in Wales; North Wales, Mid and West Wales, South West Wales (East) and South West Wales (Central).

State parties

The party in Scotland

Devolution in Scotland has given a fresh impetus to the Scottish branch of the Liberal Democrats, evident not just in the party's coalition potential in Scotland but also in the party in Scotland's organisational structure.

The party in Scotland has a president, a leader (who constitutionally must be a MSP), and deputy leader (who must be a Westminster based MP for a Scottish seat) that are all distinct from the offices of the same name in the federal party. Other office bearers in the Scottish Liberal Democrats are the positions of convener, policy convener, conference convener, campaigns and candidates convener and treasurer.

The Scottish Liberal Democrats have their own executive committee consisting of the eight office bearers plus eight members elected by the Scottish Liberal Democrat conference, parliamentary representatives from the European parliament, Westminster and the Scottish parliament plus two representatives for each of the eight Scottish regions. Members of the Scottish SAOs and AOs can attend in a non-voting capacity. (See below for a discussion of the role of associated organisations.)

The Scottish Executive Committee has the permissive authority to appoint sub-committees where it sees fit, but also has the formal power to oversee the work of the official party bodies, where members of the executive sit as chairs of the business committee, campaigns and candidates committee, conference committee, and policy committee.

There are then, parallel paths of power for the Scottish party. Firstly, there is the dedicated Scottish bureaucracy outlined above, but at the same time the Scottish party is represented in the heart of the Federal party. The Scottish Executive also has representation on the main committees of the party – the federal executive, the campaigns and candidates committee, the conference committee, the policy committee, equal opportunities and the finance and administration committee.

The impact of devolution in Scotland has transformed the relationship that the Scottish Liberal Democrats have with the rest of the federal party. Moreover, sharing power with Labour in Scotland has given an edge to the decision-making structures of the Scottish party, and has created the potential for conflict with the federal party. In government, parties have to react quickly to issues, which may not be easy if the party is designed to reach decisions through complex and formal policy-making bodies. Furthermore instant policy decisions in Scotland might contradict the less immediate policy of the Federal party in opposition. The first Labour–Liberal Democrat coalition in Scotland did create some controversy over fishery issues and genetically modified crops when the Scottish Executive adopted policies that appeared at odds with official Liberal Democrat policy for example.

A leading party official played down this potential tension and argued that the federal nature of the party neutralises this tension:

> I'd argue that the Scottish Party should only be making policy on things that are matters for the Scottish Parliament, and so we federally shouldn't be saying anything about that. This is of course becoming an issue with regard to differences between different parts of the UK, I'm quite keen to argue and I think this should be the Lib-Dem position that we will say different things in different parts of the country for different local circumstances.

Nevertheless, the same official did concede that the Federal party's line was being tempered by the reality of being involved in government in both Scotland and Wales: 'You can probably see in the GM debate differences in opinion between the compromise positions in Scotland and Wales and perhaps the more hard line that the Federal party might choose to take.'

The party in Wales

Just as in Scotland, the constitution of the Welsh Liberal Democrats provides the party with its own party officers – president, vice president, leader of the

Welsh Liberal Democrats and leader of the parliamentary group. Other officers who serve on the Welsh National Executive are the leader of the Liberal Democrats in the National Assembly, the treasurer, secretary, membership officer, as well as nine elected members, one local authority representative, two youth and student SAO representatives, one delegate from the Liberal Democrat assembly group, one Westminster MP, and the chair of the sub-committees of the executive.

The executive oversees the work of the following committees, policy, candidates, finance and administration, campaigns and elections, and conference committee, and has like its Scottish counterpart has representation on the federal party committees as well.

The party in England

The regions provide the party with membership for the English council but according to the party's constitution, and in contrast to the policy-making potential of the Scottish and Welsh branches of the party which are charged with 'placing the policies of the Federal party in a Scottish context' and 'the co-ordination of the Welsh contribution to the to policy work of the Federal Party': 'all English policy-making powers are passed up to the Federal party'.

The sovereign body of the English party is the English Council (EC), which meets bi-annually to oversee the administration and accounts of the party in England. Between meetings of the EC, the party is managed by the English Council Executive (ECE). Membership of the council and executive is determined by regional representation, election and appointment. The EC is charged by the constitution to co-ordinate and facilitate the activities of the English regional parties. There may have been an important change here. Writing in 1996, Ingle felt that there was a tension between the regions and state parties due to 'the preponderant size and financial strength of the English party' (Ingle, 1996, 129).

Furthermore, he commented that: 'From a Scottish perspective the Federal party is frequently perceived as synonymous with the English State party' (Ingle, 1996, 129). However, devolution has effected an organisational strengthening of the parties in Scotland and Wales, and given the formal passing up of policy-making powers in England to the federal party it was noteworthy that we encountered some envy from the English regional parties towards their counterparts in Scotland and Wales.

The Federal party

The Federal party is the apex of the Liberal Democrats' organisation. It is responsible for the determination of party policy and strategy, and preparation for elections to the parliaments in Westminster and Brussels, Luxembourg and Strasbourg. It is also responsible for media liaison and international relations. If the Federal party is the power base of the party, it is telling that its source of power is fairly elusive and ambiguous. It is instructive to note that the party's constitution permits the Federal Party to also: 'do anything else which is incidental to its functions'.

The Federal Executive

The Federal Party is responsible for overseeing a number of committees. The most important of these is probably the Federal Executive (FE). Formally the FE comprises the party leader, the party president (as chair), the three vice-presidents, two MPs, one peer, one MEP, two councillors, three representatives from the state parties, plus a number (one more than the number of appointments) of elected members, chosen at the party conference. One election agent we spoke to argued that the FE was essential to the workings of the party and described it as the Liberal Democrats' 'central nervous system'.

The Federal Policy Committee

Officially party policy is drawn up by the bi-annual party conference but co-ordinated and refined by the Federal Policy Committee (the FPC). The FPC has three basic constitutional roles; the researching and development of policy, preparation of the General Election manifestos, and the institution of occasional policy working groups. As such, it is possibly the most influential body within the party.

The FPC is chaired by a chosen MP and comprises the leader, MPs representing seats from Scotland, Wales and England, parliamentarians from the House of Lords and the European Parliament, the president, councillors, state party representatives and a raft of members elected by the federal conference.

A party which sees its conference as the supreme policy-making body and allows conference to elect a plurality of members to its important bureaucratic committees might be viewed as 'too democratic' to function effectively. A member of the Leader's staff implied that the democratic nature of the party was sometimes frustrating for policy-makers. Before the institution of a national minimum wage by the incoming Labour government in 1997, the Liberal Democrats were committed only to implementing a regionally variable rate. This policy seemed unnecessarily cautious as soon as the minimum wage was brought in. Plans to amend the policy were leaked to the press which led to some upset from members of the party's official policy-making bodies not that the decisions taken were wrong, but that that the proper channels had not be used. As one strategist recalled:-

> A story appeared in [a national newspaper] that FPC had approved a change of policy [whereas in fact] FPC had never discussed it. You can imagine there was some tension when it came to the next FPC meeting. We got the change through, but any major change like that the FPC does has to be approved by conference in the next report of the FPC, so we had a short debate on it in Plymouth in 2000 and you really felt that was a bit of a problem that the system wasn't able to move with the times easily. But by and large the democratic elements of the structure are very helpful because they ensure that you end up with something that the people are prepared to go out and campaign on and are happy with and it's a good message to send to the rest of the country. So that's the opportunity really, the challenge is the slowness of it.

The Federal Conference Committee

Party conference is the supreme policy-making body in the Liberal Democrats' organisation. It meets twice a year and delegates with voting rights are sent from each local party, the parliamentary parties, officers of the party and adopted candidates. The Federal Conference Committee oversees the administration of the conference. This committee is made up from the party president, the chief whip, one representative from each of the state parties, two elected representatives from the FE, two from the FPC, the Federal Chief Executive and one member of staff from the party, and 12 members elected by the Federal Conference.

Other FE committees

Two subordinate committees of the FE the Finance and Administration Committee (FAC) and the Campaign and Communications Committee (CCC) are often said to be less formal but are just as formidable bases of power in the party. The FAC is responsible for the budgeting of the party and ensures the party complies with the regulations of the 2000 Political Parties, Elections, Referendums Act.

The finances of the Liberal Democrats have been centralised since the merger between the Liberal and Social Democratic parties. The centralisation remains the cause of much distrust from the local party activist base. One long serving party worker in a Liberal heartland constituency caricatured the antipathy felt by many local party workers and the central party. '"Cowley Street, load of idiots who can't keep the membership records correctly, who keep phoning us when we don't want to be phoned, send us inappropriate literature. And then Cardiff are just as bad." The day that attitude changes Montgomeryshire will not be Montgomeryshire I can assure you.'

To many, the FAC represents the triumph of the centre of the party over the local level, and is a continuing source of resentment from the local activist base. As one MP told us: 'Around the country, grassroots object to Cowley Street – membership phone canvassing for money and things like that, but Cowley Street will tell you that for every person they upset, they get loads of quids in from others. So it's a question of trying to avoid upsetting anybody.'

However, relations between the centre and the party at large have improved from the early days of the new party. In 1989 a motion of no-confidence in the party's financial management structures was only defeated after a recount and the dawning realisation that the entire Federal Executive would be forced to resign if the motion was passed (Ingle, 1996, 115). While the *Ashdown Diaries* reveal that Ashdown's election as leader of the new party was nearly hijacked by a visit from the Inland Revenue intent on closing Cowley Street for non-payment of National Insurance contributions (Ashdown, 2000, 5).

The Campaign and Communications Committee (CCC)

The party's Campaign and Communications Committee (CCC) was designed to co-ordinate policy making, and the party's campaign strategy (Brack, 1996, 96), although it is not the sole party body that seems to have a campaign remit. The CCC was responsible for the concentration on the five Es (electoral reform, environment, Europe, economic policy, and education) in the run-up to the 1992 General Election (Ingle, 1996, 117) although the chair of the party's Communications and Campaigns Committee in the 1992 and 1997 general elections (Nick Harvey MP) had a less significant input into the running of those campaigns than the General Election managers Des Wilson in 1992 and Lord Richard Holme in 1997.

Specified Associated Organisations

Beneath the local parties there is an extra tier of organisation in the party called the Specified Associated Organisations (SAOs). These are recognised sub-groups that are resourced officially through the party centrally, and through their own fundraising activities. The eight official SAOs are Ethnic Minority Liberal Democrats (EMLD), Youth and Students (LDYS), Women Liberal Democrats (WLD), the Association of Liberal Democrat Councillors (ALDC), Liberal Democrats for Lesbian, Gay, Bisexual and Transgender Equality (DELGA), the Parliamentary Candidates Association (PCA), Agents and Organisers, and the Association of Liberal Democrat Trade Unionists (ALDTU). The influence of the SAOs is hard to map – indeed Ingle's (1996) otherwise excellent pictorial illustration of the formal structure of the party omitted their role completely – but two in particular are worthy of further investigation, the ALDC and the LDYS.

The ALDC

The strongest SAO is probably the Association of Liberal Democrat Councillors (ALDC). As well as providing a recruiting ground for prospective parliamentary candidates, agents and key local activists, the ALDC might be said to encapsulate the community politics ethos in the party. According to one 2001 PPC and ALDC member the Association: 'serves to keep the party's local roots in the forefront of the minds of those in the parliamentary party'. The ALDC is based in Hebden Bridge in Yorkshire. This in itself is important because it formalises the difference (and distance) between London and the organisation. The ALDC seems to fill a number of functions for the party, offering campaigning assistance to local parties, and training and support structures for Councillors once elected. One MP seemed to believe that the strength of the organisation lies in its campaigning activities.

> It's not compulsory for councillors to belong to it, it's voluntary membership and the ALDC get a grant from the party nationally and they get membership subscriptions from members. It's actually the Association of Liberal Democrat Councillors and Campaigners, so it's not just councillors; it's also lots of activists. I still belong to it now, but I'm not a councillor.

As such the ALDC is a very powerful organisation, as it has become part of the mainstream bureaucracy of the party as well as offering a reminder to the main party of the community politics roots of many of the activists.

As another MP pointed out, 'Most of us in the parliamentary party have seats built on local government success; most of the '97 intake were councillors previously and most of them were on councils that we were running. [There are] very few MPs who haven't won the local council, a few exceptions, but very few.' The ALDC, because of its heritage – the Association of Liberal Councillors being the campaigning wing of the Liberal party – has highlighted a structural tension between the old and new structures of the party. One party official, who admitted to feeling sceptical about the role of the ALDC confided:

> It really comes from the days of ALC, because it has got its feet under the table of so many things. It has representatives on the CCC, as do other groups, but the ALDC has a very strong presence in a lot of that sort of stuff, and it will never be taken away. We've got this two-pronged campaigning structure where we have the campaigns department in London, which deals with parliamentary elections and principally deals with MPs in target seats. Then you've got ALDC in the north that deals with council elections. We talk to each other and we exchange things with each other but we do operate as two rather separate beasts.

One council leader summed up the philosophy of community politics as central to their vision of what the Liberal Democrats should be about, and saw the work of the ALDC as vital to maintaining that philosophy:

> I was a founder member of the Association of Liberal Councillors as it then was, I've been with them ever since. The ALDC represents where the Liberals are coming from; that we are very much a grassroots party, a community-based party. We believe in local communities, we are strongly against the dead hand of traditional municipal socialism which treats everybody the same and tries to impose top down solutions.

Clearly a national party designed to move to catch-all status on the Kirchheimer (1966) 'catch-all' model is likely to 'nationalise' its policy profile and increasingly concentrate power in the leadership. The community politics ethos that permeates the Liberal Democrats, and in particular the work of the ALDC, dilutes any centralising tendency in the party.

The LDYS

The Liberal Democrat Youth and Students (LDYS) is the only SAO that is allowed to function outside the party – members can join the LDYS without officially joining the party – although due to the payment structure of the organisation this is very rare.

It is illuminating to see the extent of assistance from the central party that the LDYS is in receipt of. An office holder with the LDYS told us:

> A lot of our funding comes from the party. We get a lot of expertise from the party – they come in and support what we are doing. In turn that's created a lot of expertise. The party runs training for trainers, so almost all of the (LDYS) executive are accredited trainers. We go and train all round the country, keeping people enthused.
>
> It is a very good relationship [we have with the party]; we get money, we get expertise. In return we give a lot back. We've got PPCs in place who are members of the LDYS, we've got agents who are in LDYS. As a proportion, far more of us work for the party than people in the general membership of the party.

The LDYS has particular challenges – especially concerning recruitment and retention, and it is probably for the reason of encouraging young people under the age of 26 to stay in the party, that the LDYS has such a privileged position on so many committees. A member of the LDYS executive informed us:

> More than the party generally, we suffer from a very high turnover. When you're wandering around the Fresher's Fair you'll join anything. And people do move on after that year. We do have that problem but we also recruit much faster than the rest of the party.
>
> We must be important to the party because local parties are massively committed to us. They are all desperate to have a branch. Young people are playing individual roles on committees across the country. Every local executive has to have an under 26-year-old on the committee if they can find one.

The LDYS pride themselves on being able to initiate policy for the party at large as well as for the youth sections of the party. They are granted assistance to tailor literature to a youthful audience and the party encourages the LDYS to develop its own identity. In return the LDYS have a remarkable level of access to the leadership elite of the Liberal Democrats.

> The Liberal Democrats are much more open than the other parties. We've got far more potential to say what we think. And that doesn't just go for LDYS that goes for anyone in the party. But the LDYS – have major policy input at federal conferences. And local parties get delegates on the basis of members they have got at a conference and we get exactly the same quotas. So we've got people here who we can propose policy, and amendments to policy.

Associated Organisations

Below the SAOs in the party machine are the Associated Organisations (AOs). The recognised AOs are the Association of Liberal Democrat Engineers and Scientists, DAGGER – the organisation for the promotion of electoral reform, Green Liberal Democrats, the Christian Forum, the Liberal Democrat European Group, the Peace Group, and the Liberal International British Group.

Unlike the SAOs, AOs do not receive resources from the central party, but they are granted certain rights and privileges. For instance they are likely to be consulted by the party if a policy document infringes on their field of interest. One organiser of a particular AO revealed that the lack of support structure from the party can be a source of frustration.

> I suppose there is informal support, but in general terms there is no support, we can use meeting rooms in party headquarters but that is about it. We are not an official SAO and I'm a bit confused by what this AO business means. When a SAO has a special status in the party but an AO just seems to have a special title within the party, but no status. It is actually a little bit of a 'bugbear' of ours at the moment. I can see an argument for a SAO being restricted to organisations that reflect a certain grouping in the party, whether it is women, ethnic minorities, gays, whatever and that would be fine if we didn't have ALDC which are a SAO just by their sheer weight and size. And you know it would split the party into pieces if ALDC was ever told, 'You can't be a SAO', it's so big and powerful, that already sets a precedent for other sorts of organisations to be SAOs, so where do you draw the line and I think that has become, as people begin to question it, it's getting quite vague and there are moves around to change the whole structure.

Other sources of influence in the party

The final layer of the party to consider here are the unofficial sources of party power that might be found in intra-party pressure groups and non-specified organisations. Less specific still but even harder to map is the influence of various party outpourings. Members receive the weekly *Liberal Democrat News* and subscribers can receive daily email briefings from the Liberal Democrat website.

From the less formal strands of the party, it is worth pointing to the work of two publications that have an influential role in measuring the temperature of the party at any given time. The *Reformer*, the magazine of the think tank, the Centre for Reform (CfR). The CfR proclaims itself 'an independent, free thinking forum for new ideas and progressive debate' although its personnel are drawn predominantly from the ranks of the Liberal Democrats. The *Reformer* a quarterly publication tends to concern itself with strategic questions about the future of liberal matters such as the viability of attracting Conservative voters to the Liberal Democrats.

Liberator is far less glossy than The *Reformer* but perhaps just as important. Styling itself the 'UK-based magazine of liberal political thought and news' and 'a forum for debate among radical liberals in all parties and none'. Established in 1970 it is still run by a collective who promote the publication's less professional ethos. It has a commentary editorial that tends to plug straight into the activist mindset and *Liberator* continues to provide a crucial rallying point for the grassroots and radical liberal wing of the party capable of articulating an important counterbalance to the professional elite of the party.

Who controls the party?

Given the formal structure of the party, and the clear organisational framework imposed by the party's constitution, it might seem strange to say that it is not altogether clear who effectively controls the party. Formally the party conference has the last say on policy but day-to-day management of policy is left to FPC, and FPC is staffed by individuals who resemble people with elite like qualifications. Moreover in non-policy terms it is often very difficult to assess were power resides. Looking at the Liberal Democrat party in the run up to the 2001 General Election, it was difficult to isolate the leadership elite: This may be because the party remains relatively small and a few people can exert significant influence but it might also mean that the heart of the party does not reside in the formal structure of the party. In the run-up to the 2001 General Election campaign, it was very difficult to ascertain who did what and how. This task was not made easier by the tendency for potential elites to have confusing or overlapping job descriptions. For instance in the Leader's Office, Lord Dick Newby was Charles Kennedy's Chief of Staff. Dr Richard Grayson was Director of Policy – and was the principal author of the 2001 General Election manifesto. Former journalist, David Walter was the party's Chief Executive, Lord Chris Rennard was Campaigns and Elections Director but Lord Tim Razzall was nominally in charge of the General Election campaign. Clearly, establishing a cadre of highly professional Liberal Democrat elites is significantly less difficult than differentiating the input of individuals. The leader has considerable scope to influence the party but so do other members of the leadership elite.

As one MP told us the formal structure of the party is fairly straightforward: 'Who makes the decisions? Well [Federal] Policy Committee and the general election team and the MPs and key councillors. There's the leader of the Scots and the Welsh and the European Parliament and the House of Lords. All of these people come together.'

Whilst undeniably true in the strictest sense, the overlap of key personnel in the party makes it unclear whether power in the party rests in the institutions or the individuals who fill the key positions. One leading MP told us that regardless of the formal structure of the party, power in the Liberal Democrats really resides with an often-overlooked faction of the party – the Liberal Democrats in parliament. Moreover the MP argued that with an unprecedented number of MPs in Westminster, the parliamentary party holds a *de facto* power of veto over the design of policy that simply does not exist constitutionally.

> The policy process is theoretically the prerogative of the party policy committee out of the conference. But in fact, it is negotiated between the parliamentarians and the policy committee. At the end of the day, the policy committee has the say, but there's an intent to make sure that the MPs are in accord [with the policy]. We're the people that are going to have to deliver the message and if we don't believe it's credible, then it's wrong.

Indeed for all of his domination of the party, it is clear from his *Diaries* that some of Ashdown's most uncomfortable moments came not with the defeats at conference, or in formal FPC meetings, but often at the weekly parliamentary party meetings. The dramatic increase in size of the parliamentary party since 1997 has done nothing to diminish its effective power. Moreover, a senior party strategist seemed to say that Ashdown's initial power over the parliamentary party was the result of Westminster dynamics in the early 1990s. Having such a small parliamentary group meant that Ashdown could more easily be the dominant voice. In contrast Kennedy had to deal with a new dynamic, a bigger parliamentary party that had developed a hunger for flexing their muscles: 'Charles has got far more MPs to start with, it's easier to lead a small group of 20 and stamp your mark on them, than it is a group of 47. And he's probably much more of a team person. So Charles will probably work with other people, play to their strengths and do more, whereas Paddy was more one man band-ish.'

Conclusion

This chapter has attempted to open up for analysis the divides between the formal and informal structures of the Liberal Democrats. It has assessed the formal, federal design of the party from the local party through to the federal party via the regional and state levels, but has also highlighted the less formal routes of influence through the SAO/AO organisations, the role of the leadership and of the parliamentary party.

In the next chapter we will further explore the dual identity of the Liberal Democrats and suggest that there is a perpetual tension between the various layers of the party. We will attempt to demonstrate this by evaluating the conflict between the elite and mass level of the party in terms of decision-making and policy outcomes.

4

Dual identities: grassroots versus leadership elite

The aim of this chapter is to explore further the duality of the Liberal Democrats, in particular the tension between the activist base and the central party. It will explore the apparent paradox of a tradition of 'community politics' and the increased professionalism in the party, and the possibility of conflict between these dual forces. It will use case study illustrations of these dual identities – the controversy surrounding the naming of the new party in 1988, and the party's reaction to 'the Project' (see Chapter 2) are used to illustrate the limits of leadership power in the party; while the issue of European integration is used to highlight the tension between the edicts of the central party and the grassroots.

Their performance in the 2001 General Election and 2003 local elections notwithstanding, the Liberal Democrats are a small party, and as such the party's key identity depends to a large extent upon its leadership. According to a senior party strategist, Paddy Ashdown's 'credit rating' was such that he was able to force his 'project' on the party 'despite their natural wariness and suspicion'. This 'top-down' approach is consistent with the mainstream literature on party organisation and party systems (see Panebianco, 1988; Taagepera and Shugart, 1989; Katz and Mair, 1994, 1995; Lijphart, 1994; Mair, 1994) that suggests that modern political parties find the pressure to centralise irresistible.

On his succession to the party leadership in August 1999, Charles Kennedy needed to be mindful of the sensibilities of the party at large. Indeed it seems illustrative that in a hustings speech during the 1999 leadership campaign he told the assembled audience that: 'Leaders have to lead, but they also have to listen.'

While the tendency to catch-all status 'nationalises' political parties (Kirchheimer, 1966) the Liberal Democrats remain regionally disparate, fighting both Conservative and Labour parties in a series of micro-contests. Their best hope of challenging Conservative and Labour parties relies on the dual identity of national leadership on the one hand and 'pavement politics' on the other. This is particularly important in view of the 'credibility gap', which means that a party placed third nationally must build on local bases of support in order to achieve increases in parliamentary representation (see Chapter 7). Cox (1997) suggests third parties can break through at the local rather than the national level by establishing strong community networks and organisations. Liberal Democrats might resist Duverger's law ('the simple majority single ballot system favours the two party system', 1954, 217) by forging links with local communities.

The grassroots are widely perceived to be crucial for the party's health but, as we saw in the previous chapter, there are potential tensions between mass and elite levels. However, Brack declares that the Liberal Democrats are virtually unique in finding the source of their radicalism from the leadership rather than the membership (Brack, 1996, 99). One MP asserted that the Ashdown era epitomised a power struggle within the party that was dominated by the sheer force of the leader's personality:

> Our party tends to default towards pavement politics; towards fixing the streetlights and the cracks in the pavement . . . Once in a while we do get individuals who come along who can galvanise the whole party, but it's interesting to note when that happens, the party can get scared. The party was scared of Ashdown's very clear vision to lead us towards government and towards co-operating with government and he had a virtually 24–hour, 7–days a week struggle to maintain the party's confidence.

In terms of formal structure, power lies in the federal nature of the party (see Chapter 3). Informally, however, it is less clear where real power rests. When asked whether the party was a bottom-up or top-down organisation, many interviewees were genuinely unsure if the party could fit either, neither or both models. One PPC stressed the formal and informal bases of power:

> I'm under no illusions that the leader controls the party. We have a federal executive but ultimately one person has to take a decision. But in terms of the general flow of policy in terms of our behaviour, our attitudes, our culture, the heart of the party – that rests with the party conference and beyond that in the hearts of the people who go out delivering leaflets on a cold, wet day.

This duality has implications for how constituency parties organise and campaign. In effect the Liberal Democrats face a battle on two fronts and a series of micro-contests – the Conservatives forming the main opposition in most areas, Labour in others (see Chapter 8). This can prove problematic but the professional approach and the assistance offered by the party centrally was widely appreciated. At the grassroots level some constituencies were found to be very reliant on a small number of individuals and outside help was welcome. Ultimately, the relationship between centre and grassroots is reciprocal, with the leadership acting as a figurehead for the party more widely, giving personality and direction, yet answerable to the grassroots, with

Cowley Street offering campaign advice and resources. As one agent put it: 'I think the strength of the party – and also the weakness – is the fact that the party centrally has got a lot of power, but it doesn't get that power without the grass roots . . . That's what I like about the party, it's not afraid of saying the leadership is wrong.'

New institutional arrangements have introduced another potential arena for conflict between the different levels of the party. As we saw in Chapter 3, coalition in Scotland and Wales has meant the party is forced to make hard choices on key policy issues that can impact at the local level. The continuing professionalisation of the party is likely to further stretch this relationship between the organisational centre and the interests of the local parties. The ability to bring cohesion and achieve peaceful coexistence between the different sides of this power struggle (although not necessarily uniformity) remains a key challenge for the Liberal Democrat leadership.

The name debate

As we saw in Chapter 2, the merger between the former Alliance partners in the Liberal and Social Democratic parties was traumatic to say the least. A key feature of the difficult birth of the party was the new party's choice of name. From a desire to please both Liberal and SDP members, the party had been formed under the title 'Social and Liberal Democrats', but shortly afterwards Paddy Ashdown, the newly elected leader, pushed the party into accepting the single term 'Democrats' as its official name. However, disaffected Liberals continued to campaign for the retention of the old 'Liberal' label. In a footnote in his *Diaries* Ashdown admits he misjudged the mood – and the resilience of – the old Liberal party: 'I underestimated people's sense of insecurity about losing their old parties, and especially the importance of the 'Liberal' name and tradition. This debate, which on the surface was about the name, was in reality, about our identity and both dominated and disrupted the first year of the new Party' (Ashdown, 2000, 11).

In retrospect the process that resulted in the party changing its name again – to the Liberal Democrats – might have seemed unnecessarily painful at best and foolhardy at worst. However, the resistance from old Liberals to a name that did not include the word 'Liberal' meant that the issue was kept live for months and months. With significant proportions of the parliamentary party making it known that they were to declare themselves 'Liberal Democrats' unilaterally, Ashdown worked hard to assert the constitutional requirements before another name change could occur. On one occasion, Ashdown's Deputy leader – Alan Beith – threatened to resign the whip if permission to use the nomenclature 'Liberal Democrat' was denied him. In response, Ashdown threatened to resign as leader if the constitutional process was not properly observed.

> By now it was clear that, despite the decisions taken by the party conference last year to adopt the short title 'Democrats', the issue of the name was still an open sore. I had privately come to accept that we would probably adopt the name 'Liberal Democrats', but this had to be done through the Party's proper procedures. It could not be imposed on the Party unilaterally by the MPs, if more splits were not to be opened up. It was this question of process that now became the main issue of contention among MPs. (Ashdown, 2000, 51)

This is instructive since Ashdown, with his talk of 'an open sore', 'proper procedures' and 'this question of process', had come to appreciate that the membership of the party had a particular hold over the newly formed party – and that the party elite needed to demonstrate due respect to the procedural features of the new party.

The leadership

The clear impression from the legacy of Ashdown's leadership is that he dominated the party. In particular, Ashdown came to be seen as the party personified, a perception which both increased his power and rank and file suspicion of his role. MacIver pointed out that electorally Ashdown was the party's trump card: 'The promotion of the leader was simply a reflection of the wholehearted belief within the party that Paddy Ashdown was their strongest asset' (MacIver, 1996, 183–4).

Nevertheless his first significant act as leader – to adopt a name – was slowly pulled to the ground by the vestiges of the old Liberal activist base that had support all the way up the chain of command to the Deputy Leader. Furthermore, this was not to be the last time that Ashdown's leadership was undermined by the rank and file. His reactions to policy defeats at conference in 1994 on cannabis decriminalisation and the minimum wage suggest that he never really got the taste for this particular medicine.

Ashdown: 'running the party as much as leading it'

Between 1992 and 1999, Paddy Ashdown dominated the Liberal Democrats. MacIver (1996) devised a typology of Liberal Democrat strategies during the 1990s that claimed that the important strategic decisions that the Liberal Democrats needed to take were dependent on attitudes to realignment (long march versus quick fix) and the conception of the party (centrist or radical). Ashdown, MacIver asserted, was likely to be a 'quick-fix radical' (MacIver, 1996, 176), which might explain his ability to appeal to both fundamentalist and pragmatist tendencies in the party simultaneously. In the same anthology, McKee felt that Ashdown had united the Liberal Democrats in a way that few others might have done. Almost out of gratitude for their delivery from the dark days of 1988 Ashdown enjoyed the wholehearted support of most of the party (McKee, 1996, 167). A senior party official who believed that Ashdown's approach to politics was the epitome of brinkmanship supported this view.

> Paddy Ashdown's leadership was characterised by building up a huge amount of credit with the activists by going to all the back-waters and talking to them, stroking them, and spending a lot of time at by-elections and so on. And every now and then just spending all his credits in one go by talking to Tony Blair and agreeing something and then he'd build up all the credit all over again.

Another party strategist gave the following assessment of Ashdown's control over the party.

> Paddy was so hands on as leader, that I would actually characterise his leadership as being Paddy largely running the party as well as leading it, because he spent a long time in his first years as leader attending so many of the party committees, making all the key appointments that would be made in the party in terms of members of staff or personally writing or rewriting manifestos.
>
> But he may have wanted to move the party in a way where ultimately the party wouldn't let him. He was keener on more aggressively selling the case for us being part of a coalition with Labour and ultimately I think he perhaps realised that that parliamentary party would have to have some say in this, as would the party at large, not necessarily in any party committee, but you couldn't buck a trend in the party completely. You don't have a free hand as Lib-Dem leader. But he ran it as much as led it.

The interesting thing about both of these assessments is that as well as underlining Ashdown's domination of the party; his scope for pushing through what he wanted; they also clearly demonstrate the limits of his power.

The end of the line: the Project and Ashdown's legacy

Several of our interviewees drew a line between the old style of leadership under Ashdown and the 'new' leadership of Kennedy, suggesting that the power of the leader stemmed as much from personality traits as from institutional guarantees. One MP spoke of the change in leadership style: 'Charles is far less anxious to control the whole agenda than Paddy was, but Charles has only been leader for a short time, and 5 years down the line he might be a control freak as well.'

We certainly found evidence that Ashdown's project of closer relations with Labour had caused discomfort in the party at large. One council leader, based in northern England, felt uneasy with the entire project:

> [Liberal Democrats in the south are] not used to seeing Labour as unacceptable. They're used to seeing a benign, third party, Labour party. Leading councillors in places like Oldham and Liverpool and Sheffield, have to punch above our weight to make sure the party doesn't get into bed with Labour and we were constantly telling Paddy – 'You're getting too close. In areas like ours it's the kiss of death because we've been fighting these people for a generation, you don't understand what they're like.'

Reflecting on the differences between the two Liberal Democrat leaders, one constituency activist told us: 'Paddy did pull us in certain directions, upset activists from time to time. That's what leaders are for and as long as they recognise when they've gone too far. Charles hasn't yet got the authority to do that.'

One election agent claimed that the Ashdown leadership was tempered by the need to keep activists on board but that he did not accept that the debates that many activists saw the necessary were good for the party. 'When Paddy was trying to convince us we all ought to be part of the Labour party or something, he didn't succeed totally. He had to take it step by step, and he had to put up with the rows and in the end of it we had a good debate and we had a better view of where we were going.'

Another leading councillor and candidate in the 2001 election highlighted a degree of resentment from the party's activist base during the Ashdown years:

> You always have to be humble in our party to actually go and explain to some people why you're doing some things. And it is to explain, not to ask their permission. I think Charles has been a lot better at that, than Paddy was in his last couple of years and that's no disrespect to him because that bloke dragged us from the brink of death in the opinion polls, didn't he? . . . If there's one thing Liberal Democrats like to know, they like to know what's going on, they get really worked up if they think something's going on and they don't know about it.

One PPC complained: 'Paddy lost the plot a bit, if a strong leader wishes to lead, you can only move as fast as the slowest troop and he moved (too quickly). He got his legs kicked from underneath him once or twice for trying to run.' Ashdown's *Diaries* make it clear that his resignation announcement in 1999 was not the result of a snap decision to retire (see Chapter 2). However, we did encounter a strong feeling in the party that Ashdown's stock had been diminished significantly by the lack of tangible results from the Project. In particular, Labour's decision not to act on the recommendations of the Jenkins Commission – or to honour their manifesto pledge to hold a referendum on electoral reform – seemed to have galvanised large sections of the party into further opposition to co-operation with Labour.

What we suggest then, is that just as the debacle over the naming of the new party in 1988 taught Ashdown the lesson that there were limits to his influence as party leader, this lesson was re-learnt in 1999. Ashdown may have felt that he had no further avenues to explore after the recommendations of the Jenkins Commission had been shelved, and this may have strengthened his determination to go, and to have influenced the timing of his departure.

The strength of activist base

So far we have collected a wealth of data that suggests that the party activist base could not be ignored by the Liberal Democrat leadership. There is a tendency to down play the role of activists in modern political parties. Membership studies of modern parties have noted the decreasing role of activism in modern British politics, and even where party memberships do not seem to be in terminal decline, a different type of party member – a less active membership has abounded (see Seyd and Whiteley, 1992; Whiteley *et al.* 1994; Whiteley and Seyd, 1999). However, our evidence suggests that the bottom line for the Liberal Democrat leadership is that the base of the party cannot be neglected.

We did find evidence to suggest that the Liberal Democrats had undergone a professionalisation of its membership, although many would reject the notion that the new professional membership was less active than their predecessors. One MSP admitted that the professionalisation of the party personnel might have been the legacy of the original merger between the Liberal and Social Democratic parties: 'To be taken seriously we have to be no longer a bunch of sandal wearing anarchists. I suppose there was the input of the SDP into the merged party, and although they were not that numerous, a fair number of them were prominent in the new party and they come from, you might say, the managerial wing of the sort of credit card and claret school of thought.'

Others concurred that the party had undergone a process of professionalisation at the edges of the party's decision-making core. In the run-up to the 2001 General Election, a senior party strategist asserted:

> One of the things that will be very different in this general election from the 1997 election, is that we have hugely more people working professionally paid for the party. In the past we always relied heavily on volunteers. And undoubtedly there are a number of people with a lot of experience who we will want to involve at the centre in the general election campaign. But we do, before we get them in, have a much bigger cadre of people who work professionally for the party.
>
> Our researchers, in particular, have a much better database of all kinds of research, on subject areas and what the other parties are doing in those areas,

> which we can use. On the other hand, [at] Tory Central Office you're talking about 200–300 employees. Here we're talking about 30 or 40. So there is a very big difference.

Although we found near consensus that the party was operating on a more 'professional' basis than in previous times, we also highlighted a continuing tension between the forces of professionalism and activism. Some interviewees even saw hostility to the centre as the defining characteristic of their Liberal activism. One election agent claimed: 'If we ever lose our ability to embarrass the leadership as a party, even when we are in government, then we won't be the Liberal party I joined.'

It would be unfair to paint a one-sided story here however. We have uncovered the potential for conflict between the local grassroots and the centre of the party, but overwhelmingly the local attitude to assistance from the centre is fairly positive.

The professionals: 'without Cowley Street, I would not have won'

In fact, locating the Liberal Democrat leadership elite is easier said than done. The constitution readily identifies the structure of the party but there are a series of parallel routes to influence in the party. With his secret talks with Labour forging ahead in the 1990s, Ashdown created an influential subcommittee of trusted advisers and strategists – the Jo Group (Ashdown, 2000, 278). The Jo Group managed to influence the course of British politics (not just Liberal Democrat) for a number of years without ever having to answer to the constitutional strictures of the party.

Nowhere is this move evident than in the role of election campaigning. Lord Chris Rennard – now the party's chief executive but more famous as the party's director of campaigns and elections – has a reputation as the most effective election campaigner in Britain today. The point here is that he is outside the parliamentary party and his power is hard to detect through a paper trail of the party's organisational structure. Rennard represents an informal power base that is invisible to the type of investigation carried out in Chapter 3 but is evident from a more qualitative exploration of the way the party is run.

One MP who won a seat for the first time in 1997 highlighted the benefit of the highly professional elite assisting the battle for seats at the local level:

> Without Cowley Street I would not have won, it's as simple as that. Not just the campaign itself; if anything, we'd won it before the campaign had started. It was in the two years beforehand, the training weekends at Peterborough for target seats and for agents, the briefing material, the constituency-wide questionnaires which they funded and had printed and all we had to do was put together and deliver – I mean that was a hell of a job, but I mean, you know, it was all that back-

> up and support. Also the fact the message went out that if we wanted to get a Lib-Dem MP in the region we ought to do as we were told. And because people trust our elections strategists, Rennard and Co. at Cowley Street, we played it by the book. People don't query – generally – his judgement because of his track record.

One strategist felt in no doubt that the campaigning wing of the party held the real power in the Liberal Democrats.

> Basically I think the balance lies primarily with the campaigners. Chris Rennard. I think that's primarily because they win the seats, they set the messages that are used to win the seats, which are then transformed into the parliament. I think there's a big force there now and I think in terms of the balance, Chris Rennard's gained a hell of a lot of power in recent years. '97 boosted his stock. Now he's running the whole general election campaign rather than just doing the campaign stuff. His power has developed tremendously and it amazing because he can say anything!

In fact this does Rennard an injustice since the Ashdown *Diaries* show that he felt able to express very forthright views as early as 1990. With the Eastbourne by-election looming, Ashdown had doubted whether the Liberal Democrats should contest the seat left vacant after the assassination of Conservative MP Ian Gow. Rennard responded with the now legendary fax that as Ashdown admitted 'could have got him sacked':

> Dear Paddy,
> I'm appalled if I understand correctly that you were thinking of issuing a statement about the Eastbourne by-election without consulting the person responsible for organising the party's by-election campaigns, i.e. me . . . Your job is not to do what the Labour and Tory Parties want but to stand up to them. (Cited in Ashdown, 2000, 92–3)

The extent to which Rennard's success (especially in by-elections) has increased his stock was evident from our selection of interviews with more than 70 of the party personnel, from officers, parliamentarians, and activists. All interviewees were asked who they felt controlled the party. Not only was Rennard the most popular answer, but more than twice as many of our non-representative, but carefully selected, sample mentioned Rennard than Ashdown and Kennedy combined.

One PPC might have had his tongue in his cheek but did reveal:

> Obviously the leader thinks he controls the party, but I'm sure Chris Rennard (also) thinks he controls the party. And he does. He probably actually has more influence than Charles Kennedy does. I know if they both rang me up once, one said 'Jump right', the other said 'Jump left', I'd jump the way Chris said.

This seems to suggest that the party is mostly concerned with winning seats in parliament, and that the architects of the seat winning strategy are revered because of the success of that strategy perceived as a surrogate for being a successful party.

Resisting centralisation and limited resources – making a virtue out of necessity

So far we have seen that the dual identity in the British Liberal Democrats as a virtue. That the differing agenda of the local and national, the centre and the grassroots, the leadership and the councillor base could be seen as an essential outcome of the philosophical drive of the party. The federal party expects to organise itself along federal lines, sharing decision-making practices according to the party's defining principles.

Nevertheless, there is another school of thought – one that concentrates on the use of resources. This draws attention to the essential lack of choice that the party has in the matter, that the Liberal Democrats have made a virtue out of necessity. In other words, the freedom from the centre that is so precious to the local parties is as much a result of political reality than of a victory for the grassroots. The central party simply do not have the resources or personnel to control the local branches even if they so desired.

The Liberal Democrats suffer a number of electoral handicaps. As the third party in a two-party system, the Liberal Democrats find themselves marginalised in the British media. Trapped in a polity that works under a majoritarian electoral system, rather than a proportional one, such a third party is destined not to punch its weight electorally – unless like the SNP or Plaid Cymru, it has a significant geographic bias in the nature of its support (see Johnston *et al.*, 1988, 2001). Being a third force that draws support fairly evenly from all geographic regions (until recently anyway) the Liberal Democrats are thus disadvantaged. Finally, the absence of state funding, and the lack of significant financial backing from trade unions or big business leaves the party comparatively short of funds. The upshot of the media, electoral and funding biases against the Liberal Democrats are that they are seriously disadvantaged as a party. As such there might be an irresistible tendency for the centre to attempt to gain control over the party at large, but such a tendency can only be acted upon if the centre has the means to exert such a control. Most of our evidence shows that ideologically the party tends to resist overt central control, but also that the resources do not exist that would facilitate such control in any case. Local constituencies are allowed their head in the Liberal Democrats not just because that is the 'liberal' course of action but also because the party has no choice in the matter.

One of the party's senior officials and respected campaigners concluded that the party had developed more centrist tendencies but had managed to assimilate these into a set of core liberal beliefs.

> A by-election in Liberal party days, that was bottom up. Trevor Jones from Liverpool would go to Sutton and Cheam and say, 'We've got to win this!' And he'd raise the money, run the campaign, print the leaflets in Liverpool, put them in his car, drive them down to Sutton and Cheam, get them delivered, drive back to Liverpool, write another leaflet, drive down to Sutton and Cheam and so on.
>
> In Romsey (in 2000) we had a local base, but a team from around the country with by-election experience, piling in from the centre to go up to Romsey to do it. So actually we've become more centralised than we were 25 years ago. It's much more effective, but actually to be effective we've got to work both ways.

The parliamentary party

Downs (1957) assumed that parties are motivated by the prospect of gaining office. How then do we explain the behaviour of the British Liberal Democrats a third party in a two party system? Clearly, they are far away from forming the next government (gaining 18% of the popular vote in 2001). Downsian analysis might suppose that such a party is motivated by the prospect of getting closer to office either singularly or jointly. Of course it might be claimed that the third party in British politics might seek other means of extending their influence rather than the straightforward search for votes and Westminster seats. However, the potential for influence was intrinsically linked with the size of the parliamentary party. The *Diaries* of the party's former leader make clear that the Liberal Democrats saw their potential for influencing the government of Britain linked to their capability to hold the balance of power in parliament – or to form part of a new axis of the 'progressive left' (Ashdown, 2000). As one senior strategist told us:

> Perhaps the lesson for the party in the future is, that we could have even greater power over say a Labour government on a lot of issues, but that power would derive not from the fact that we necessarily have Cabinet ministers ourselves in a coalition agreement, but from the fact that we would have the balance of power or more power than we have at the moment actually in Westminster, in the House of Commons.

In truth without the benefits of a partisan press, state funding or widespread media exposure, the party came to believe that influence was linked with increasing Liberal Democrat representation in parliament. The influx of new Liberal Democrat MPs in 1997, resulted in a surge in party morale while political developments made a realignment of the centre-left more likely. The common perception is that the Ashdown-Blair project foundered not because the Liberal Democrats failed to win enough seats but because Tony Blair's

Labour party was unexpectedly over-represented in the landslide of 1997. Furthermore coalitions were secured between the Liberal Democrats and Labour party in the devolved parliament in Scotland and assembly in Wales because the Liberal Democrats held the balance of power in those institutions. Sartori (1976) suggests that the political relevance of a political party is measured by its ability to enter coalition and its blackmail potential. In abandoning equidistance (see Chapter 8) the Liberal Democrats might have reduced their coalition potential (since they rejected the possibility of entering coalition with the Conservatives), but by halving their possible coalition partners the Liberal Democrats were defining their realistic potential for coalition with Labour. The Ashdown *Diaries* reveal that the leaders of both Liberal Democrat and Labour parties were planning a quasi-coalition and even talking about formal merger in the medium to long term. The Liberal Democrat potential for coalition was focused on the ability to deliver a sizeable section of Westminster MPs to the equation.

The growth of the parliamentary party has brought with it interesting new challenges for the management of the party. As we have already pointed out controlling a Westminster party of 47 or 53 is a different proposition entirely to the management of a rump parliamentary party of around 20 MPs. Moreover the parliamentary Liberal Democrats, and those in the Scottish parliament and National Assembly for Wales are able to exert an influence outside their constitutional role (see Chapter 3). Furthermore, the new influx of Liberal Democrat MPs from 1997 had a markedly distinct profile. Overwhelmingly male and typically victorious over the Conservatives, a significant proportion of them had a background in local Liberal Democrat politics. Consequently they were more likely to have a set of shared ideologies with the expanding power base of the party from local government.

Meanwhile the extension of Liberal Democrat MPs has naturally reduced the number of multiple portfolios for party spokespeople. This has allowed greater concentration on a wider set of themes in parliament and has consequently reasserted the influence of the parliamentary party (since after 1997 the parliamentarians have swallowed up issues that would have been devolved outside the parliamentary party in the 1980s).

Local strength

We have seen how the local strength of the party has been reiterated in recent years. However, not only has the influence of the ALDC grown in recent times, local electoral success has become the blueprint for Westminster based success in general elections. (see Chapter 7).

One party official revealed an interesting strand of thought in the party.

> I think comparing councillors with leadership is a different exercise from activists and leadership. The councillors actually brought an awful lot of professionalism to the party because of going to meetings, making decisions, being responsible; the activists have that more radical edge. The activist/leadership thing – there's always tension in that. The councillors' side is slightly more understanding of each other's position.

Moreover, if the parliamentary party is increasingly drawn from this slice of party personnel, it is likely to affect the political behaviour of the party itself. Furthermore, the party continues to attempt to recruit from a local issue base rather than from national issues. One senior activist revealed how this might work:

> If you get people concerned about the local hospital closure and they understand that the process of saving it is not raising money it's a political process. Our most successful recent event was centred on local issues – the threat of post office closure. When we invited people to come and talk about the issues of the day we had a full room. But we did get activists out of that . . . we've got to be clever about getting those people in because otherwise the political process, irrespective of the Liberal Democrats, will die in this country.

There is also significant scope for the party to engage in politics through the local level. Some have even suggested that the expansion of Liberal Democrat council seats has created a new intermediary level of party activity. One local council leader revealed:

> When I first got elected to the council in 1973 we only had 300 councillors nationally. Now it's quite astonishing to see how the party has grown in numbers of elected people, grown in terms of real influence, you know, controlling everything from big cities down to small shire districts. Far more powerful than the MPs have been since the Second World War and that's where the strength of the party lies. The parliamentary numbers, it's welcome to see them going up, but unless there is a balance of power or a coalition government, the MPs are not the most important part of our party.
>
> [The party's] gone from being a rather ephemeral debating society which bounced a few good ideas into the national political arena and had very little impact on everyday life to one where we are in charge politically of local council services for several million people and hold the balance for many million more than that and the parliamentary party is larger, largely as a result of that. It's not the other way round. It's very much the local government strength has allowed the parliamentary strength to expand and hopefully will continue to allow it to expand.

Europe: dualism in policy?

So far this chapter has demonstrated the dualism in the power structure and ideology of the Liberal Democrats. The final task of this chapter is to investigate this dualism in the arena of policy making. In particular, we will look at the Liberal Democrats' commitment to European integration, which is on the one hand part of the national identity of the party, but which curiously seems less popular in some of the geographic heartlands of Liberal Democrat voting.

Initially, we want to establish that the leadership of the Liberal Democrats see Europe as one of their defining issues. In 1888 Gladstone had talked of being 'part of the community of Europe' although his commitment to Europe was made under completely different circumstances to those that face the contemporary Liberal Democrats. Nevertheless, they do show an ongoing concern with international affairs and towards a common goal shared between Britain and the rest of Europe.

The community of Europe has been a central concern for Liberal leaders since Gladstone, and has been one of the defining characteristics of Liberalism since World War II. Moreover it seems to have been one of the party's guiding principles in many ways.

Britain's entry to the European Community

As early as 1950 the Liberals, under the leadership of Clement Davies, advocated British membership of the European Coal and Steel Community. By 1955, they were lamenting British reluctance to play a full role in the Messina talks that proved to be the birth of the European Economic Community, by the 1957 Treaty of Rome, the Liberals had established their position as the advocates of European unity.

In February 1972 the Second Reading of the European Communities bill – paving the way for British entry to the EEC – came to the House and Conservative Prime Minister Edward Heath was in trouble. Labour decided to vote against the bill (treating it as a vote of confidence in the Tory regime) and a small rebellion from the Conservative benches was likely. In the event 20 Conservatives failed to support the government in the lobby. In the end, Liberal support for the bill could have helped defeat the government but the party chose to vote for the bill – which passed with a majority of eight. In the pandemonium that followed the vote in the House, a Labour MP physically accosted Thorpe and Labour Chief Whip Bob Mellish denounced the Liberals as 'a gutter party'.

Thorpe's resultant statement made the case for seeing the vote as a statement of ideology rather than a matter of grubby politics.

> This is not a matter of arithmetic, but one of principle. This is not the first time we in the Liberal Party have borne the brunt of Europe, nor will it be the last . . . The Liberal party pioneered the movement towards European unity in this

> country, and it is a sign of the cynicism to which politics has now sunk that we should have been expected to throttle it tonight. (Thorpe, 1999, 187)

Curiously the events of 1972 were to be repeated in near identical fashion 20 years later with the Maastricht Paving Bill. This time the Conservative Prime Minister in trouble was John Major, his slim majority threatened by a sizeable rebellion from the Conservatives benches. Labour, under John Smith, were treating the bill as a vote of confidence in the Conservative regime, and the Liberal Democrats had to decide whether to vote for the Treaty or against the government of the day. In the end the two votes on the bill went the way of the government by six and two votes – the Conservatives were reliant on the Liberal Democrats – who with only one exception had voted with the government – and as the political cartoonists had it Ashdown had come to Major's aid like the US cavalry in a Western movie. Labour's anger with the Liberal Democrats was manifest and a Labour Party whip – Lady Patricia Hollis – called Ashdown 'a traitor' (see Ashdown, 2000, 197–202).

Here then were two events, 20 years apart when the Liberals (and the Liberal Democrats) could have sought political advantage by subverting their European interests for their domestic ones. On each occasion they chose to go with their pro-European instincts despite the consequences. For a party in search of an identifiable stance, European integration was becoming part of the Liberal Democrats unique selling points. When the party's campaign for the 1992 election hit upon the theme of 5Es it was no surprise that 'Europe' should be one.

Europe: some qualifications and addenda

Nevertheless, it would be a mistake to see the Liberal Democrat commitment to Europe as unconditional. Future leader Charles Kennedy's speech at the 1999 European Movement Conference spelt out that there were limits to the party's pro-European stance: 'The tide of history is in favour of European integration – but we must ensure that it is diverted down the right channels to ensure that British interests and democratic values are not drowned. Only by taking a lead in Europe can we achieve our worthy goal.' Coupled with the 2001 manifesto it is possible that the Liberal Democrat commitment to Europe is less strident than popularly supposed. Indeed Europe is seen as a collection of sovereign states that is sometimes undemocratic and ineffective.

Europe and the voters

In their study of Liberal Democrat members, Bennie, Curtice and Rudig highlighted that the pro-European line of the party's leadership was not necessarily reflected in the rank and file members of the party: 'Liberal Democrats are, it seems, scarcely more pro-European than the electorate as a whole' (Bennie *et al.*, 1996, 141).

Extending this to voters, we find that the Liberal Democrat reservoir of support was largely unaffected by the party's stance on Europe. In Chapter 6 we reveal that the issue of EU integration appears to play a very small role in the issue-based mobilisation of Liberal Democrat voters. Far fewer voters were prepared to say that their views on EU integration were closer to the Liberal Democrats' position than Conservative or Labour parties (Table 6.4). At the same time, less than 45 percent of reported Liberal Democrat voters in 1997 were in favour of the party's stance on EU integration – whereas more than 70 percent of them supported the Liberal Democrat policies on education, health, proportional representation and unemployment and inflation (Figure 6.3). Moreover of those who were in favour of EU integration only 20 percent actually voted for the Liberal Democrats, nearly 60 percent of them voted Labour and 18 percent voted Conservative in 1997 (see Table 6.6).

Liberal Democrat heartlands and Eurosceptism

It is a curious feature of the electoral geography of the Liberal Democrats that their areas of strength are often associated with the farming, fishing and tourist industries – where hostility to the European project seems particularly high. This is an important research question: how can we explain the sustained support for the most Euro-friendly party in a region of consistent hostility to the matter of Europe?

One MP told us that there was a large gap between the 'obsessions' of the party and those who vote for it.

> It's quite interesting when you look at Europe and the parties standing on Europe, it's a phenomenally pro-European party, but I mean the party's voters are at least as Eurosceptic as the Tories, slightly more so in each case than Labour.
>
> And then you get to the party conference and the MPs and you've got a completely different view. Now I'm not raising this thing with you to make a thing about the Euro I'm just using it as an exemplar of how there can be a difference between the national party and the federal organisation.

This would seem to support the view of Bennie *et al.* who claimed with some justification that: 'Europe is capable of dividing the Liberal Democrats just as it does the Conservatives' (Bennie *et al.*, 1996, 142).

However, the fact that this divisive potential remains latent rather than active requires further investigation. The 1992 Maastricht vote saw the Liberal Democrats vote for the Treaty with one exception. It is instructive to know that the one Liberal Democrat who voted against the Treaty was Nick Harvey, (MP for Devon North), one of the Liberal Democrats heartland seats in a Eurosceptical region.

One MP from an area of traditional Liberal voting informed us that the duality of the party permitted the local campaign to differ greatly in texture from the national campaign: 'There's quite a big culture gap between the federal party and the party out in the constituencies. It's not conflict; it's just a big gap.'

This is not to say that the Liberal Democrats could ignore the issue of Europe in these heartland regions – after all voters were typically hostile to the European project rather than indifferent to it. One election agent told us that the secret of campaigning in such a locality was to play up the Liberal heritage of the region and highlight the 'room to manoeuvre' on the European issue granted by party pronouncements on the need to reform the EU. Furthermore the local culture of scepticism could also be found in the local party and this played a role in compensating for any disadvantage that the national focal point of the party might provide. In particular the success of the Liberal Democrat controlled council in securing EU funding for the region could offset some of the apparent demerits of association with Europe. The region's MP went on: 'In the election here in 1997 Europe was, certainly along with hunting, the two things that were raised most on the doorstep. Of that I haven't the slightest doubt at all, but whether or not (Europe) really shifted that many votes on polling day I can't tell. I'm not so sure it did.'

Finally we were given a glimpse of how the reality of an anti-European local electorate could be persuaded that the Liberal Democrats – regardless of the national identity of the party – might be a viable electoral outlet for local sentiment: 'The farmers were in a most appalling situation (and) the biggest culprits in the situation that the farmers find themselves in are the Tories through the grotesque mishandling of the whole BSE fiasco and their complete inability to talk serious turkey with the European community in terms of the common agricultural policy during their 18 years in office.'

Our investigation of campaigning in the Liberal heartland areas revealed that the dual identity of the party became a virtual necessity in converting a general local hostility to Europe into specific support for the local Liberal Democrats. This is illuminating since it reveals that the dual identity of the party is advantageous on a number of levels. The distinctions between the national central machine and the local nuances of Liberalism are practical – the party does not have the resources to control all of the local branches from the centre, partly ideological – the party's ethos of federalism and community politics mean there is little desire to 'control' the localities, but also necessary to allow local parties to campaign effectively on local issues.

Top-down, bottom-up?

By way of conclusion, we return to the question of locating the foci of power in the British Liberal Democrats. One MP declared that the party was a tripartite alliance: 'There's a delightful tension between the leadership and the grassroots and the activists – a triumvirate of tension if you like! Which is probably healthy, although it doesn't always feel like it to whichever particular group is trying to convince the other two.'

When asked who controlled the party, another MP declared:

> I know it's daft, but simultaneously both (top-down and bottom-up) observations are correct. I mean, yes it is top-down on occasions – it must be, it's inevitable if you've got a leader and national headquarters, but equally we are very much grassroots pushing up through policies, Lib Dem News, conferences, regional conferences and all the rest of it, so yes, we're obviously far stronger at grassroots than we are at national level because at national level they don't have the resources of the other parties. The other two parties are very much top-down. We seem almost a twin track.

Similarly, the party's Chair of Campaigning told us that campaigning was a two way process. Electioneering was both a top-down and a bottom-up process.

> If you were to say to me, 'You should be targeting this and you should be moving your resources and your troops to win these seats, because I've identified in the demographics and we can win.' I'd say, 'Hold on a minute, you've got this wrong' . . . I can't go off and say, we should win in say Gainsborough, but if the activists within Gainsborough say 'We want to be a target seat, what we'll do is we'll win every council seat within this constituency, we'll select a candidate that's determined to win and get a high profile.' That candidate is in the *Gainsborough News* every single week without fail, that candidate gets on to the regional TV on a regular basis, that candidate builds up to a large membership – I'll say 'Hey, from the bottom, they've decided they're going to build this up.' Now from the top what I will do is I will try and train their activists, their councillors and their prospective MP to be more effective. I'll give them some money from the centre. I will try and steer their campaign, I'll try and advise them on everything like tactical voting techniques to media techniques, but they will do the bulk of the work. Now, last time round, the combination of the two, the bottom-up working on the seat to start with, and me coming in on the top, was very effective. Helped us win a lot of seats but it couldn't happen without both.

Finally one former MP gave us a valuable insight into the *realpolitik* of the modern party – and a compelling feature of tension between different aspects of the party. The dual identity of the party is secured by the very ideology of the Liberal Democrats:

I think leadership would like (the party) to be top down because they persuade themselves that undisciplined parties don't get elected, although philosophically they believe in decentralisation. The grassroots would certainly like it to be bottom-up and I think there is always, and always will be, a tension between the two and the balances shift a bit depending on how clever the people in the leadership are, how well they read what's going on and all sorts of things like that.

Liberalism as a philosophy has inbuilt tensions which will never be resolved. You know, the inbuilt tensions between the need for leadership and the strength, and democracy going down to the lowest level; between the need for discipline and the valuing individuality. I've been the leader of a council group of 40– odd people and you're facing those tensions all the time. You need the group all to vote in the same way so you'll win the vote and so you'll look like you're disciplined, so people will trust you to run the council; but on the other hand, you recognise that they're 40 individuals and you don't want to start heavy-handedly whipping people, because you wouldn't be a Liberal if you didn't think they were entitled to have their own views. Those tensions cannot be resolved. You find local resolutions to individual situations, but there isn't a global resolution of those tensions, that's the nature of the philosophy.

Figure II:1 **Liberal Democrat support**

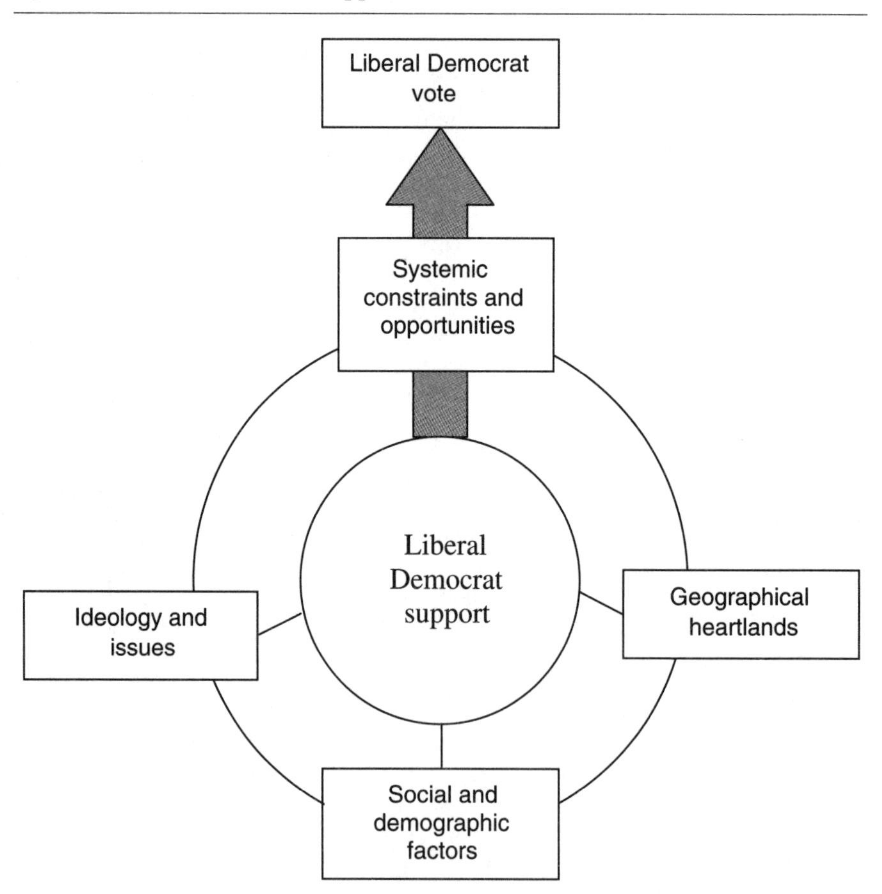

Part II

The Liberal Democrats and the electorate

There are many approaches to understanding voting behaviour, but most commonly these can be reduced to either socio-demographic or expressive models and instrumental models. The latter vary to the extent to which they focus on ideology and issues (see for example Franklin, 1984; Scarbrough, 1984; Rose and McAllister, 1990) or on rational choice or economic models (see for example Sanders *et al.*, 1987; Dunleavy, 1991). To that we should add, especially in the context of Liberal Democrat voting, the importance of contextual influences (e.g. see Johnston et al., 1988). Given this, perhaps not surprisingly when we asked respondents who they thought voted Liberal Democrat some referred to the social groups, some to like-minded voters and others to the geographical heartlands. This is illustrated in Figure II.1 which reflects the pattern of responses to this particular question, but also feeds into the structure of the empirical analyses presented in this section. Thus in the following three chapters we explore these three components and build a model of Liberal Democrat voting which incorporates these three elements, starting with the social basis of Liberal Democrat voting (Chapter 5) to which we then add the attitudinal basis of Liberal Democrat support (Chapter 6) and in Chapter 7 we incorporate contextual and geographical influences into the model.

5

The profile of Liberal support

The aim of this part of the book is to investigate the relationship between the Liberal Democrats and the electorate. This chapter will begin this process by exploring the bases of support for the Liberal Democrats – and their predecessors, the Liberals and the Alliance. In our analysis here the terms 'Liberal' and 'Liberals' are used as generic labels for all permutations of the third party.

Although third party voting is a regular feature in British elections, the nature and source of their support remains elusive. This chapter uses data from the *British Election Study* (BES) series and qualitative data from interviews with key party personnel to investigate the social and political basis of Liberal support in Britain. The chapter is divided into two main sections: the first investigates the social basis of Liberal support since the 1970s. The second section examines the nature and linkage between the party and its supporters – the strength of party identification, the loyalty of voters – and explores the changing relationship between the Liberals and the other main parties. The implications of our findings for the party's electoral strategy will be discussed at length in the third part of the book.

The analysis is restricted to elections from February 1974 onwards; the number of Liberal voting respondents – and Liberal candidates – in earlier BES surveys is simply too small for meaningful analysis.

The social and demographic profile of Liberal voting

Traditionally at least, the Conservative Party has been seen as the party of the middle classes and the Labour Party of the working class (although see Chapter 1). By contrast, social and demographic modelling of the Liberal vote has shown that Liberal voters are distinct only in their indistinctive nature (Johnston *et al.*, 1998). It is often suggested that one of the features that prevented the Alliance from making a substantial breakthrough in terms of Westminster representation was that the party appealed across all classes and almost uniformly across all regions of Britain (see Johnston and Pattie, 1988). In short, the Liberals continued to be hampered by an electoral system that rewarded parties with support concentrated in geographic and/or social strongholds (see Chapter 7 for a fuller discussion). Indeed, the continued ability of the party to come second in a large number of parliamentary seats strengthened support within the party for a system of proportional representation. However, the 1997 and 2001 General Elections saw the party's best electoral returns, in terms of seats won, since 1929 (despite the share of the vote remaining well below that achieved by the Alliance in the 1980s). We wish to investigate whether or not these results point to the development of a more coherent core support for the contemporary Liberal Democrats.

Before the 1997 election Curtice (1996) argued that the traditional view of Liberal voting as coming from no single section of the electorate was misplaced. He argued that Liberal Democrat voters were drawn disproportionately from certain groups of voters: 'Support for the party is not classless, but is distinctly stronger amongst the educated middle class than in the less well educated working class . . . Rather than having a geographically even spread vote, the party has developed an area of concentration in the south west of England' (Curtice, 1996, 200).

We can investigate the validity of this assertion by examining a range of social demographic variables, including age, class, education and religion. These variables can then be entered into the appropriate regression equation in order that their relative importance in explaining Liberal voting can be established. It should be remembered that the data we are using here, from the *British Election Study* (BES) series, relate to the individual level (we explore constituency level relationships in more detail in Chapter 7).

Age and sex

Two age related effects might be important in determining voting patterns. The first is absolute age with the youngest sections of society generally being the most liberal; the eldest sections the most conservative. The second concerns lifecycle events or cohort effects that leave an indelible stamp on an individual's political and electoral behaviour (Lipset and Rokkan, 1967). Our analysis shows that at every General Election since February 1974 the mean age of Liberal voters was lower than that for the Conservatives and lower in all but one election (1987) than for Labour. However, these differences are relatively small and have narrowed since 1974.

Following the work of Lipset and Rokkan we attempted to investigate the propensity of certain cohort groups to vote Liberal by separating the electorate into four political generations according to when they were first eligible to vote. The four cohort groups were: those first eligible to vote between 1918–35 (the rise of the organised working-class vote and start of the Liberal decline); 1936–50 (the immediate pre and post-war era); 1951–70 (the nadir of the party's electoral fortunes) and after 1970 (the gradual resurgence of the party) reveals that the Liberals do not perform particularly well in any of the four cohorts. Generally speaking, the cohort group most likely to support the Liberals are those who reached the age of majority after 1970. One possible explanation revolves around party organisation. Older voters may have had less opportunity to vote Liberal due to the very limited number of candidates the Liberals were able to field prior to 1974. Whereas those sections of the electorate who were first eligible to vote after 1970 would have been politically socialised during or after the Liberal resurgence of the late 1960s which resulted in the reinvigoration of local party machinery and the party contested the great majority of parliamentary seats from 1974 onwards. However, the patterns observed are not consistent and do not point to a concentration of support in any particular age group or cohort.

An analysis of Liberal vote by sex reveals that women tend to support the party in slightly higher proportions than men, but again the differences are small and inconsistent. Little discernible pattern emerges from combining sex with age; although the party traditionally performs best among younger women.

Social class

There are considerable problems in achieving a consistent measure of class over the period of interest. However, collapsing occupational grade in the 1974 and 1979 *BES* and Registrar-General's social class in the *BES* from 1979 to 2001 (for guidelines on this procedure see Crewe *et al.*, 1995) produces the following three class categories: professional and managerial; intermediate and routine non-manual; and manual working class. Table 5.1 shows that although the Liberals have consistently performed best in the professional and managerial class, this group are more likely to vote Conservative (with the exception of 1997 – when they were most likely to vote Labour). While the two main parties have traditionally had clear class heartlands of support, among the professional and managerial for the Conservatives and the manual working class for Labour, the Liberals have been unable to win anything like a majority of any class.

A simple way of summarising the class basis of Liberal support is through odds ratios[1]. Table 5.2 seems to support Curtice's case for describing the Liberal Democrats as a middle-class party. This is seen by the similarity in the class profiles of Conservative and Liberal voters, particular in the 1980s and 1990s (indeed, the Liberal Democrats were the most middle-class party in term of voter profile in 1992). The odds ratios also show, however, that the class distinctions between all three parties have blurred over time (see Franklin, 1984; Robertson, 1984; Heath *et al.* 1985; Crewe, 1986). For

Table 5.1 **Vote by class, 1974–2001 (%)**

	1974 F	*1974 O*	*1979*	*1983*	*1987*	*1992*	*1997*	*2001*
Professional/managerial								
Con	56.5	52.3	62.1	54.9	53.6	53.2	36.2	40.8
Lab	18.8	18.5	20.9	13.8	17.2	19.9	38.5	31.3
Lib	*22.7*	*25.8*	*15.5*	*30.5*	*28.3*	*23.8*	*21.0*	*24.7*
Intermediate								
Con	45.8	44.7	54.8	54.4	54.5	55.3	33.9	29.2
Lab	30.3	32.6	27.5	19.2	21.5	26.0	43.2	43.3
Lib	*22.4*	*19.5*	*15.8*	*25.1*	*22.7*	*16.2*	*17.1*	*21.9*
Manual working class								
Con	24.6	23.5	35.5	34.9	34.0	34.3	28.5	19.8
Lab	57.1	58.2	50.7	41.9	44.1	49.3	48.9	61.3
Lib	*15.0*	*14.2*	*12.2*	*21.7*	*21.1*	*13.1*	*17.5*	*14.2*

Source: Derived from *British Election Study* surveys 1974–2001.

Table 5.2 **Odds ratios, 1974–2001**

	1974 F	*1974 O*	*1979*	*1983*	*1987*	*1992*	*1997*	*2001*
Con vs. Lab	7.0	7.0	4.2	4.8	4.0	3.8	2.9	4.0
Con vs. Lib	1.5	1.2	1.4	1.1	1.2	0.9	1.3	1.2
Lib vs. Lab	4.6	5.7	3.1	4.3	3.4	4.5	2.2	3.4

example, the ratio of difference between Conservative and Labour parties fell from 7.0 to just 2.9 between 1974 and 1997, although the ratios widened somewhat in 2001 (the Conservatives re-established themselves as the most popular party among the professional and managerial class).

If class is combined with employment sector (private or public) the Liberals appear to do particularly well among public sector professionals, such as teachers and university lecturers. The party won over a third of this group in the elections of 1983 and 1987 and 27 per cent in 1997 (dropping slightly to 25 per cent in 2001). Generally, the party enjoys around 10 per cent more support from public sector professionals than from their counterparts in the private sector. The reasons for this pattern is unclear, but it could stem from such Liberal Democrat policies as hypothecated taxation and increased resources for the health service, which are likely to be particularly popular among public sector workers.

Education

Analysing the effect of education on voting behaviour reveals that Liberal voters are the most educated of all voters in the British electorate. In every election since 1974 the Liberals have enjoyed the highest proportion of degrees holders in their party vote. In 1997, for example, 16 per cent of those who voted for the Liberal Democrats held a degree, compared to 10 per cent for both the Conservative and Labour parties.

Although the Liberals have a greater proportion of degree holders in their party vote, this does not necessarily mean that they are favoured by degree holders generally. Figure 5.1 details the voting pattern of degree holders and shows the party does in fact perform well within this group. Indeed, in 1987 the Alliance was actually the largest party in terms of the popular vote among voters educated to degree level and in 2001 they out-polled the Conservatives within this group (although perhaps the most interesting finding relates to the very large increase in the educated Labour vote in 1997). Comparing degree and non-degree holders shows that the Liberals receive, on average, 10–15 per cent more votes from those with a university qualification.

But what is it about education that makes the Liberals attractive? Forslund's (1980) study of attitudes to delinquency in the USA suggested that exposure to formal education was positively associated with the popularity of liberal measures (see Babbie (1995) for a full discussion). Or could it be that the Liberal Party appeals to those liberal minded middle classes tradi-

Figure 5.1 **Vote by degree holders**

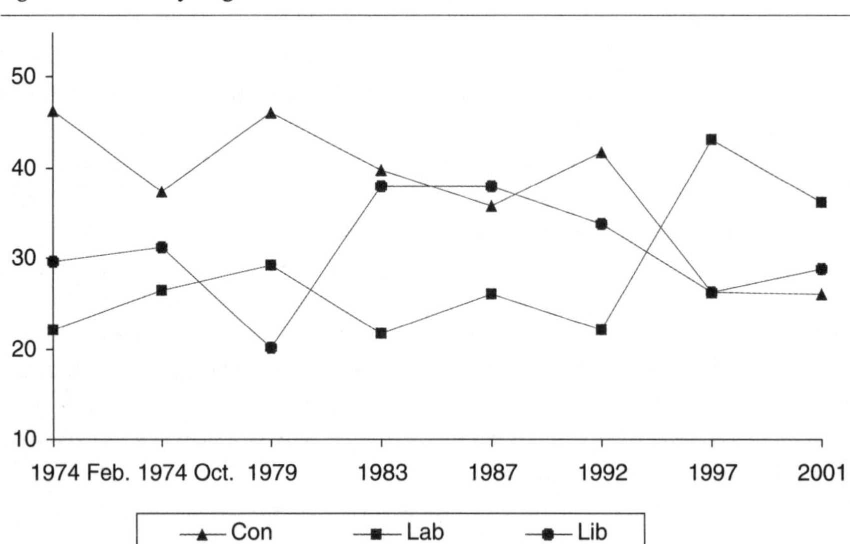

tionally disinclined to vote Labour because of their class or employment background?

When educational level is linked to employment sector some interesting patterns emerge (Table 5.3). The Liberals have traditionally recruited particularly well among those with university degrees and public sector jobs (adding weight to our finding of the party's support among public sector professionals). In fact, between 1983 and 1992 the party actually won the largest share of the vote amongst this section of the electorate (due to small numbers we have excluded the 1974 and 1979 elections). Although still doing relatively well in 1997, the party lost further ground within this group in 2001 and, for the first time, actually performed better among private sector degree holders. It is too early to be certain whether this signals a real change, but it is certainly a development worth noting.

The image of the traditional Liberal voter as an educated, public sector professional that has emerged from the analysis above is certainly supported by many in the party. One local campaign co-ordinator felt that the party had a natural electoral heartland among the 'thinking middle class', while a PPC noted:

Table 5.3 **Vote of degree holders by employment sector, 1983–2001 (%)**

	1983	*1987*	*1992*	*1997*	*2001*
Private sector					
Con	49	45	60	29	20
Lab	19	18	19	45	42
Lib	33	36	18	21	29
Public sector					
Con	34	31	30	18	34
Lab	21	29	26	48	29
Lib	44	39	41	30	28

Source: *British Election Study* surveys 1983–2001.

> It is not unusual to find, within the Liberal Democrats, large numbers of teachers, university lecturers, doctors, often self-made individuals, who have the time and the energy and the intellect to see there are alternatives and the world isn't full of arguments with only two points of view.

Although this may be an idealised view of the Liberal voter our analysis would seem to lend some weight to this assertion.

Religion

While Curtice (1996) felt that the historical link between nonconformism and Liberal voting atrophied with the formation of the Liberal Democrats this does not seem to be the case (see Chapter 7 for a fuller discussion of the historical link between Liberal voting and nonconformism). Our analysis of vote by religious affiliation (Figure 5.2) shows that there is still a positive association between support for the Liberals and nonconformity. The shortfall in nonconformist Liberal Democrat voters in 1992 (that encouraged Curtice to announce the death of the nonconformist Liberal vote) was reasserted in 1997. In 2001, however, the Liberal Democrats fared best among voters with no religious affiliation, while the figure for nonconformists fell slightly. The party continues to perform badly among Catholic voters, a group with a strong association with Labour voting – for example Labour won 60 per cent of the Catholic vote in 2001.

Figure 5.2 **Liberal vote by religious denominations, 1974–2001 (%)**

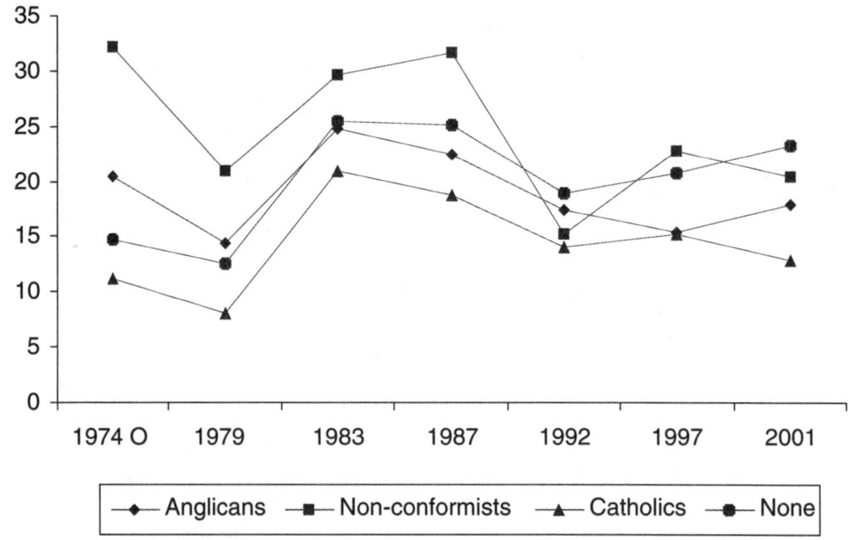

35
30
25
20
15
10
5
0

1974 O 1979 1983 1987 1992 1997 2001

Anglicans Non-conformists Catholics None

Source: *British Election Study* surveys 1974–2001.
Note: Due to the small number of cases all other denominations are excluded.

Even if the link between nonconformity and Liberal voting is weaker than in the past, many in the party believe it survives. For instance, a PPC pointed to the strength of the modern party in the 'Celtic fringe', an area with a particularly strong history of nonconformity. Although at the individual level the statistical relationship is not particularly strong, a more powerful relationship exists at the constituency level (see Chapter 7). Indeed, there are a number of seats where nonconformity still plays a very important role in explaining Liberal Democrat support. One activist in Montgomeryshire summed it up:

'If you come to Montgomeryshire and say "Where is our vote?" the heartland vote does come from a nonconformist tradition and that's the same in all the Celtic fringe. You would still see the chapel people, over sixty, naturally, thinking of doing nothing else than voting Liberal Democrat.'

Region

Analysing the Liberal vote by standard region since 1974 (Table 5.4) shows that the party tends to perform well in the south west of England, typically garnering around one-third of all votes cast in the region (this data is derived from General Election results and is not based on individual-level data). There are other areas of strength but, by and large, the electoral performance of the party varies little around the country. This is not to say that the party has not performed particularly well, or badly, in certain regions at certain elections but that the overall pattern of Liberal support is evenly spread. What does vary, however, is the party's ability to convert this support into seats in Westminster. Indeed, within regions there are substantial concentrations of support that may provide a base for expansion (we examine the Liberals geographical distribution of the vote in much greater detail in chapter 7).

It is noticeable that an identical share of the vote in the south west at the 1992, 1997 and 2001 elections has resulted in remarkably different outcomes. In 1992, the Liberal Democrats' 31 per cent of the regional vote gave the party victory in 6 of the 48 seats, while in 2001 the concentration of resources on winnable seats meant that 31 per cent across the region allowed the Liberal Democrats to win 15 of the 51 seats (an increase of one from 1997). The same pattern emerges in the south east, where the party's share of the vote fell by 1 per cent in 1997 but due to targeting the party was able to win an additional 13 seats (all of them at the expense of the Conservatives). The party added a further seat to this total in 2001 (winning Guildford and Romsey but losing the Isle of Wight). Interestingly, the best 'pound-for-pound' return from Liberal Democrat vote share in any of the standard regions was in Scotland where, even in a four-party system, the party won 10 of the 72 Scottish seats in 2001 from only 16 per cent of the vote. We will return to the reasons for these geographical patterns in chapters 7 and 9.

While class, employment sector, education, religion and region appear to play some role in explaining Liberal voting, the figures may suggest that the Liberal Democrats still cannot rely on a distinct heartland of support. To test this theory, the independent effect of all these factors on the Liberal vote was assessed using a series of logistic regression models.

Table 5.4 **Liberal vote and seats by region, 1974–2001**

	1974 F	*1974 0*	*1979*	*1983*	*1987*	*1992*	*1997*	*2001*
South east	25	21	15	27	25	20	19	19
Seats/total	1/193	1/193	1/193	3/192	3/192	1/193	14/191	15/191
South west	30	27	23	33	33	31	31	31
Seats/total	3/43	3/43	1/43	3/48	3/48	6/48	14/51	15/51
East Anglia	25	21	16	28	26	20	18	19
Seats/total	1/17	1/17	1/17	1/20	0/20	0/20	0/22	1/22
East Midlands	22	17	13	24	21	15	14	15
Seats/total	0/36	0/36	0/36	0/42	0/42	0/42	0/44	1/44
West Midlands	22	18	12	23	21	15	14	15
Seats/total	0/56	0/56	0/56	0/58	0/58	0/58	1/59	2/59
York/Humberside	24	20	15	26	23	17	16	17
Seats/total	1/54	1/54	1/54	2/54	0/54	0/54	2/56	2/56
North west	22	18	13	23	21	16	14	17
Seats/total	2/78	2/78	2/78	2/73	3/73	2/73	2/70	3/70
North	22	17	13	25	21	16	13	17
Seats/total	1/39	1/39	1/39	2/36	1/36	1/36	1/36	1/36
Wales	19	16	11	23	18	12	12	13
Seats/total	2/36	2/36	2/36	2/38	3/38	1/38	2/40	2/40
Scotland	17	8	9	25	19	14	13	16
Seats/total	3/71	3/71	3/71	8/72	9/72	9/72	10/72	10/72

Source: Nuffield Series, 1974–2001.

Modelling Liberal support

Three separate models were run for the elections of 1979, 1987 and 1997: Liberal voters against all other voters; Liberal voters against Conservative voters; and Liberal voters against Labour voters.[2] This allows us to determine how Liberal voters differ from voters of the two other major parties.

Table 5.5 shows that in 1979, 1987 and 1997 social class was a significant factor in shaping voting behaviour, as would be expected from the odds ratios above. In all three elections Liberal voters were significantly more middle class than Labour voters. Although the gap narrowed in 1997, the Liberal Democrats were still more than twice as likely than Labour to receive support from the professional and managerial class than from the manual working class. Unsurprisingly, the Conservatives were the most middle class of all the parties, significantly more so than the Liberals in 1987 and 1997 but not in 1979. Comparing Liberal voters with all non-Liberal voters reveals that those from the professional and managerial classes were about 1.5 times more likely to vote Liberal Democrat in 1997 than voters from the manual working class, all other variables remaining constant.

Holding a degree is only a significant influence in Liberal voting in the 1987 election (those with a degree being around twice as likely to vote for the Liberals than those without). The fact that education does not play a more prominent role in the models is probably due to the relationship between class and educational qualification (the variables are highly correlated). Indeed, if class is removed from the 1997 model educational qualification is significant (those with a degree being 1.5 times more likely to vote Liberal Democrat).

The link between nonconformist religious denominations and Liberal voting, as discussed above, is supported by the models. In both the elections of 1987 and 1997 the Liberals did significantly better amongst nonconformists than Anglicans (or Church of Scotland). The relative weakness of the party in relation to Labour among Catholic voters is particularly clear.

A regional variable was also included in the model to assess the geographical profile of Liberal support. Looking at Liberal voters versus all voters we see the party's strength in the south west. Voters in that region were 1.4 times more likely to vote for the Alliance in 1987 and 3.2 times more like to vote for the Liberal Democrats in 1997 than their Scottish counterparts, all else being equal. The party also does particularly well in the south east in 1997. However, the models also clearly show the party's weakness in many regions, particularly in Wales against Labour and even, despite their advances in 1997, in the south against the Conservatives.

When other variables are held constant, sector of employment, sex and

Table 5.5 **Logistic regression model of Liberal voting 1979, 1987 and 1997**

Variable	*1979 Exp(B)*			*1987 Exp(B)*			*1997 Exp(B)*		
	All	*Con*	*Lab*	*All*	*Con*	*Lab*	*All*	*Con*	*Lab*
Region (vs. Scotland)									
South east						2.6**	2.1**	0.5*	2.7**
East Anglia						2.1*		0.4*	
Greater London					0.5**				
South west						2.9**	3.2**		
West Midlands								0.4*	4.4**
East Midlands					0.6**	1.7*			
York-Humberside								0.2*	
North west				0.6*	0.4**				
North				0.6*	0.5*				
Wales						0.4**			0.4*
Class (vs. manual work)									
Professional/managerial			3.2**		0.7**	3.2**	1.5**	0.7*	2.1**
Intermediate			2.6**		0.6**	2.2*		0.6**	1.6**
Education (vs. no degree)									
Degree					2.0**				
Religion (vs. Anglican/Church of Scotland)									
Nonconformist				1.4*	1.6**		1.7*		2.1**
Roman Catholic	0.5*		0.4**			0.4**			
None	0.7*		0.5**		1.5**	0.8*	1.5**	2.4**	
R^2	*0.01*	*0.00*	*0.10*	*0.05*	*0.06*	*0.20*	*0.07*	*0.09*	*0.14*
-2 * *Log likelihood*	*1015*	*819*	*722*	*2801*	*2210*	*1762*	*1887*	*1198*	*1487*

Notes: ** = $p < 0.01$; * = $p < 0.05$. Empty cells represent insignificant coefficients.

age have no significant effect on Liberal Democrat voting and are therefore not included in the table.

However, the models perform poorly in explaining the variance in Liberal voting in all three elections, suggesting that there is little distinctive about Liberal supporters. It is only able to explain a maximum of 9 per cent of the variance in the three models of Liberal against Conservative voting, indicating there is little difference in the social and demographic make-up of the supporters of the two parties. Nevertheless, the model performs considerably better in accounting for Liberal versus Labour voting, explaining 20 per cent and 14 per cent of the variance in the 1987 and 1997 elections respectively.

The political profile of Liberal support

As Curtice (1996) has asserted, the Liberals may not be *the* party of the middle class, but as the odds ratios and regression equations show, their voters have a similar social profile to that of the Conservatives. Given the similarity, this raises the interesting question of why Liberal voters chose to support a third party and not their 'natural' party, the Conservatives? However, as we will show in Chapter 6, the policy positions of Liberal Democrat supporters at the 1997 and 2001 General Elections were much closer to Labour then the Conservatives. Using data from the BES we can demonstrate that on four major policy dimensions – government spending, internationalism, economic choices and egalitarianism – Liberal Democrats voters occupied a position closer to Labour. Indeed, on two issues, law and order and environmentalism, the party was the most 'left' of all three major parties. The law and order dimension, while representing a traditional touchstone of liberalism, may also reflect the Labour Party's move to the right on the issue. The Liberal Democrats' radicalism on the environmentalist dimension reflects the party's history of campaigning on ecological and environmental issues. Along with non-traditional concerns, such as constitutional and electoral reform, these dimensions might provide policy arenas around which the party may mobilise support. In short, Liberal Democrat voters may be more like Conservative supporters in terms of class, but ideologically – at least in recent elections – they are more similar to Labour voters

The Liberals appear to garner support from certain sections of the electorate but is this a temporary expression of dissatisfaction with the other parties or a stable core support? There may be little unique about the social profile of Liberal voters but is there anything distinctive about their political profile? To answer such questions we must explore how Liberal voters feel about the other parties (and vice versa), where they perceive their party in relation to Labour and the Conservatives and examine the party's ability to retain and recruit voters. A first step, however, is to look at the level and strength of identification with the party.

Party identification

One of the key characteristics of Liberal voting is perhaps the perceived lack of a firm attachment to the party. One way of measuring this to look at the levels of party identification (Butler and Stokes, 1974) and at how successful the party is in converting identification into votes. Crewe's study of the 'soft' Liberal vote concluded that the party suffered from lower levels of identification amongst the electorate, both in terms of absolute numbers and in the strength of identification (Crewe, 1985, 121).

An analysis of the *BES* shows that the trends identified by Crewe in 1985 have continued to the present day (Table 5.6). Only 13 per cent of voters in 2001 identified with the Liberal Democrats, compared to 47 per cent and 26 per cent for Labour and the Conservatives respectively. Moreover, the percentage of those who identify 'very strongly' with the Liberal Democrat is much lower than the percentages for the Conservative and Labour parties. Although the numbers who identify very strongly with the two major parties has fallen since 1974 (and particularly so for Labour in 2001), they still enjoy a much higher level of support than the Liberals. Indeed, the percentage of identifiers with a very strong Liberal identification has fallen from a peak of 14 per cent in 1979 to just 7 per cent in 2001 (despite an increase in the Liberal vote over this period).

Weaker party identification among Liberal voters has an important effect on voting. Crewe (1985) and Norris (1997, 108) found that Liberal identifiers were not only fewer in number but less likely to vote for their 'natural'

Table 5.6 **Party identification and strength of identification, 1974–2001 (%)**

	1974 F	*1974 O*	*1979*	*1983*	*1987*	*1992*	*1997*	*2001*
With party identification								
Con	35	34	38	36	37	42	28	26
Lab	40	40	36	31	30	31	42	47
Lib	13	14	11	17	16	12	12	13
None	7	8	10	11	11	10	12	10
Identifiers with very strong ID								
Con	32	28	24	26	23	22	15	14
Lab	41	36	29	28	26	25	24	16
Lib	12	14	14	12	10	9	6	7

Source: *British Election Study* surveys 1974–2001.
Note: 'Others' are excluded from the analysis.

party than identifiers of the two major parties. Consequently, whilst the level of identification with the Conservative and Labour parties is closely related to their electoral success, Liberal identification is consistently lower than the party's election showing (as seen in Table 5.6). Indeed, as Table 5.7 shows, around one-fifth of Liberal identifiers have generally voted for other parties (although 86 per cent of Liberal identifiers voted for the party in 2001 – the highest figure in the entire series). Some authors have concluded that this lack of a strong and committed Liberal identification means that any improvements in their electoral fortunes would be short-lived (see for example, Studlar and McAllister, 1987; Rose and McAllister, 1990; Lutz, 1991)

Table 5.7 **Votes of Liberal identifiers, 1974–2001 (%)**

	1974 F	*1974 O*	*1979*	*1983*	*1987*	*1992*	*1997*	*2001*
Lib	78	79	70	84	82	85	79	86
Con	12	13	19	12	13	10	3	2
Lab	8	8	9	3	5	4	13	10
Other	2	1	2	0	0	1	5	1

Source: *British Election Study* surveys 1974–2001.

Table 5.7 also reveals another important feature of the political profile of Liberal Democrat identifiers: the party that 'defectors' (Liberal identifiers who vote for a different party) choose to support. Until 1997 the majority of Liberal defectors voted Conservative (this may seem the natural choice given the social profile), yet in 1997 and 2001 only tiny proportions of Liberal Democrat defectors voted for the Conservatives (while 13 and 10 per cent voted Labour in 1997 and 2001 respectively). This undoubtedly reflects the anti-Conservative alliance between the Liberal Democrats and Labour at the 1997 election and, perhaps to a lesser extent, in 2001. This is, of course, also associated with Labour's shift to the centre ground under Tony Blair.

Retention of support

It is particularly vital for smaller parties to retain supporters between elections. The Liberal Democrats are certainly aware of this and active Liberal Democrat constituencies attempt to retain a high visibility between elections (for example, through the *Focus* newsletter). Nevertheless, Crewe (1985) showed that Liberal voters were the most likely of all partisans to switch between parties from one election to the next. Our analysis of the British Household Panel Study (BHPS) also shows that the Liberal Democrats are more likely to lose support in inter-election years. For example, less than three-quarters of those respondents who said they supported the Liberal Democrats in the 1994 BHPS stayed loyal to the party in the survey of the following year (this compares to around 90 per cent for the other two major parties). Data from the British Election Studies from 1974 to 1997 appears to support Crewe's case and reveals that the trend he identified in 1985 has continued. As Table 5.8 shows, the Liberal vote is less secure than the Conservative and Labour vote, they generally retain far fewer voters than the two main parties between elections.[3]

Table 5.8 **Retention rates, 1974–2001 (%)**

	Conservative	*Labour*	*Liberal*
1974 F–1974 O	86	91	67
1974 O–1979	92	78	58
1979–83	85	67	81
1983–87	84	80	74
1987–92	85	86	67
1992–97	66	89	59
1997–2001	79	80	75

Source: *British Election Study* surveys 1974–2001.
Note: The retention rate is defined as the proportion of voters who had reported voting for a party at successive elections.

During the height of Alliance voting in the mid-1980s the party was relatively successful in retaining support (more so than Labour between the elections of 1979 and 1983). However, the retention rate has fallen since then, standing at less that 60 per cent by 1997, although climbing again to 75 per cent in 2001. It is interesting to examine which party these defectors switched to. Until 1997 if Liberal voters choose to support a different party in a subsequent election it was generally the Conservatives who benefited (and particularly so in 1979). However, in 1997 no fewer than 31 per cent of those who had supported the Liberal Democrats in 1992 switched their allegiance to the Labour Party (while only 5 per cent moved to the Conservatives). In 2001 Labour again benefited most from Liberal Democrat defections, but to nowhere near the same extent as in 1997. These patterns are consistent with the flows of Liberal identifying defectors described above.

Using the British Election Panel Study (BEPS) it was possible to construct an actual flow of the vote matrix for the 1997 and 2001 General Elections (Table 5.9). This gives us more reliable information for the 1997–2001 flow than Table 5.8 derived from the BES series since that is reliant on voters at election B accurately remembering their vote choice at election A. The BEPS

Table 5.9 **1997–2001 flow of the vote based on 1997 electorate (row %)**

Vote, 1997	*Vote, 2001*				
	Conservatives	*Labour*	*Liberal Democrat*	*Other*	*Non-voter*
Conservatives	66	7	10	3	15
Labour	4	67	8	4	17
Liberal Democrat	12	14	54	3	17
Non-voter	15	16	8	3	58

Source: British Election Panel Study, 1997–2001.

panel allows us to match contemporaneous records of individuals' votes at both elections.

As Table 5.9 reveals only 54 per cent of Liberal Democrat voters from 1997 stayed loyal to the party at the next election, whereas 66 per cent of Conservatives and 67 per cent of Labour voters stuck with their party of choice in 2001. Of the Liberal Democrat defectors 12 per cent went to the Conservatives, 14 per cent chose Labour and 17 per cent did not vote in 2001. It is important to remember that this differs from the retention rate as it is based on the percentage of 1997 Liberal Democrat voters who supported them again in 2001, rather than the percentage of 2001 Liberal Democrats who recalled voting for them previously. Clearly even in the context of unprecedented numbers in the House of Commons, the Liberal Democrats still found it comparatively difficult to retain their voters from election to election, and they leaked support almost equally to both the major parties as well as to abstention.

Recruitment

The Liberals share of the vote has been relatively stable since 1974 but the retention rates show the net figures hide a very great deal of gross volatility. Low retention rates have presented the party with real problems, as they must recruit large numbers of voters between elections in order to counteract the advantage of the relative voter stability enjoyed by the two major parties. This means that the local parties must work particularly hard. One senior councillor revealed what this involves: 'You've constantly got to convince people that you're doing the right thing . . . You have to repeat the message, but you have to try and repeat that message in a different way so that it keeps registering. You've got to keep on putting that piece of paper through the door with the right messages on it.'

As Table 5.10 shows, the Liberals have relied most heavily on recruiting 'new' voters. Typically, the party recruits over half of its voters between elections, indeed, according to the BES, no less than 59 per cent of the Liberal Democrat vote in 2001 came from new recruits.

Table 5.10 **Recruitment rates, 1974–2001 (%)**

	Conservative	*Labour*	*Liberal*
1974 Feb.–1974 Oct.	18	20	36
1974 Oct.–1979	33	21	56
1979–83	25	21	70
1983–87	22	28	57
1987–92	22	28	55
1992–97	16	36	62
1997–2001	24	20	59

Source: *British Election Study* surveys 1974–2001.
Note: The recruitment rate is defined as the proportion of the party's vote coming from voters who had not supported the party at the previous election.

The Liberals have been successful in attracting support from both the major parties and from those who abstained or were too young to vote at the previous election (Figure 5.3). It is perhaps not surprising that a third of the SDP/Liberal Alliance's votes in 1983 came from people who had voted Labour in 1979. Similarly, the Liberal Democrats were able to profit from the

Figure 5.3 **Liberal recruitment, 1974–2001 (%)**

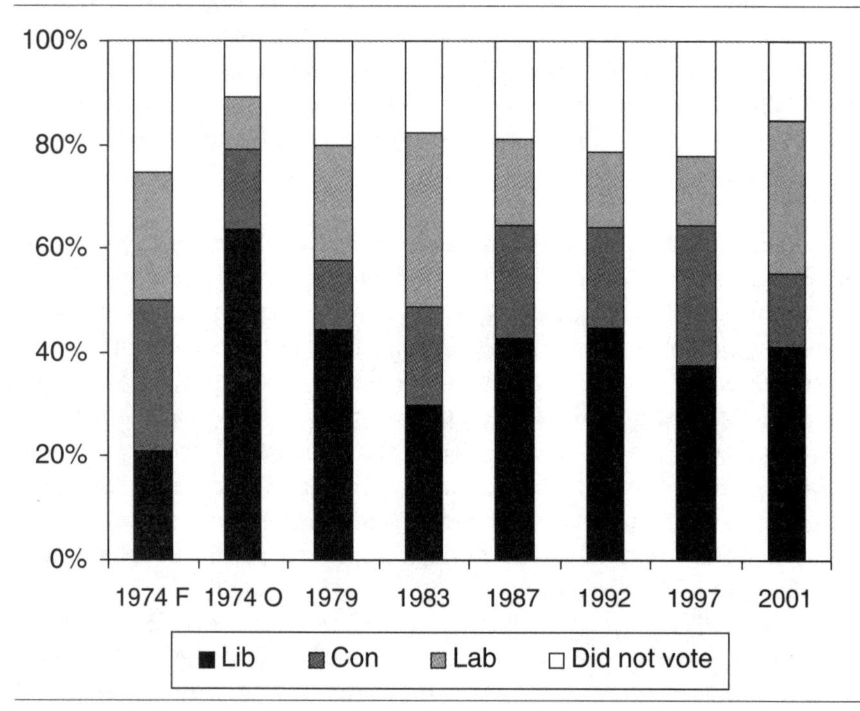

Source: *British Election Study Surveys* 1974–2001.

collapse of the Conservative vote between 1992 and 1997, with over a quarter of Liberal Democrat voters having voted Conservative at the 1992 election. However, it is perhaps even more significant that it was Labour who were able to capture the majority of those voters who defected from the Conservatives in 1997 (almost half of Conservative defectors switched directly to Labour). In 2001 the relationship changed again, with a large proportion of new Liberal Democrat recruits having voted Labour in 1997. This might be because the Conservative vote in 1997 and 2001 came disproportionately from Tory diehards who were less likely to defect than 'softer' Conservatives who had already defected. Nevertheless, Table 5.9 revealed that 10 per cent of this small core Conservative vote moved to the Liberal Democrats in 2001, whereas 8 per cent of the larger Labour vote switched to the Liberal Democrats in 2001. The retention and recruitment figures would certainly seem to add weight to those who suggest that Liberal voting remains, by and large, a temporary expression of dissatisfaction with one or both of the major parties.

Perceptions of the Party

Given the 'softness' and instability of the Liberal vote, the political perceptions of Liberal sympathisers are especially important to the success of the party. Moreover, how supporters of other parties perceive the Liberals has important implications for the party's electoral strategy. If we examine public assessments of the party in 1997 we find that were favourable across the political spectrum – although once again there appeared to be a particular affinity between the Liberal Democrats and Labour voters (Figure 5.4). While

Figure 5.4 **Assessments of the Liberal Democrats**

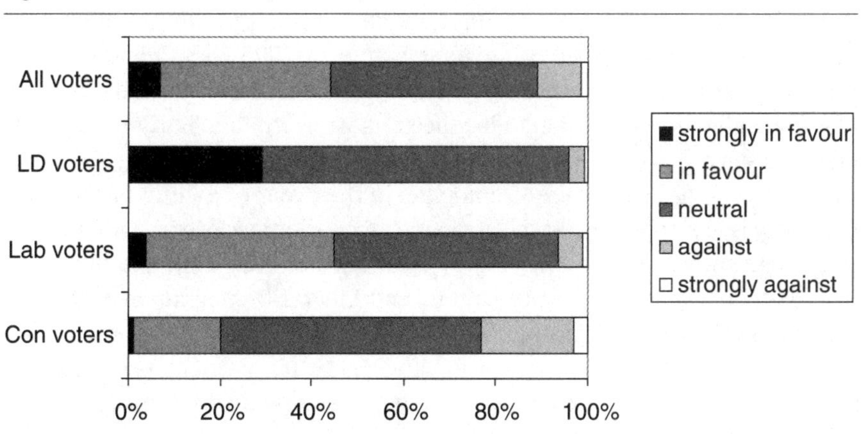

Source: 1997 *British Election Survey* cross-section.

40 per cent of the electorate were either 'in favour of' or 'strongly in favour of' the Liberal Democrats, only 12 per cent said that they were 'against' – or 'strongly against' the party. The ratio of the electorate 'in favour of' vs. 'against the party' of 40:12 for the Liberal Democrats compares to a ratio of 56:14 for the Labour party and 24:47 for the Conservatives in 1997.

Between February 1974 and 1997 the *BES* has asked respondents to assess which of the other two parties the Liberals were closest to. Breaking down these perceptions by reported vote shows that the Liberals have traditionally been seen as closer to the Conservatives than Labour (Figures 5.5 and 5.6). The one notable exception is the 1979 election – directly after the Lib–Lab pact – when voters of both the Liberal and Labour parties tended to believe theirs was a mutually close relationship (although even in 1979 Conservative voters felt the Liberals were closer to their party). For the most part, this was a view generally shared by Liberal voters themselves, although not to the same degree. However, the general perception of a closer link between the Liberals and Conservatives began to alter in 1992. Liberal Democrat voters were now almost evenly split, while Labour voters believed the Liberal Democrats were closer to them than to the Tories.

The real change occurred in 1997, however, with voters of all three parties now believing the Liberal Democrats were closer to New Labour than to John Major's Conservative Party. The change, even from 1992, was dramatic. Nearly half of Conservative voters thought the Liberals were closest to Labour; the corresponding figure for Labour voters was 68 per cent (an increase of 23 per cent since 1992). The most interesting change though was among Liberal Democrat voters, with nearly 60 per cent saying that their party were closer to Labour (only around 20 per cent considered the party closer to the Conservatives).

This changing pattern was undoubtedly encouraged by the abandonment of the party's official 'equidistant' stance in 1995 (see Chapter 2 for a fuller discussion). The succession of Tony Blair as leader of the Labour Party made the abandonment of equidistance almost inevitable. Early in his leadership, Blair called for a 'dialogue of ideas' and expressed his party's willingness to work with the Liberal Democrats in the event of a hung parliament. On policy issues too, the Liberal Democrats were clearly closer to Labour than the Conservatives, particularly in key areas such as education and health.

The perceived closeness of Labour and Liberal Democrats in 1997 was manifested in tactical voting, with the best-positioned anti-Conservative party normally being the beneficiary (Table 5.11). It is particularly noticeable from Table 5.11 that the smallest increase in the Labour vote came in constituencies where the Liberal Democrats were either a close second to the Conservatives (a majority of under 10,000) or holding the seat. Similarly, in

Figure 5.5 **Liberal Party is closer to the Conservative or Labour Party?**

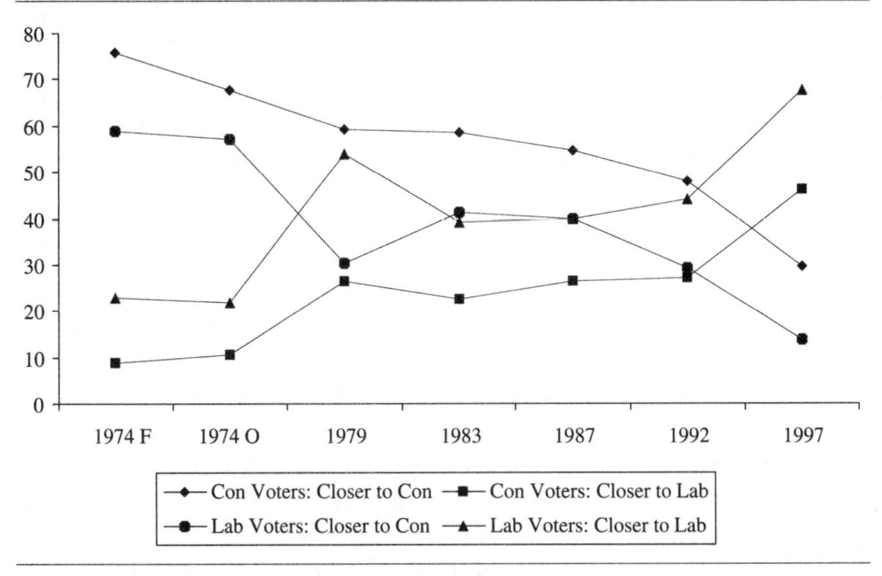

Source: *British Election Study surveys* 1974–97.
Note: The question was not asked in 2001.

Figure 5.6 **Liberal Party is closer to the Conservative or Labour Party (Liberal voters)?**

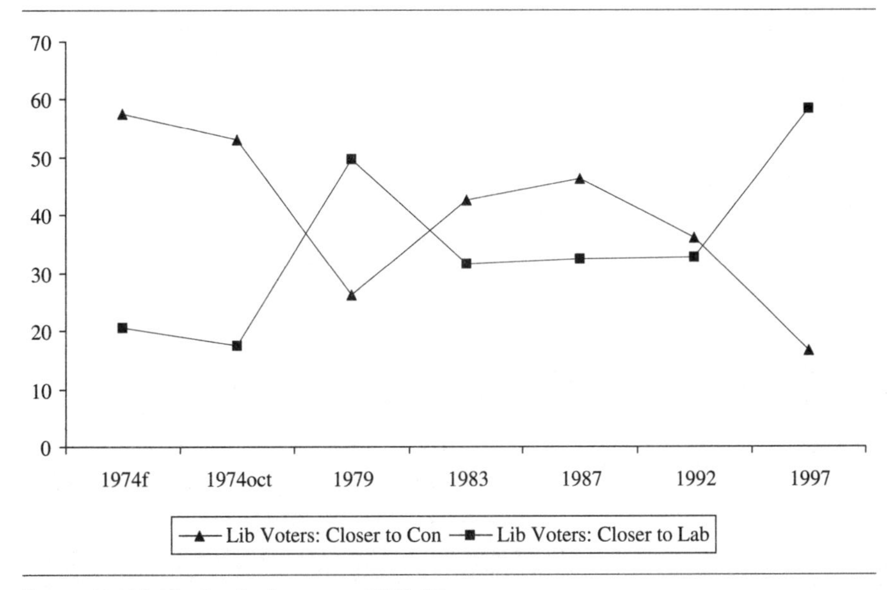

Source: *British Election Study* surveys 1974–97.
Note: The question was not asked in 2001.

Table 5.11 **Tactical voting and change in vote share, 1997**

Tactical situation	*Con*	*Lab*	*Lib-Dem*	*No.*
Con: Lab seats	−12.7	+12.8	−3.1	182
Lab: Con seats	−11.1	+8.5	−0.9	230
Con: LD (maj. <10,000) seats	−11.5	+6.1	+2.1	47
Con: LD (maj. >10,000) seats	−12.8	+9.2	−0.3	111
LD held seats	−9.7	+6.2	0.0	18

Note: Due to the small numbers involved, other tactical scenarios are excluded from the analysis.

constituencies where Labour were second to the Conservatives the Liberal Democrat vote fell considerably regardless of the marginality of the seat. The campaign case studies in Chapter 10 discusses the importance of tactical voting in different constituency contexts in much greater depth.

This increasingly close relationship between Labour and the Liberal Democrats is also reflected in the second choice party of Liberal voters (Figure 5.7). While the Conservatives were the second choice party of Liberal supporters in every election from February 1974 until 1992 – peaking in 1987 – a dramatic shift occurred in 1997. Labour became by far the favoured

Figure 5.7 **Second choice party of Liberal voters, 1974–97 (%)**

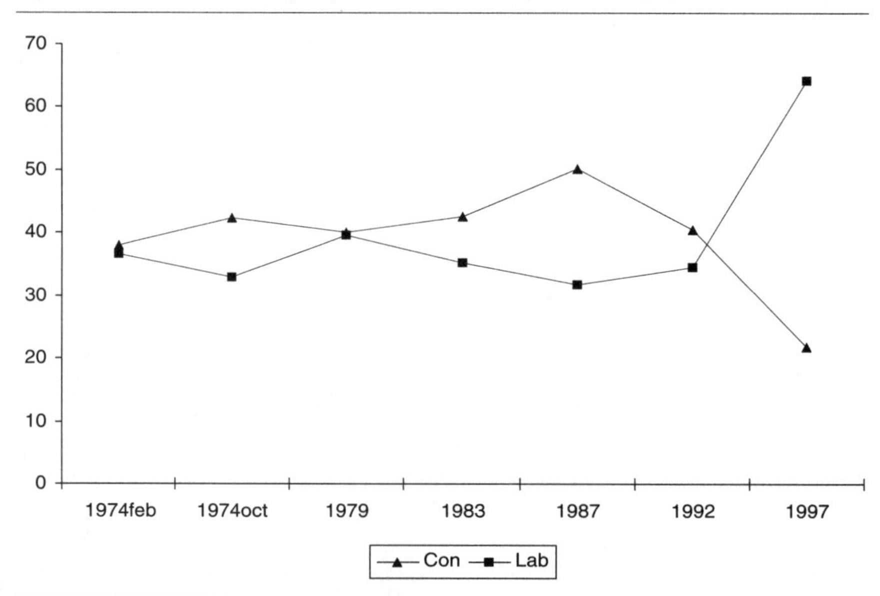

Source: *British Election Study* surveys 1974–97.
Note: The question was not asked in 2001.

second choice party, with nearly two-thirds of Liberal Democrat voters preferring them to the Conservatives.

Analysing the second choice party of Conservative and Labour voters confirms these findings and highlights the exceptionally close links between Labour and the Liberal Democrats after 1992 (Figure 5.8). Moreover, the Liberals have been the clear second choice party of both Conservative and Labour voters since 1979, or in other words, the least disliked party. However, an obvious shift occurred in the 1990s. Conservative voters have traditionally been the most sympathetic towards the Liberals but this changed in 1997 with just over a half now saying they would vote for the Liberal Democrats as their second choice party (a fall of around 13 per cent from 1992). The corresponding figure for Labour voters increased by 10 per cent between the two elections.

But have these perceptions changed since 1997? Is there still a close relationship between Labour and the Liberal Democrats? Since 1987 the BES have asked respondents whether they approve, disapprove or neither approve or disapprove of the major parties. Table 5.12 shows the results broken down by party voted for.

Table 5.12 reaffirms the anti-Conservative alliance that formed between

Figure 5.8 **Conservative and Labour voters choosing Liberals as second choice, 1979–97 (%)**

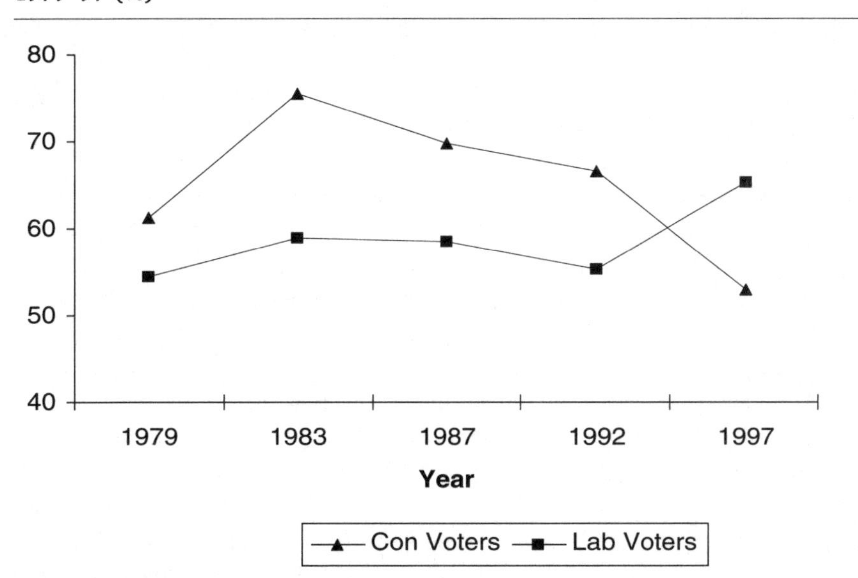

Source: *British Election Study* surveys 1979–97.

Table 5.12 **Disapprove (or not in favour) of party, 1987–2001 (%)**

	1987	*1992*	*1997*	*2001*
Conservative voters				
Lab	84	83	43	59
Lib	25	19	23	31
Labour voters				
Con	74	72	74	69
Lib	28	16	6	19
Liberal voters				
Con	42	43	56	67
Lab	56	44	13	28

Source: *British Election Study* surveys 1974–2001.
Note: The 2001 BES question is slightly different from previous questions. The 2001 figures have been derived from a 11–point scale ranging from 0 (strongly disapprove) to 10 (strongly approve). Consequently, 0–3 has been coded as disapprove, 4–6 as neither approve nor disapprove and 7–10 as approve.

the Liberal Democrats and Labour in 1997. While negative assessments of the Liberals remained constant – at around 20 to 25 per cent – among Conservative voters between 1987 and 1997, the percentage of Labour voters offering a negative assessment of the Liberals fell from 28 per cent in 1987 to just 6 per cent in 1997. Liberal voters themselves became increasingly hostile to the Conservatives during this period and increasingly sympathetic to Labour. Indeed, the proportion of Liberal voters hostile to the Labour Party fell from 56 per cent in 1987 to 13 per cent in 1997. However, there are signs that this very close relationship cooled somewhat in 2001. The percentage of Labour voters with a negative perception of the Liberals increased to 19 per cent, while the equivalent figure for the Liberals' view of Labour stood at 28 per cent (more than double the 1997 figure). This is not to say, however, that Liberal voters are becoming more sympathetic towards the Conservatives – the percentage of Liberal Democrat voters with a negative perception of the Tories increased for the third election in a row, standing at no less than 67 per cent in 2001.

Another perspective on the political closeness of Labour and Liberal Democrat supporters can be obtained from the British Election Panel Study. In 1997 and 2001 the survey asked (the same) respondents about their strength of feeling for all the major parties (ranging form strongly in favour to strongly against). An examination of the patterns of feelings of Liberal Democrat and Labour supporters for each of the parties in 2001 shows that both sets of voters are strongly anti-Conservative, but are relatively close, not only of their own party, but to the other (see Figure 5.9). This implies that in terms of political affiliations, there is a strong negative relationship between being Conservative and being 'centre-left' (Liberal Democrat or Labour), but a positive relationship between having approval for either of the 'centre-left' parties. This is confirmed in Table 5.13, which shows the correlations between the strength of feeling scores for the three main parties in 1997 and 2001. The table also confirms that Liberal Democrats are slightly less anti-Conservative than Labour supporters.

Figure 5.9 **Strength of feeling, by vote, 2001**

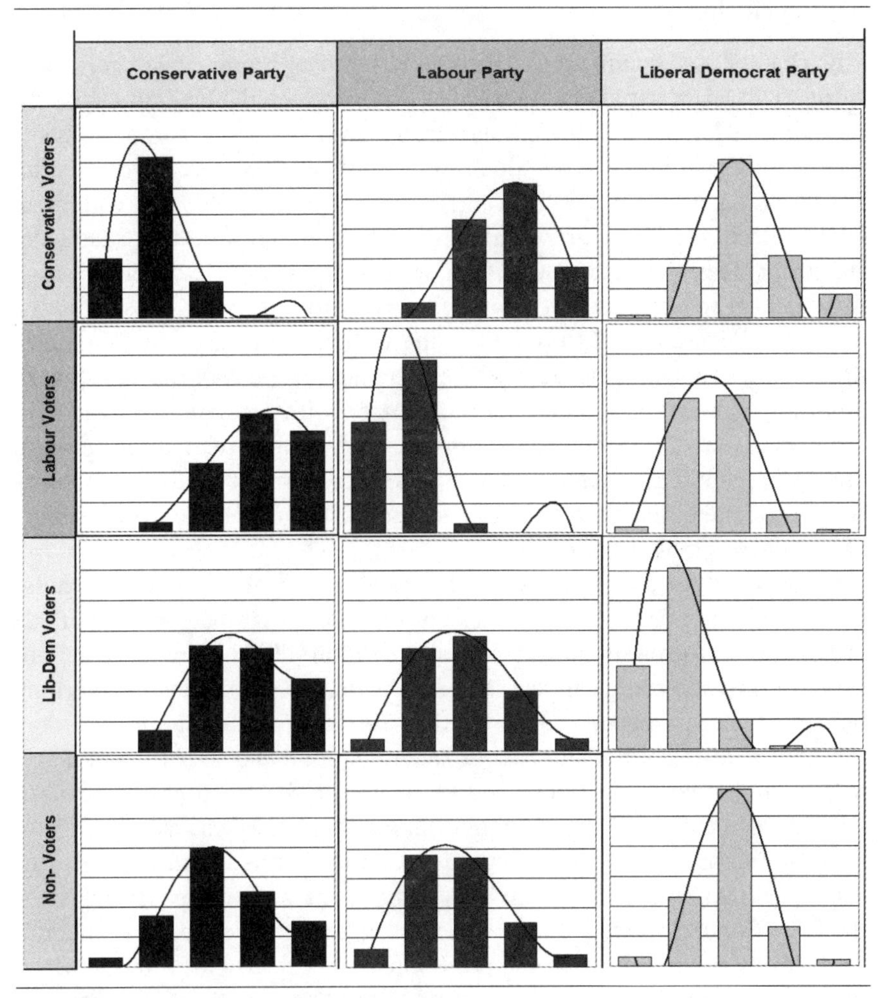

Source: BEPS 1997–2001, Wave 8. N=2331.
Respondents were asked to express their feelings for each party from 'strongly in favour' (left of scale) to 'strongly against' (right of scale).

Table 5.13 **Bivariate correlations between strength of feeling for main parties, 1997 and 2001**

Contrast	*Pearson's R 1997*	*Pearson's R 2001*
Conservative–Labour	−0.47	−.50
Conservative–Liberal Democrats	−.10	−0.22
Liberal Democrat–Labour	+0.26	+0.26

Source: British Election Panel study, 1997–2001. All correlations significant at p=0.005.

Conclusion

This chapter has examined the social and political profile of Liberal voters since 1974. From our analysis it is clear that although the Liberals cannot be described as *the* party of the middle classes, they perform disproportionably well among that group. The odds ratio show that they have a very similar class profile to the Conservatives and that this has remained fairly consistent across elections. The party also has increasingly distinct heartlands of support, at least in terms of seats won, in several regions. However, although there appear to be variations in support among the educated, those working in the public sector and those belonging to nonconformist denominations, logistic regression models are unable to account for much of the party's variation in support, particularly when compared with Conservative voters. In other words Liberal Democrats voting was very weakly related to the social and demographic characteristics of voters. If the party is unable to mobilise support on the basis of social divisions, instead it must look to the possibility of issue-based mobilisation.

Given that the social profile of the Liberal Democrat vote remains similar to the profile of Conservative voters, it is interesting that the political outlook of Liberal Democrat supporters has become more like the profile of Labour supporters over recent years. As we have shown, Liberal Democrat voters are now much more likely to believe that they are closer to the Labour Party than the Conservatives, nominate Labour as their second choice party and defect to Labour between elections. The closeness of the relationship between Liberal Democrats and Labour supporters in the 1990s was clearly encouraged by the party leadership. Although Charles Kennedy did not have the same personal relationship with Tony Blair as his predecessor, events since the 2001 General Election would seem to suggest that the Liberal Democrats are unlikely to move back to the position they occupied in the 1980s where they were generally perceived as closest to the Conservatives. However, the leadership has signalled a move back towards equidistance (or at least a growing disatisfaction with Labour), and this has been reinforced by the promotion of more conservative members to positions of prominence since post-2001.[4] Coalition partnerships with Labour in the Scottish parliament and the Welsh Assembly government probably added to the perception that the Liberal Democrats are closest to Labour (although Cowley (2002) has pointed out that in Westminster the parliamentary party moved away from Labour after 1999).

Perhaps the most interesting finding that have come out of the above analysis is the continued 'softness' of the Liberal Democrat vote. Crewe (1985) found that the Liberals suffered from low levels of party identification, both in terms of absolute numbers and in the strength of identification, and were generally poor at retaining their supporters between elections. Our figures suggest that these trends have continued, the Liberal Democrats have been unable to attract a loyal and committed group of voters who stay with the party from one election to the next. The party's national share of the vote may have changed little since the 1990s but this hides a great deal of gross volatility – the party must typically recruit over half of its voters between elections to counteract the large scale defections.

We will discuss the implications of these findings for the party's electoral strategy in more detail in the third part of the book. Before doing so, however, we will first examine the attitudinal basis of Liberal support to discover whether there is a clear ideological heartland of support.

Notes

1 The odds ratios were calculated by dividing the ratio of voting in the professional and managerial classes by the ratio of voting in the manual working class for each pair of parties (for a discussion of odds ratio see Crewe, 1986).

2 Regression models for all elections were run and the results found to be similar. Due to constraints of space only three models are reported here. The three elections chosen represented the three phases the party went through: from Liberal to Alliance to Liberal Democrat.

3 The *BES* asks respondents to recall their voting (where applicable) in the previous General Election. Analysis shows that there is a significant mismatch between voter recall in 1997 of the 1992 vote and the actual 1992 vote. For our purposes, the amount of Liberal Democrat voting in 1992 seems under-represented. Nevertheless, the general pattern of recruitment and retention remains consistent with the pattern found by Crewe's study and our analysis of the BHPS.

4 For example, Vincent Cable replaced Mathew Taylor as Treasury spokesperson in the 2003 reshuffle.

6

Sympathy and support for the Liberal Democrat agenda

Introduction

One of the most fundamental problems facing the Liberal Democrats is asserting themselves in a predominantly two party system. In particular a crucial task facing the modern third party is to maintain an identity that is distinctive from that of the two major parties (Dunleavy, 1993; Crewe and King, 1995; Russell and Fieldhouse, 2000). In the days of the Alliance, many commentators concluded that the lack of identity of the third party caused a shortfall in public support and precipitated only short-lived improvements in the fortunes of the third party and a relatively unstable or 'soft' core of the Liberal vote, as described in the previous chapter. It has been argued that, the Liberal Democrats, like their predecessors, continue to suffer from a failure to communicate a distinctive identity (Rose and McAllister, 1990; Crewe and King, 1995). In Downsian terminology (Downs 1957) a party of the centre is likely to be squeezed from both left and right. Essentially, whilst being the least unpopular of the three largest parties on many issues, the centre party may be the most popular on very few. Whilst this may make the party a safe haven for protest votes, it does little to provide a long-term basis of support (Crewe, 1985; Studlar and McAllister, 1987; Clarke and Zuk, 1989; Huang, 1999).

As we argued in Chapter 5, unlike the British Conservative and Labour parties, the Liberal Democrats do not have a clear heartland of support in terms of social or demographic characteristics. In this chapter we examine the attitudinal basis of Liberal Democrat support and consider whether the party is able to mobilise voters on the basis of their political attitudes in absence of a powerful social basis of mobilisation. We provide evidence from the 1997 and 2001 British General Election Studies, and investigate the extent to which the Liberal Democrats have developed a distinct attitudinal heartland and analyse how successful the party was in converting sympathy into votes. It is hypothesised that because of the 'softness' of their support and the lack of a social heartland, the Liberal Democrats are forced to mobilise voters by campaigning around policy issues and through creating electoral credibility in a geographically disparate fashion (this is further developed in Chapter 7). However, they continue to find themselves trapped in a two party system, and whilst they may be *less unpopular* than the other main parties, only a small minority of voters are actually 'closest' to their position. Furthermore, because of structural obstacles (in particular the electoral system), the Liberal Democrats are less able to convert sympathy (or latent support) into actual votes (see Chapter 7 and also Rae, 1971; Taagepera and Shugart, 1989; or Gallagher, 1991 for a fuller discussion of the reasons for the structural inhibitors to electoral progress). This is likely to be particularly important in areas where the Liberal Democrats have little hope of victory. The implications for electoral strategy are picked up later in Chapter 8.

A centre party?

Traditionally the third force in British politics has struggled to impose its identity on the electorate (see Dunleavy, 1993). During the campaigns of 1992, 1997 and 2001, the need to establish a distinctive image appeared to be one of the main challenges facing the Liberal Democrats. As the party's campaign director and his assistant in 1997 wrote:

> The party's message also needed to be more focused to deal with the "Nobody knows what they stand for" problem. Education remained the priority . . . Our advocacy of [hypothecated taxation] which had the danger of having us portrayed as the high-tax party, nevertheless succeeded both in placing a burr beneath Labour's saddle and in assisting in our strategy of differentiation. (Holme and Holmes, 1998, 18)

The success or failure of this strategy would largely determine the outcome of the party's electoral fortunes. In his account of the 1997 campaign, Jones reports that key Liberal Democrat personnel felt that the party profited from a more radical stance than that proposed by the other parties (Jones, 1997, 256). Having distinctive policies however, is not in itself a guarantee of maximising electoral support. A 'centre' party is always vulnerable to a 'squeeze' from both left and right (see Duverger, 1954). As Rose and McAllister put it: 'Because the median voter tends to have centrist values, centre parties are always vulnerable. The Conservative and Labour parties can both compete for their votes. The resulting squeeze leaves the centre party with little middle-of-the-road support and fewer votes still from the left or the right' (Rose and McAllister, 1990; 192).

But are the Liberal Democrats really a party of the centre? As we shall see in Chapter 8, the party elite prefer to talk about the 'radical centre', strategically placing themselves neither both in the mainstream of political opinion nor on the radical edge of British party politics. In the previous chapter we showed that since 1992, Liberal Democrat voters have come to regard themselves as closer to Labour voters than to Conservatives (and vice versa). But where do voters place the Liberal Democrats on a left–right continuum in comparison with the other parties, and perhaps more importantly in comparison with themselves?

Figures 6.1a and 6.1b show the overall distribution of the electorate on a left–right scale in 1997 and 2001 respectively. The familiar bell shaped ('normal') distribution with a peak in the centre confirms that by and large the electorate conforms to classical spatial model predictions of voter distributions – that is, with the majority of voters clustering around the centre with fewer and fewer voters found as we move towards the extremes. If we examine the same distribution form the perspective of voters of each party separately (Figures 6.1c and 6.1d), we find, as we might expect, that Liberal Democrat voters (in 1997 and 2001) have a stronger peak in the centre, with Labour voters placing themselves rather more to the left and Conservative voters placing themselves rather more to the right. The Liberal Democrats were placed slightly more to the left in 2001 than in 1997, no doubt reflecting their more radical stance on the issues discussed below.

Figure 6.2 examines how the voters perceive the different parties. Figure 6.2a and 6.2b show that in 1997 and 2001 the Conservatives were perceived to be on the right of the scale, whereas Labour in 1997 was placed towards the left-hand end of the scale. In 1997 and 2001 (Figures 6.2c, and 6.2d) Labour had been perceived to have shifted towards the centre thus potentially squeezing Liberal Democrat support. The Liberal Democrats, however, were perceived by the electorate to have remained very much in the centre ground (Figures 6.2e and 6.2f) with a strong peak at the centre of the distribution. This supports the idea that any abandonment of equidistance was more the inevitable consequence of Labour changing image, rather than any movement of the Liberal Democrats. Thus, however the party perceives itself (which is discussed in detail in Chapter 8) the electorate very much identifies it as a party of the centre. This poses the problem identified above, namely that they face a squeeze as the Labour Party in particular seeks to win over voters from the centre ground.

One way to avoid this centre party squeeze is to outflank one of the major parties (on left or right) or to step outside the left–right spectrum, by appealing on the basis of new issue agenda. Later we will examine how one of the central objectives of Liberal Democrat electoral strategy has been to overcome this problem and to develop a distinctive image (Chapter 8 below).

In terms of policy positions, in 1997 and in 2001 the Liberal Democrats occupied distinctive ground in a number of policy arenas, including education and taxation, constitutional issues (such as electoral reform and the reforming of political institutions), public spending and the environment. Below we explore whether voters who sympathise with the Liberal Democrats on these issues convert this into electoral support for the party. First, however, we consider the role of attitudes in determining Liberal Democrat voting in the context of the model of Liberal voting as introduced in the previous chapter.

Issue based mobilisation? Political attitudes and Liberal Democrat voting

There is plentiful evidence that as class has become less potent in influencing voting behaviour, the electorate has become increasingly inclined to vote on the basis of policy preferences (see, for example, Franklin, 1984; Robertson, 1984; and Crewe, 1986; but also Heath *et al.*, 1991). Furthermore, rather than holding randomly assorted attitudes towards these issues, voters tend to structure their attitudes around common ideological themes (see Scarbrough 1984; Heath and Evans, 1988; Fieldhouse, 1995). Certainly the Liberal Democrats have never enjoyed the same potential for mobilising support on the basis of social divisions as the other main parties in British politics (see Chapter 5 above). So if the party is unable to mobilise support on the basis of social divisions, it must look, instead, to the possibility of issue-based mobilisation. In brief, the issues-based mobilisation hypothesis states that the basis for appealing to voters cannot be along class lines or based on the tradition of party identification, but, rather, the Liberal Democrats must appeal to voters on the basis of the major issues of the day. Certainly, many of our interviewees referred to people's political beliefs when they were asked 'Who do you think votes for the Liberal Democrats?' As one MP replied: 'I don't think there is any economic group fits the position we take and what differentiates us in our political positioning, so in that sense I don't think there is one group, unless you talk about the group of people who are perhaps more, I mean naturally, liberal with a small "l".'

Appeal to voters beliefs and policy preferences means their votes are likely to be conditional and potentially subject to lower retention rates as was demonstrated in the previous chapter. As another MP put it, this means 'winning every vote on merit'. Even if the party succeeds in identifying a popular appeal, as we have argued, simply having popular policies alone does not guarantee success. That latent popularity must be converted to real support at the polling booth. If attitudes are important in determining voting behaviour, then a successful party must have policies that are not only popular but also distinctive from those of their main competitors. As

Figure 6.1 **Left–right scales: self-perception**

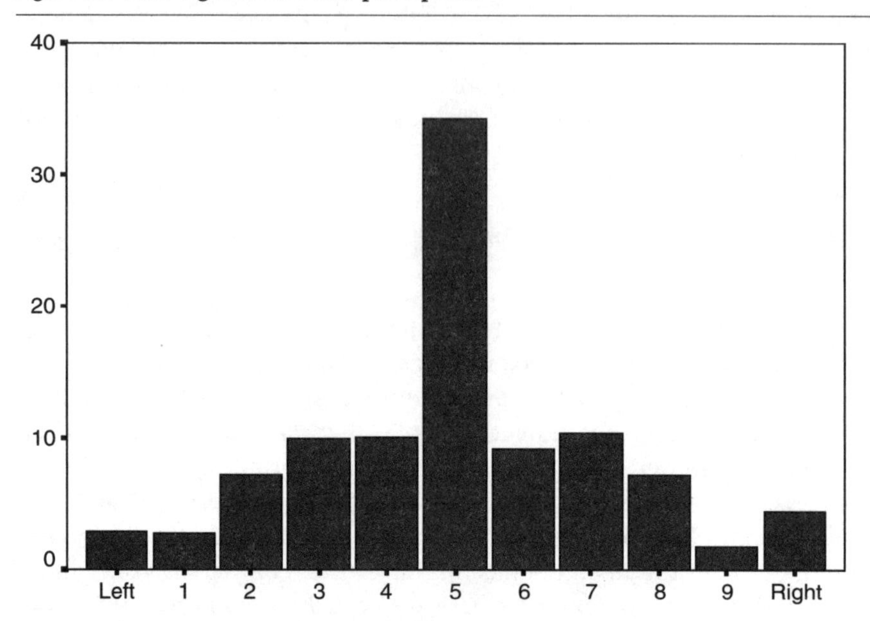

Figure 6.1a **Place yourself on left–right scale? (1997)**

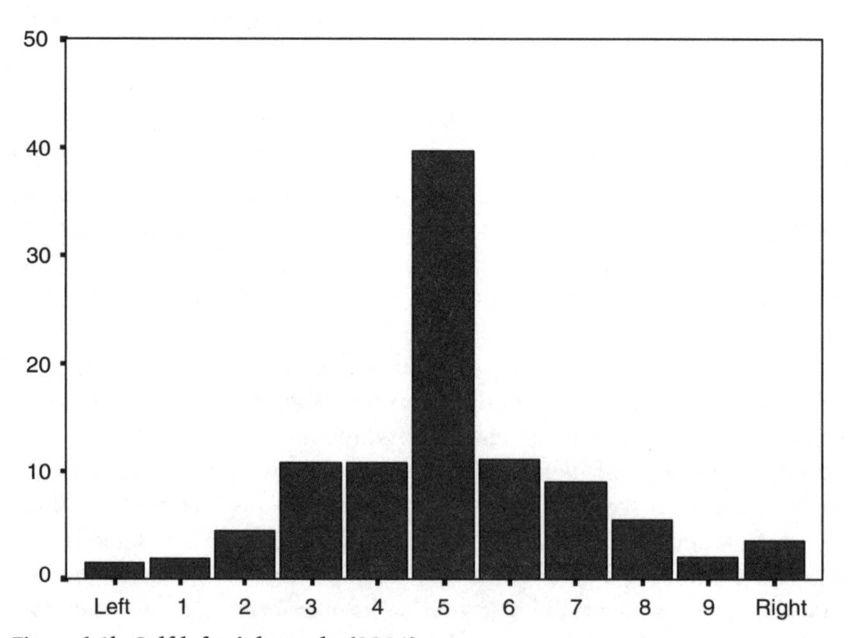

Figure 6.1b **Self left–right scale (2001)**

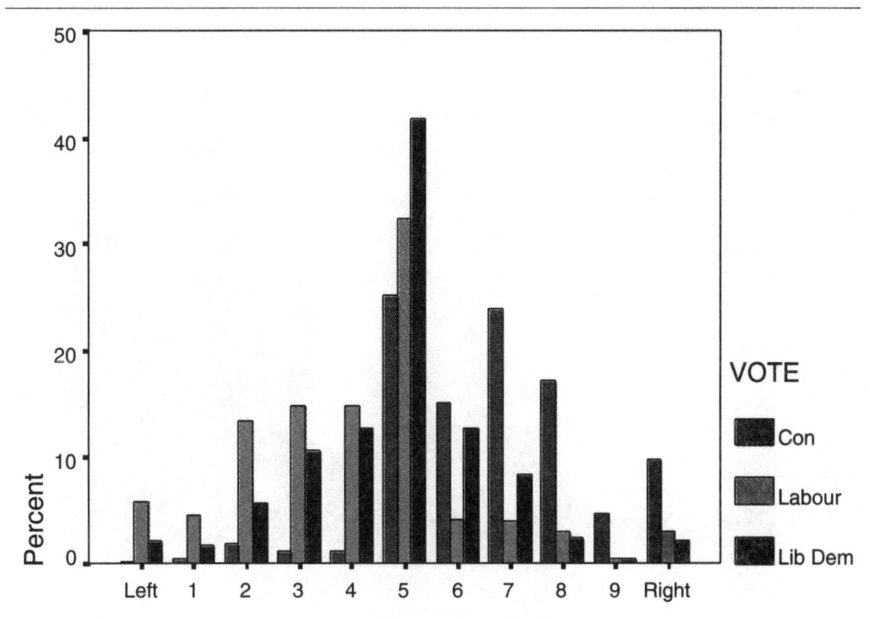

Figure 6.1c **Place yourself on left–right scale? (1997)**

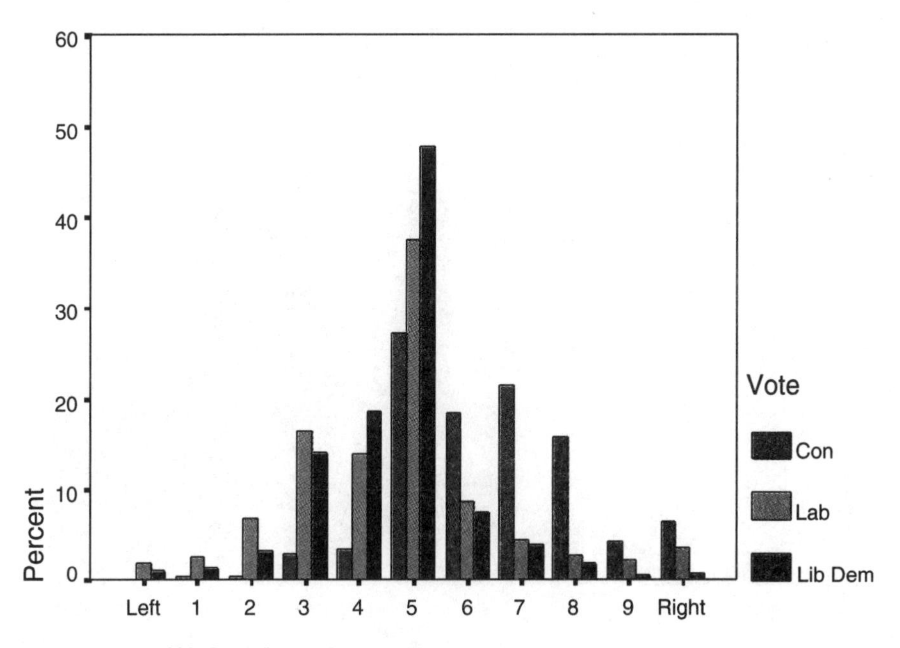

Figure 6.1d **Self left–right scale (2001)**

Figure 6.2 **Left–right scales: perception of parties**

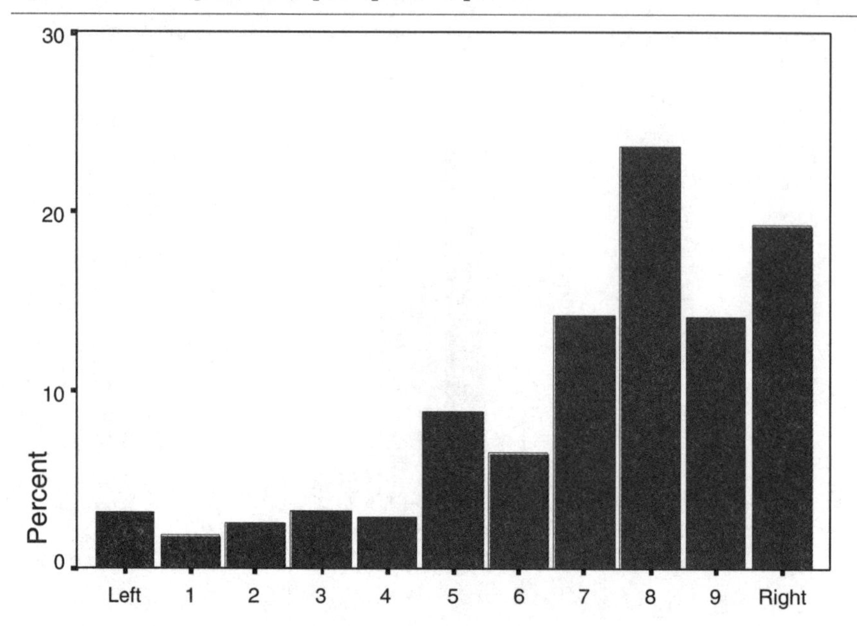

Figure 6.2a **Place Conservative Party on left–right scale? (1997)**

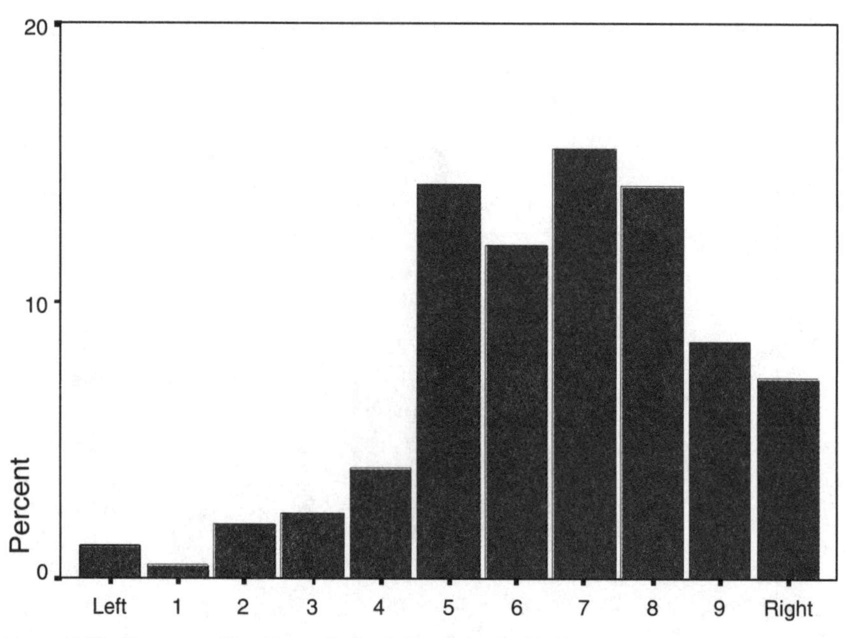

Figure 6.2b **Conservative Party left–right scale (2001)**

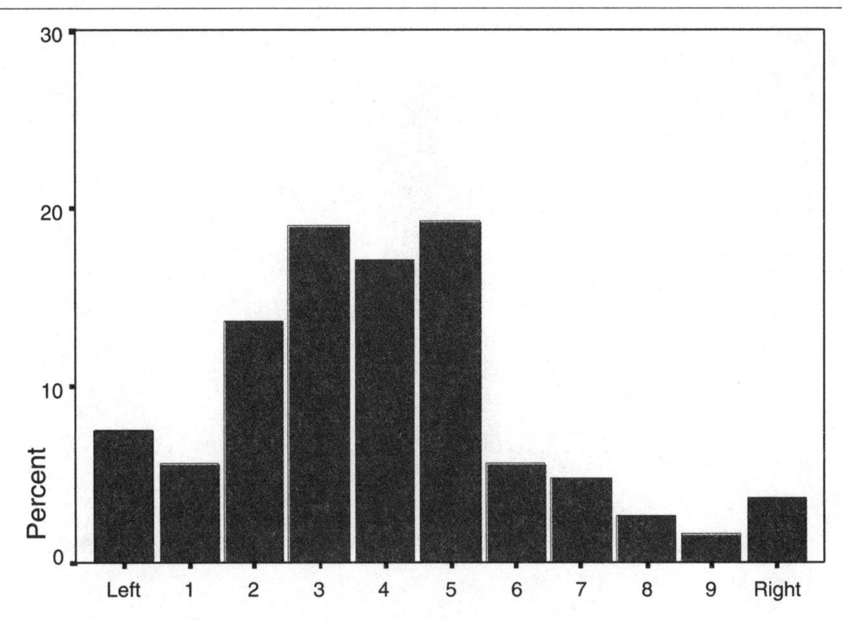

Figure 6.2c **Place Labour Party on left–right scale? (1997)**

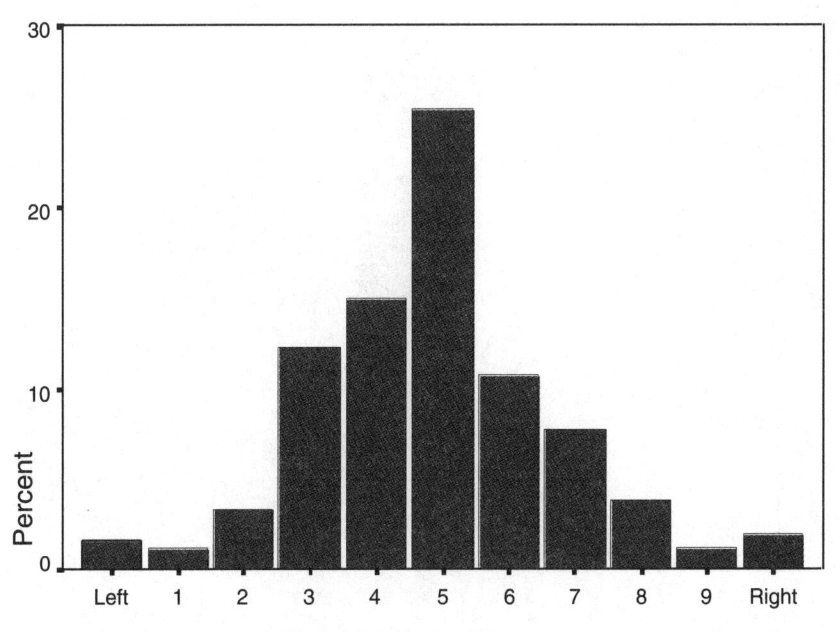

Figure 6.2d **Labour Party left–right scale (2001)**

Figure 6.2 (continued)

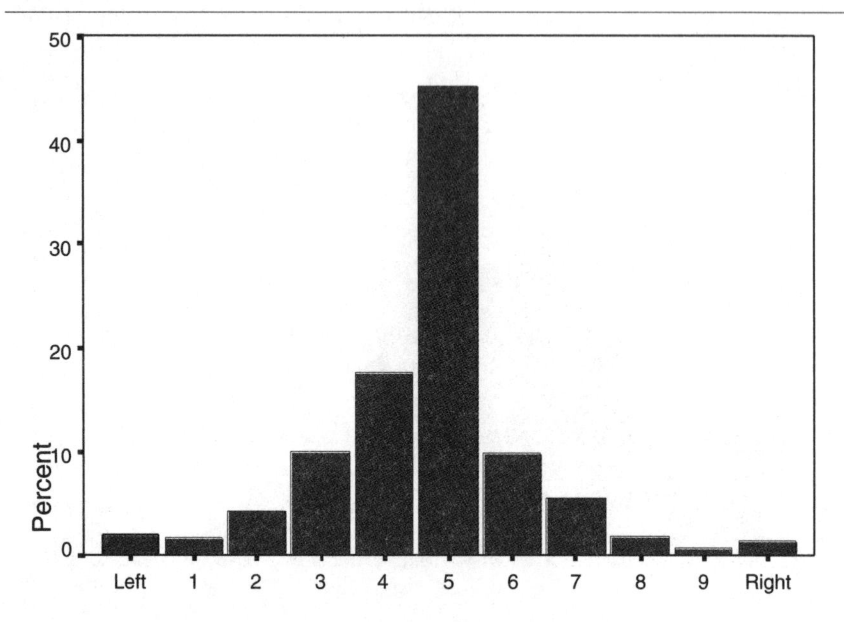

Figure 6.2e **Place Lib Dem Party on left–right scale? (1997)**

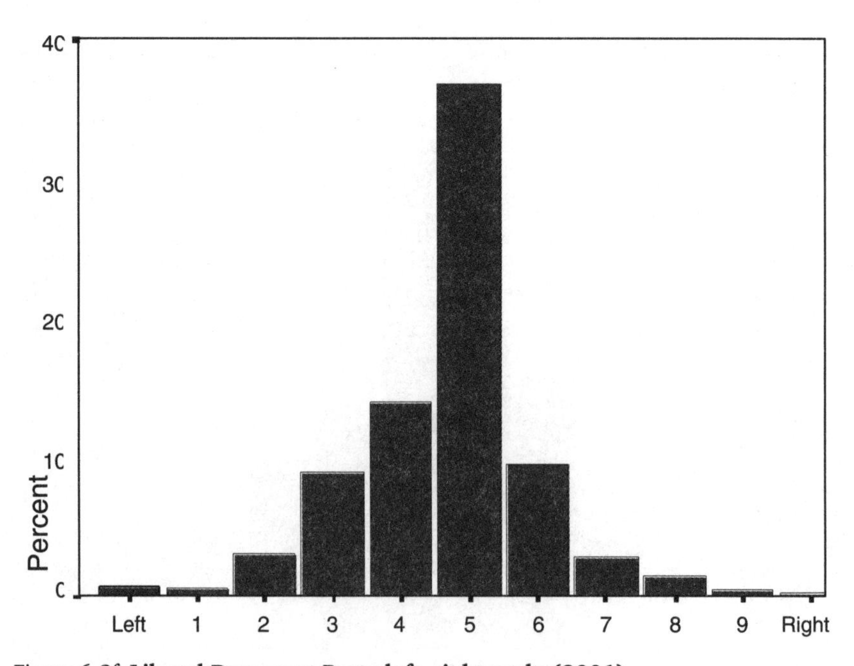

Figure 6.2f **Liberal Democrat Party left–right scale (2001)**

indicated above one of the major problems faced by the Liberal Democrats is to achieve this distinctiveness and avoid being squeezed from both left and right. The following sections examine whether the Liberal Democrat party and Liberal Democrat voters were characterised by any particular set of values; the popularity of the Liberal Democrat position on major issues of the day is assessed; and finally the success of the party in converting sympathy into votes is examined.

A Liberal Democrat agenda

Although widely perceived as a party of the centre, there are a number of key policy areas where the Liberal Democrats have striven to be distinct from the two major parties. These include the future of Britain in Europe, public services, the environment, constitutional issues, the economy and social liberalism. In the run up to the 2001 General Election campaign when most of our interviews were conducted, the almost unanimous perception was that the key election issues would be education and health, both of which would be potentially strong areas for the party. The third most commonly identified issue was crime and policing. These three issues also featured heavily in campaign literature and in the party election manifesto, under the broader banner of 'Freedom, Justice and Honesty'. Other key issues that were identified were social justice, pensions and poverty. However, our interviewees themselves also identified a much wider range of issues of concern more explicitly to Liberal Democrats voters than the electorate as a whole: these included personal freedom, European integration, the environment and constitutional reform or democratic principles. These can be considered cornerstones of the party's political identity, but not necessarily thought of as vote winners. Thus whereas health and education were both important to the party and popular with the electorate and consequently had a high profile in the campaign; other policy areas were regarded as potential voter losers (such as Europe, asylum seekers and prison reform).

The position of Liberal Democrat voters at the 1997 General Election on a wide selection of issues measured in the BES is detailed in Figure 6.3. All the issues presented in Figure 6.3 were coded into a simple three way categorisation – those who favoured the position advocated by the Liberal Democrat manifesto in 1997, those who were against the official Liberal Democrat policy and those who responded neutrally (including don't knows and not answered). In broad terms, most Liberal Democrat voters generally agreed with the party position on most issues. Unfortunately comparable questions were not asked in 2001 except in the case of closer European integration for which data is presented for both elections. Each issue is discussed further below.

Figure 6.3 **What do Liberal Democrat voters think, 1997–2001?**

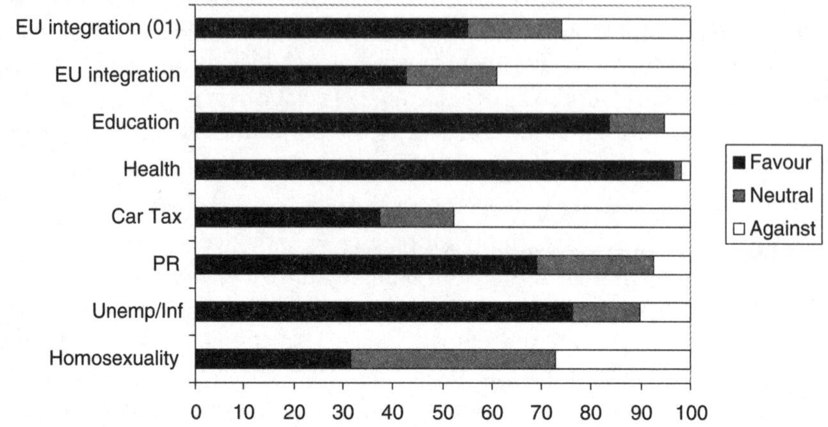

EU integration (01)
EU integration
Education
Health
Car Tax
PR
Unemp/Inf
Homosexuality
0 10 20 30 40 50 60 70 80 90 100
Favour
Neutral
Against

Source: *1997 British Election Survey* cross-section.

That Liberal Democrats voters should agree with the party on the issues is not a sufficient condition of issue-based mobilisation. Rather than looking at the position of Liberal Democrat voters, a different perspective was required using analysis of how voters who shared the Liberal Democrat position on each issue, actually voted (Table 6.1). Although the Liberal Democrats may have shared each policy position with one of the other parties (usually Labour), it would be reasonable to expect them to do relatively well amongst this sympathetic section of the electorate. However in 1997, the Liberal Democrats won no more than 24 per cent of the vote amongst voters agreeing with their policy position on any single issue.

Table 6.1 **Vote of individuals agreeing with Liberal Democrat position on selected issues, 1997**

	Con vote (%)	*Labour vote (%)*	*LD vote (%)*	*Others (%)*	*N No.*
EU integration (in favour)	18	59	20	4	1007
Education (for hypothecated taxation)	23	51	21	5	1694
NHS spending (increase)	27	50	18	3	2640
Prohibitive car tax (agree)	23	50	22	4	528
PR for British elections (agree)	23	49	23	5	1410
Prioritise employment over inflation	25	52	18	5	1994
Homosexual rights (not gone far enough)	16	56	24	4	515
Total (BES)	29	49	17	5	

Source: 1997 *British Election Study* Survey cross-section.

Britain and Europe

Perhaps above all else, the Liberal Democrats are identified as a pro-European party. This was an issue on which the Liberal Democrats could clearly be identified as distinct from the other mainstream parties: advocacy for the single currency was unmatched by any other party in the 1997 and 2001 General Elections.

Voters' attitudes towards Europe were measured by their views on closer European integration. Like the electorate as a whole, Liberal Democrat voters were split on the issue. Less than half positively endorsed a policy of closer integration, with a similar proportion being against it (Figure 6.3). In 2001 slightly more than half endorsed the pro-European message, but a significant number still opposed it.

But do attitudes towards European integration influence voting behaviour? Examining how voters with different views voted in 1997 reveals very little difference in Liberal Democrat voting between Europhiles (20 per cent) and Eurosceptics (15 per cent). A large majority of pro-Europeans voted Labour, but the Liberal Democrats were only two points ahead of the more Eurosceptic Conservative party even amongst this group (Table 6.1) In 2001 one-quarter of Europhiles voted Liberal Democrat compared to 17 per cent of the remainder of the BES sample. As in 1997, however, the majority (over 50 per cent) voted Labour and almost 20 per cent voted Conservative.

Public services

A second area in which the Liberal Democrats were distinct in 1997 was on the issue of public spending and public service provision. The party had a unique policy of hypothecated taxation, with funds generated from an increase in income tax to be earmarked for education. Together with a commitment to increased funds for the NHS, hypothecated taxation was a cornerstone of the Liberal Democrat manifesto in 1997. The manifesto clearly stated that the Liberal Democrats favoured increasing the burden of tax in order to fund the party's spending pledges. For example, on the principle of hypothecated taxation: 'Liberal Democrats will make education the next government's top priority. We will invest an additional £2 billion per year in education, funded by an extra 1p in the pound on the basic rate of income tax' (*Make the Difference* – the Liberal Democrat Manifesto 1997, 'Education' Section: 1).

A similar pledge, this time worth £3 billion was made in 2001. Likewise, the commitment to increased funding for the NHS was explicit in both 1997 and 2001 manifestos: 'Health is a fundamental freedom. No one can fulfil their potential without the best possible health. We will prioritise investment to cut waiting times. But we also believe that it is best to improve health by preventing illness, tackling pollution and reducing poverty' (*Freedom, Justice, Honesty* – the Liberal Democrat Manifesto 2001, 3).

Attitudes to public services in 1997 were measured by analysing the views of voters towards increasing government spending on the National Health Service and support for the Liberal Democrat hypothecated tax plans of raising income tax by a penny in the pound in order to raise funds for education. There was a remarkable consensus amongst Liberal Democrat voters in favour of the party's policies on these issues (Figure 6.3). Over 90 per cent were in favour of increased spending on the health service and over 80 per cent supported the principle of hypothecated taxation. However, these policies were also popular with the voters of other parties. Indeed although Liberal Democrat voters were hugely in favour of these policies, this provided no guarantee that they would reap the electoral reward from those policies. Although the issue of education remained high on the public's list of important factors influencing their voting choice throughout the 1997 campaign, the support for hypothecated taxation failed to deliver votes. Half of all respondents who favoured a rise in income tax to pay for education actually voted Labour in 1997 and only 21 per cent voted Liberal Democrat (Table 6.1). It is surprising that more respondents who favoured the Liberal Democrat solution to education funding voted Conservative than Liberal Democrat in 1997.

Similarly, those who favoured increased spending on the NHS were more likely to vote Labour or Conservative than Liberal Democrat. Although Conservative voting overwhelmingly characterised that small section of the electorate that disagreed with the desirability of both hypothecated taxation for education and spending on the NHS, the Conservatives were still able to perform better than the Liberal Democrats amongst the many who supported these policies.

In both 1997 and 2001, respondents were asked to place themselves on an eleven point scale, where a value of zero represents favouring increasing taxes to fund better public services and a value of ten represents cutting taxes. In 1997 Labour voters were narrowly more likely to favour increased spending compared to the Liberal Democrats (see Table 6.2 below). In 2001 Liberal Democrat voters were the most in favour of increasing taxes rather than cutting taxes (see Table 6.3 below). They were also perceived by voters of all parties (including Labour voters) to be the party most in favour of increasing spending (see Table 6.2 below)

The environment

The Liberal Democrats have had a long-standing commitment to environmental protection. Their formation in 1988, coincided with the surge in popularity of the Greens, and the Liberal Democrats were quick to demonstrate a commitment to environmental issues. This was reflected in the manifesto in 1997, which stated that the priorities were to tax pollution (a 'carbon tax') and to set targets on the reduction of traffic and waste. In 2001 all Liberal Democrat policies had a green dimension, with an environmental section in every chapter of the manifesto.

In 1997 attitudes to the environment were measured by responses to the suggestion that prohibitive taxation should be imposed on the use of motor cars in order to protect the environment. Only a minority of Liberal Democrat voters supported this position (Figure 6.3) and attitudes to the environment were very weakly related to vote, perhaps reflecting its lack of salience at the election (Table 6.1). Exactly half of all respondents who favoured the imposition of taxes on car use to benefit the environment actually voted Labour, compared to only 22 per cent for the Liberal Democrats. In fact, nearly half of those who were neutral or against this proposition also voted Labour leading to the conclusion that the issues of the environment failed to influence voting behaviour to any noticeable extent in 1997. Comparable questions were not asked in 2001.

Constitutional issues

The great Liberal governments of a century ago had a reforming zeal at their very heart. Their willingness to tackle institutional reform was a characteristic of Liberalism that survived the wilderness years of the party. The party remains committed to constitutional reform. Most obviously the party has strongly advocated the need to reform the electoral process that tends to hamper the Liberal Democrats. As Crewe and King note, under a system of proportional representation the Alliance would have won 161 seats in 1983 and 143 in 1987 and almost certainly formed part of a coalition government. Under the British electoral system it won only 23 seats in 1983 and 22 in 1987 (Crewe and King, 1995, 285).

The 1997 election manifesto promised a holistic approach to constitutional reform, promising to 'modernise' the House of Commons, 'transform' the House of Lords and to: 'introduce proportional representation for all elections, to put more power in the hands of voters and make government more representative' (*Make the Difference* – the Liberal Democrat Manifesto 1997, 'Reforming Politics', Section: 1–2). In 2001 the Liberal Democrats pledged to reform the voting system for Westminster, to give parliament more power to hold government to account and to devolve more power to nations, regions and local government.

Indeed the issue of proportional representation (around which attitudes towards constitutional reform can be measured for 1997) is perhaps one of the single most important issues facing the party. Liberal Democrat voters were in broad agreement that the electoral system should be reformed, with nearly 70 per cent in favour and less than 10 per cent opposed to the notion that proportional representation should be introduced for all elections in Britain (Figure 6.3). However, as with other issues, the reverse is not true; only 23 per cent of those supporting this view voted Liberal Democrat (Table 6.1). This was not only considerably less than those voting Labour but also less than those supporting the Conservatives.

The economy

Not only were the Liberal Democrats alone in 1997 in promising to raise taxes, they had developed a critique of the British economy that required an overhaul of post-war economic consensus. The 1997 election manifesto chapter entitled 'Jobs and the Economy' seemed to offer solutions to both unemployment and inflation but contained more detailed plans for treating unemployment than for solving inflation. In short, the party promised to reduce inflation by joining a singe currency, and to tackle unemployment through a system of working benefits designed to break the poverty trap. In 2001 the manifesto promised to create a competitive economy within the context of an integrated Europe, to implement a more open and accountable system of taxation (largely though hypothecation) and to strengthen the independence of the Bank of England.

The 1997 *BES* asked people to prioritise solving unemployment and inflation. Most Liberal Democrat voters (70 per cent) supported the party's manifesto commitment to prioritise unemployment (Figure 6.3). However, once again, attitudes to the economy did not provide a base of support for the Liberal Democrats. The vast majority of those that favoured creating jobs over controlling prices failed to vote for the Liberal Democrats (Table 6.1).

Social liberalism

Perhaps by definition, Liberals ought to be liberal and, as such, a touchstone of the social-liberal agenda might be the 'liberation' campaigns. On the issue of the extension of homosexual rights, the 1997 Election manifesto put a surprising amount of space between the Liberal Democrats and the other two parties. In particular the party vowed to repeal 'Section 28' and create a common age of consent regardless of gender or sexual orientation. However, Liberal Democrat voters were not unified on the issue, with less than one-third believing that rights for homosexuals had not gone far enough (Figure 6.3). While 24 per cent of those who favoured the Liberal Democrat policy position voted for the Liberal Democrats, 56 per cent of them voted Labour (Table 6.1). Attitudes of the contrary position (that homosexual rights had gone too far) did seem to inhibit Liberal Democrat voting.

In 2001, one chapter of the Liberal Democrat manifesto was dedicated to civil liberties, with pledges to introduce an Equality Act (outlawing all discrimination), reform of the asylum system and the extension of freedom of information. Law and order also featured heavily, particularly in the party's perceptions of what would matter to the electorate. In keeping with the theme of freedom, this was couched in terms of freedom from crime, with promises to provide increased frontline and community policing, but also to tackle the causes of crime. In 2001 Liberal Democrat voters were similar to, or slightly more liberal than, other voters with regard to their views on a whole range of measures relating to views about crime and punishment and to immigration.

Overall, it is evident that whilst Liberal Democrat voters did appear to agree with the party on a wide range of issues, the party could not command anything like a majority amongst voters agreeing with their policy position. In other words, Liberal Democrat voters were liberal but liberals were not necessarily Liberal Democrats. Perhaps this is not surprising when Labour and the Liberal Democrats shared much of the social agenda.

Public attitudes and perceptions of party positions

To investigate the mismatch between liberal values and Liberal Democrat voting it is important to look at the relationship between how voters perceive the standpoint of the parties in relation to their own views. The 1997 and 2001 BES allowed the analysis of respondents' positions on certain policy issues and attitudinal core values (though the selection of issues was more limited in the 2001 BES). Crucially it also permitted the analysis of voters' perceptions of the position of the three main political parties. Hence not only can public opinion be gauged on attitudes to key issues, the public's perception of the positions of the Conservative, Labour and Liberal Democrat parties can also be measured. Five political themes (measured by questions in the BES) covering key attitudes towards taxation and spending, jobs and prices, nationalisation and privatisation, redistribution of income levels, and the future of Britain in the EU, are analysed in Table 6.4. For each of these themes respondents were asked to place themselves on an eleven-point scale, they were also invited to place the three main political parties on the same scale.

The mean scores for all respondents and for the perceptions of the party's positions on the same issues are disaggregated by reported vote for each of the three main parties (Table 6.3). On two of the six issues (income redistribution and privatisation), the Liberal Democrats were closer to the *average* position of the electorate than the other major parties. Whilst this does provide further evidence that the Liberal Democrats had developed popular policies by 1997, there are important caveats to this. The Liberal Democrats are generally regarded to be in the centre ground. Indeed, on all of the issues in Table 6.2 they are perceived to lie somewhere between Labour and the Conservatives. Consequently, the Liberal Democrats appear *on average* to occupy the most popular position, because the more extreme supporters of the two major parties average each other out. For example, if half the electorate occupy the most right-wing position and the other half the most left-wing position, the average position will be the centre, which may appear to be the position that the Liberal Democrats are perceived to occupy. However, in reality such a conclusion would clearly be fallacious as the distribution of preferences is 'bimodal' (twin-peaked) rather than 'unimodal' (single peaked) (see Riker, 1982). Fortunately, in reality, most of the issues we are measuring are not bimodally distributed (see Figure 6.4). In these examples we see that views on tax and spending seem to be skewed to the pro-spending end of the scale and views on European integration (1997) and the Euro (2001) are skewed towards the Eurosceptic end of the scale, but in each case there is a peak in the middle, representing those who sit on the fence (and note missing cases – don't knows – are excluded). This is a fairly typical pattern if we look at a large number of issue scales, though in some there is a less pronounced skew to one side or another and the distribution might be quite flat (even) with a peak in the centre. If we look back at left–right scales (Figure 6.1) the irregularities associated with specific issues tend to cancel each other out, and there is a relatively normal (bell-shaped) distribution with a peak in the centre.

To circumvent this problem we can look at supporters of each party separately and to compare how they view the parties' positions with their own views. This means we are no longer making any assumption that the arithmetic mean is also potentially the most populist position. In doing so we find that the Liberal Democrats were closest to their own supporters on all the issues examined, with the exception of European integration (where the Conservatives were more popular). However, Conservative voters appeared closer to their perception of the Liberal Democrats' position than their perception of Conservative positions in three key policy arenas – attitudes to taxation and spending, unemployment and prices, and nationalisation and privatisation. This indicates that a potential recruiting ground for Liberal Democrats lies amongst Conservative voters who are at odds with the party. Perhaps the most remarkable facet of this analysis, however, is that there is often a large disparity between the voter's own position and the voter's perception of the position of the party that they supported at the 1997 General Election. However, this is hardly surprising given that some issues have little salience in the minds of voters when it comes to voting, and also some issues

Table 6.2 **1997 mean scores: respondents' views and views of policy positions of the parties**

	R's view[a]	R's view of Labour	R's view of Conservatives	R's view of Liberal Democrats
Tax/spend				
Conservative	4.44	3.53	5.96	3.70
Labour	3.20	3.38	7.43	3.83
Liberal Democrat	3.26	3.85	7.47	3.17
All respondents	3.56	3.51	7.03	3.66
Inflation/unemployment				
Conservative	4.40	3.11	5.33	4.14
Labour	3.01	2.92	6.53	4.04
Liberal Democrat	3.63	3.31	6.59	3.78
All respondents	3.50	3.03	6.22	4.02
Nat./privatisation				
Conservative	6.45	4.66	7.54	5.53
Labour	4.59	4.53	8.20	5.42
Liberal Democrat	5.36	4.82	8.43	5.27
All respondents	5.23	4.60	8.08	5.40
Redistribution				
Conservative	5.98	3.66	7.09	4.67
Labour	3.05	3.17	8.74	4.44
Liberal Democrat	4.22	3.61	8.58	4.20
All respondents	4.09	3.41	8.26	4.48
EU Integrate				
Conservative	7.87	4.30	6.91	4.74
Labour	5.87	4.82	6.43	5.04
Liberal Democrat	6.06	4.87	6.51	4.79
All respondents	6.55	4.65	6.58	4.89

Note: [a] All variables are 11 point scales. A score of 6 represents the mid-point.
Source: *British Election Study* 1997.

do not separate the parties sufficiently to make an important contribution to voter choice. Also, whilst the findings may seem inconsistent with classical models of spatial competition (e.g. Downs, 1957; Black, 1958), modifications of spatial theory also consider other issue-based factors such as the direction between a party and a voter (i.e. is the party on the 'same side' as the voter) (e.g. see Reynolds, 1974; Mathews, 1979) and the intensity with which attitude positions are held (e.g. Rabinowitz and Macdonald, 1989). These models have different implications for voter choice and also for optimal party strategies (see Chapter 8).

Figure 6.4 **Issue scales, 1997 and 2001 (note: tax–spend scales are transposed in 2001)**

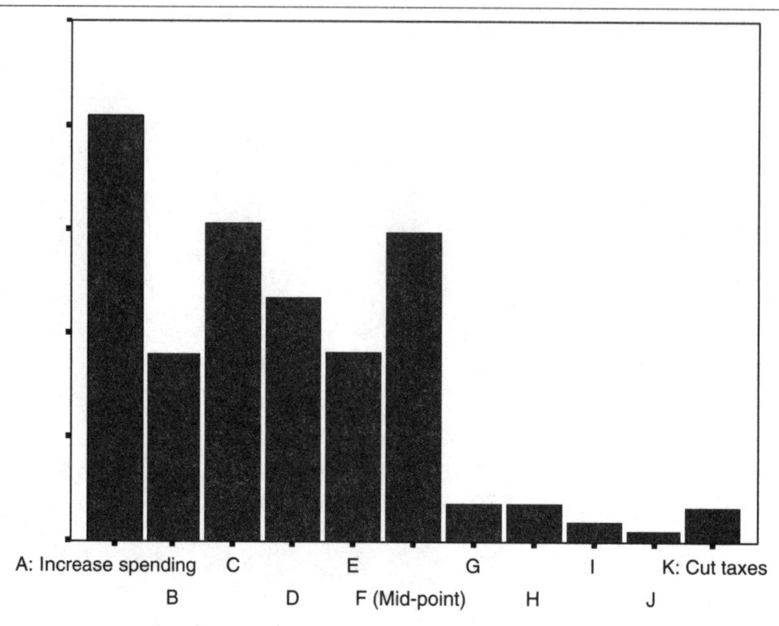

Figure 6.4a **Increase taxes and spend more (1997)**

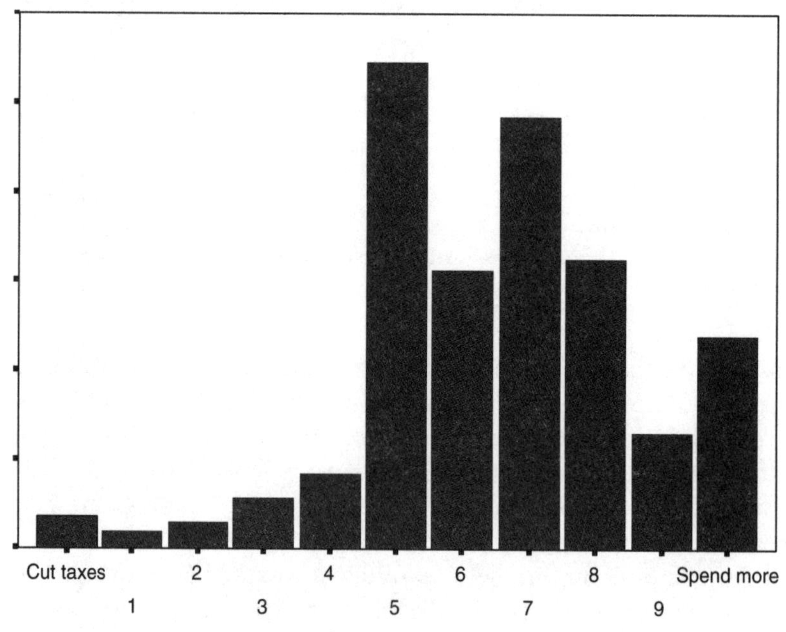

Figure 6.4b **Increase taxes and spend more (2001)**

Figure 6.4 (continued)

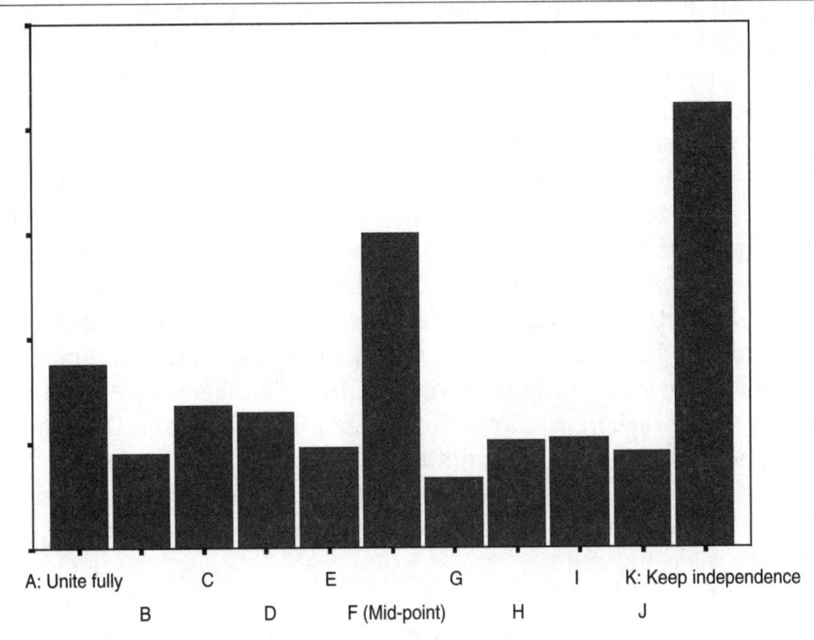

Figure 6.4c **R's v. unite fully with EU/prot.self interests? (1997)**

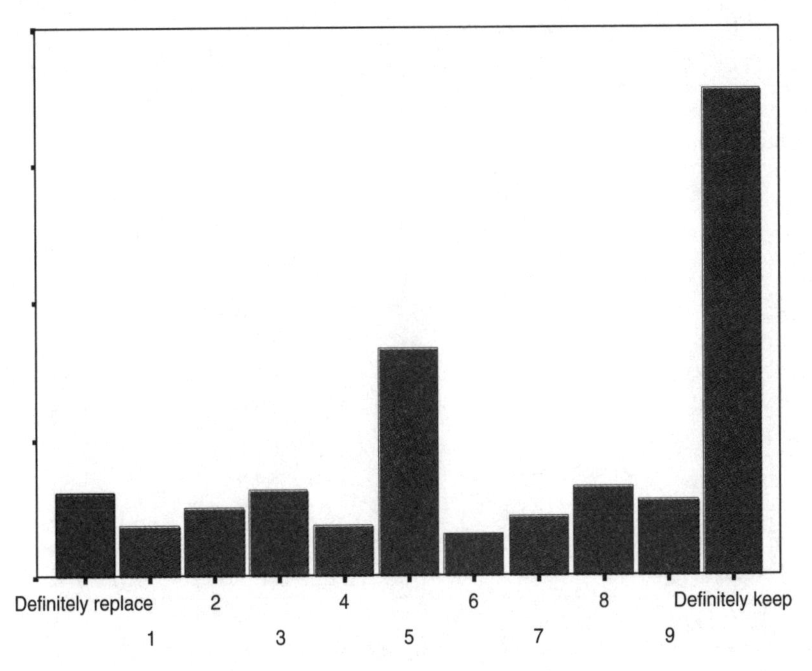

Figure 6.4d **Replace–Keep Pound-Respondent (2001)**

Unfortunately in the 2001 BES there are only a small number of issues measured on similar scales. On the issue of tax and spending the Liberal Democrats were perceived to be the most radical (spending) party, and were closest to the average voter position. Indeed voters of all parties perceived the Liberal Democrats to be left of Labour. Thus by moving away from the centre, the Liberal Democrats' ability to attract erstwhile Labour voters may have been enhanced, but the party may have jeopardised their potential appeal to Conservative voters. On the issues of balancing the rights of defendants against reducing crime, it the Conservatives who take the most popular position on average, and the Liberal Democrats are perceived to be similar to Labour. Similarly on the issue of the single European currency, the Liberal Democrats find themselves in a relatively unpopular position, outflanking even their own voters in support for the Euro (see Table 6.3). Both of these issues are ones that are, according to a senior MP, 'unpopular with the public, but right'. They may be perceived to be voter losers but are so central to liberal values that they cannot be compromised for short-term gain. In Chapter 8 we explore the importance of being true to principles in the wider context of electoral strategy.

Table 6.3 **2001 mean scores: respondents' views and views of policy positions of the parties**

	R's view[a]	*R's view of Labour*	*R's view of Conservatives*	*R's view of Liberal Democrats*
Tax/spend[b]				
Conservative	4.10	4.10	4.78	3.22
Labour	3.01	3.71	5.67	3.50
Liberal Democrat	2.90	4.36	5.90	2.84
All respondents	3.48	4.04	5.40	3.40
Crime/rights of accused				
Conservative	2.84	5.77	3.98	5.15
Labour	3.85	4.61	4.04	4.73
Liberal Democrat	3.79	4.44	3.31	4.58
All respondents	3.56	4.93	3.96	4.84
Replace/keep £				
Conservative	7.97	2.66	6.97	3.65
Labour	6.03	4.53	6.79	4.52
Liberal Democrat	5.41	3.76	6.88	3.73
All respondents	6.61	3.94	6.71	4.23

Source: *British Election Study* 2001.

Notes: [a] All variables are 11 point scales. A score of 6 represents the mid-point. [b] Tax/spend variable has been transposed to make score comparable with 1997 (10=0, 0=10).

Natural supporters?

The preceding section that the average position of the median elector is remarkably close to the average of the Liberal Democrats position on many issues, indicates that an apparent reservoir of support exists for the party. However, it was also noted that although the mean or *average* position may be in the centre, this does not mean that most (or even any) voters support this view. On some issues respondents from the BES in 1997 were asked to give their personal view and also to give their perception of the position of the three main political parties. Thus it was possible to classify respondents according to the party with which their views on each issue corresponded most closely. For the analysis presented here proximity scores were calculated for the following issues: taxation and spending, EU integration, inflation and unemployment, the redistribution of wealth and nationalisation. It was then possible to see which party each individual voter was closest to on these issues thus overcoming the limitations of aggregate data.[1]

On the issue of taxation and spending (Table 6.4) 19 per cent of voters placed themselves closer to the Liberal Democrats than any other party. This compared favourably to the percentage that placed themselves closest to the Conservatives (12 per cent) and Labour (25 per cent). A further 21 per cent placed themselves equally between Labour and the Liberal Democrats and 12 per cent were equally close to all three parties. Across the remaining four issues a similar pattern emerged. On no issue did the Liberal Democrats score more than 20 per cent or less than 13 per cent. On every issue a substantial proportion of voters were found to be equidistant between Liberal Democrats and Labour and between 6 per cent and 9 per cent were equally close to all three parties. These figures suggest that, although the scenario was not as favourable to the Liberal Democrats as aggregate analysis suggested, there was still a considerable section of potential Liberal Democrat voters with liberal inclinations. Secondly, a large proportion of voters either could not separate the parties, or did not have strong clear preferences and a large proportion of voters failed to place themselves closest to any single party. Clearly, voters either had a problem distinguishing between the parties' positions on the major issues, or were uncertain as to where they stood. One of the key challenges for the Liberal Democrats must be to appear more distinct from Labour. Overall a larger proportion of the electorate were equally near two or more parties than were closest to the Liberal Democrats. Even the Labour Party scored no more than 26 per cent on any single issue. In other words, 'natural supporters' rarely existed, and even where they did, there was no guarantee that they would support the party with which they most closely agreed.

Table 6.4 **Proximity to party's positions on five key issues (%)**

Respondent's own view is . . .	*Tax vs. Spend*	*EU integration*	*Inflation vs. unemployment*	*Redistribution*	*Nationalisation*
nearest to perceived view of Conservatives	12	22	12	18	14
nearest to view of Labour party	25	16	23	24	17
nearest to view of Liberal Democrats	19	14	14	13	20
nearest to both Conservative and Labour parties	2	3	2	1	2
nearest to both Conservatives and LibDems	3	3	5	3	2
nearest to both Labour and Liberal Democrats	21	17	22	24	26
same distance from all Conservatives, Labour and Liberal Democrats	12	17	16	11	11
Insufficient information	6	9	7	7	9
Total	100	100	100	100	100

Source: 1997 *British Election Study* survey cross-section.

Conversion of sympathy to vote

The preceding analysis has shown that a minority of voters positioned themselves closest to the Liberal Democrats, though a large section had no clear 'natural party'. However, it was noted above that even where voters were in agreement with the party's policy position, there was no guarantee that this sympathy would be converted into votes. Using two policy positions we illustrate how voters with different degrees of proximity to the Liberal Democrats actually voted. Tax and spending and European integration were chosen because it was clear from manifesto pledges that the Liberal Democrats had been able to distinguish themselves from the other parties.

Voters' proximity positions in relation to tax and spending described in Table 6.5 are broken down by vote at the 1997 General Election. In Table 6.4 we saw that less than 19 per cent of all respondents were unequivocally closest to the Liberal Democrats in their views on taxation and spending. Table 6.5 shows that only 28 per cent of these actually voted for the party. In contrast, Labour and the Conservatives won 65 per cent and 68 per cent of their natural supporters respectively. Furthermore when respondents

Table 6.5 **Tax vs. spending: proximity and vote**

	Cons (%)	*Labour (%)*	*LibDem (%)*	*Other/ none*	*Total (n)*
Own view nearest to perceived view of Conservatives	68	22	8	3	12 (331)
Own view nearest to view of Labour party	17	65	13	5	25 (703)
Own view nearest to view of Liberal Democrats	25	41	28	6	19 (518)
Own view nearest to both Conservative and Labour parties	38	42	13	7	2 (55)
Own view nearest to both Conservatives and LibDems	58	23	15	4	3 (78)
Own view nearest to both Labour and Liberal Democrats	16	55	23	6	21 (593)
Own view same distance from all Conservatives, Labour and Liberal Democrats	31	49	14	6	12 (328)
Insufficient information	32	54	10	4	6 (174)
Total % (n)	29 (791)	49 (1364)	17 (482)	5 (143)	100 (2780)

Source: 1997 *British Election Study* cross-section.

Table 6.6 **EU integration: proximity and vote**

	Cons (%)	*Labour (%)*	*LibDem (%)*	*Other/ none*	*Total (n)*
Own view nearest to perceived view of Conservatives	59	24	12	6	22 (610)
Own view nearest to view of Labour party	13	69	14	4	16 (432)
Own view nearest to view of Liberal Democrats	20	44	29	8	14 (378)
Own view nearest to both Conservative and Labour parties	31	47	20	1	3 (70)
Own view nearest to both Conservatives and LibDems	35	37	19	9	3 (79)
Own view nearest to both Labour and Liberal Democrats	10	66	21	4	17 (475)
Own view same distance from all Conservatives, Labour and Liberal Democrats	27	53	16	5	17 (484)
Insufficient information	31	50	15	4	9 (250)
Total % (n)	29 (792)	49 (1363)	17 (482)	5 (141)	100 (2778)

Source: 1997 *British Election Study* cross-section.

were equally close to the Liberal Democrats and either the Conservatives or Labour, they tended to support the other party rather than the Liberal Democrats. Fifty-seven per cent who were equally close to the Conservatives and Liberal Democrats voted Conservative and 55 per cent of those equidistant from Labour–Liberal Democrats voted Labour. Winning the argument on any issue was insufficient to persuade voters to support the party. When proximity to two parties was equal, the Liberal Democrats tended to lose out.

Analysing the issue of closer integration with Europe reveals a similar pattern (Table 6.6). Of the 14 per cent of the electorate closest to the Liberal Democrats only 28 per cent voted for the party compared to comparable figures of 59 per cent and 69 per cent for the Conservatives and Labour respectively. Voters who were equidistant from Labour and the Liberal Democrats were much more likely to vote Labour (66 per cent) than the Liberal Democrats (21 per cent). Similarly, voters equidistant from the all three major parties were most likely to vote Labour, but more likely to vote Conservative than Liberal Democrat. Similar analysis was performed using the remaining three issues described in Table 6.5 and the results were very similar. The Liberal Democrats failed to win anything like a majority of votes even amongst voters who classed themselves as in step with party policies.

In summary there was a small but significant electorate that identified closely with the Liberal Democrats on key policy issues. However, not only were these a minority of voters, but most of them did not vote for the party. Nevertheless, typically the Liberal Democrats would get double the support from those sections of the electorate who most closely agreed with the party on each of the issues. To assess the impact of issue based mobilisation on Liberal Democrat support, the logistic regression model introduced in Chapter 5 is extended to include the proximity positions as described in Tables 6.4, 6.5 and 6.6. This is shown in Table 6.7.

Adding voter proximity to their assessment of Liberal Democrat policy, attitudes to core Liberal Democrat values such as PR, and assessments of the party's leadership improves the goodness of fit of the model significantly and the variance explained by the model increases to 16 per cent (from 3 per cent). Model II also correctly predicts 21 per cent of the Liberal Democrat voters. The background characteristics introduced in Model I are hardly affected, with south-west voters and degree holders being particularly prone to vote Liberal Democrat, Anglicans being reluctant to do so.

Throughout model II the proximity measures are statistically significant and in the direction hypothesized. Again respondents who were nearest the Liberal Democrat position on each issue were nearly twice as likely to vote Liberal Democrat as those who were nearer another party or none at all (as in Tables 6.5 and 6.6). This is after holding other factors constant. In addition, favouring PR in British elections made individuals 2.8 times more likely to vote Liberal Democrat than those who did not favour PR. Public approval of the Liberal Democrat leader was important in encouraging support. Those who felt Paddy Ashdown would make a very good Prime Minister were nearly ten times more likely to vote Liberal Democrat than those who felt he would do a poor job. Overall model II greatly improved model I, but still lacks explanatory power.

In summary, not only did the Liberal Democrats have a popular leader and enjoy a fairly positive image amongst the electorate, their policies were more popular than their electoral performance would suggest. So why might people sympathising with the Liberal Democrats on the major issues of the day, be disinclined to vote for the party? The failure to capitalise on public sympathy and convert favourable ratings into votes may be due to structural obstacles, particularly the electoral system.

Table 6.7 **Determinants of Liberal Democrat voting. Logistic regression model stage II: social and demographic characteristics, attitudes and feelings towards party and leadership**

Variable	*Model II Exp(B)*
Region (vs. Scotland)	
South east	2.0*
East Anglia	—
Greater London	—
South west	3.4*
West Midlands	—
East Midlands	—
York-Humberside	—
North west	—
North	—
Class (vs. manual work)	—
Professional/managerial	1.5*
Intermediate	
Religion (vs. Anglican/Church of Scotland)	
Nonconformist	—
Roman Catholic	—
None	1.4*
Education (vs. no degree)	
Degree/higher education	1.7*
Proximity EU integration (vs. nearer others/none)	
Nearest LDs	2.0*
Nearest LDs and other(s)	—
Proximity Inflation vs unemployment (vs. nearer others/none)	
Nearest LDs	1.9*
Nearest LDs and other(s)	—
Proximity nationalisation (vs. nearer others/none)	
Nearest LDs	2.1*
Nearest LDs and other(s)	—
Proximity Redistribution (vs. nearer others/none)	
Nearest LDs	1.8*
Nearest LDs and other(s)	1.3*
Proximity Tax and spend (vs Nearer others/none)	
Nearest LDs	1.8*
Nearest LDs and other(s)	1.3
Proportional representation (against PR)	
In favour	2.8*
Neutral/neither	2.2*
Ashdown as PM (vs. No good)	
Very good	9.7*
Quite good	3.5*
Neutral/Don't know	2.0
% Liberal Democrats correctly predicted	20.9
% Total correctly predicted	84.2
Cox and Snell R^2	0.16
−2 * Log likelihood	2018

Note: * = 0.01 significance level (else = 0.05), – denotes insignificant at 0.05.
Source: 1997 *British Election Study* cross-section.

Why can't the Liberal Democrats convert latent support?

The problem of converting sympathy into votes may have its roots in the operation of the electoral system. As Crewe (1985) argued, 'unable to convert votes into seats, the Liberal party (and SDP) are unable to convert sympathy into votes' (Crewe, 1985, 120–1). Unless the party can convince potential supporters that it has a chance of winning, it remains unlikely to win their votes. This is most apparent at constituency level where Liberal Democrats were observed to perform best where they had been able to demonstrate that they were capable of winning. This wasted vote syndrome or '*credibility gap*' has to be overcome in order for the party to benefit electorally. Sympathisers are unlikely to vote for a party if they feel it has no chance of winning the seat in which they are registered. An electoral system that favours a two party system forces voters to choose between the two most likely winners (see for example the classic accounts of Duverger, 1954; Rae, 1971; and Lijphart, 1994). Rather than delivering a nationwide two party system, the country splinters into a series of different two-way competitions, depending on which two parties are best established in an area. For example in much of England in 1997, Conservatives competing against Labour typified the electoral battle. In parts of Scotland the practical choice was between Labour and the SNP. By contrast, in the south west of England the competition was frequently fought out between the Conservatives and the Liberal Democrats. Indeed the Liberal Party (in all its guises) has performed best where the Labour party has been least established, especially the Celtic and rural fringe. Significantly, when asked 'who do you see as core Liberal Democrat supporters' most of our respondents couched their answers in terms of geography: that is, by describing the types of area that Liberal Democrats do well in. Some did refer explicitly to how the party appeals to voters of particular political viewpoints (as the issue based mobilisation hypothesis suggests) but this was often qualified by statements such as 'in areas where Conservatives are unpopular'. The geographical basis of Liberal Democrat support, and how this reflects the electoral constraints created by the operation of the electoral system are explored further in the following chapter, where the models presented above are extended to include constituency context.

Conclusions

The Liberal Democrats seemingly occupy a popular position in the middle ground, and on average they may represent the position of the 'average' voter. However, as a strategy for maximising support, this has two fundamental problems. First, the 'average voter' does not necessarily exist. Analysis of proximity on key issues shows that the Liberal Democrats were not the most popular party even though they occupied the 'average' position. Those placing themselves closer to the Liberal Democrat than to any other party, on a range of issues, made up less than a fifth of the electorate. Those closer to Labour than to any other party, on the same issues, represented around one-quarter of the electorate. This lack of a natural base of Liberal support is also reflected in small number of identifiers. Second, being the least unpopular party does not guarantee any votes. Even those sections of the electorate which placed themselves closer to the Liberal Democrats than any other party, were more likely to vote Labour or Conservative in 1997. Perhaps equally telling is the lack of success of the Liberal Democrats in transforming identifiers into Liberal Democrat voters.

These two phenomena probably have a common cause: structural factors that disadvantage the party, most notably the electoral system and the consequent credibility gap. An electorate which sees little difference between the parties, faced with a perceived choice of returning a Labour MP or a Conservative MP is unlikely to vote for a third party, even if it does feel marginally closer to that party's policy positions. Duverger's Law – 'the simple-majority single-ballot system favours the two party system' (Duverger 1954: 217) – appears to remain a serious obstacle for the third party in British politics. Despite their best attempts, therefore, the Liberal Democrats seem unable to mobilise a regular body of support on the basis of winning the political arguments alone. Thus the idea of issues-based mobilisation is problematic. Clearly, Liberal Democrat voters are largely liberal in their views but they also come from certain types of area and certain types of social background. Thus in reality it is likely to be the intersection of these various influences which determines Liberal Democrat voting. In the next chapter we explore why geographical factors might play an important part in moderating the relationship between social background, attitudes and votes.

Note

1 Note that here and in subsequent models, simple proximity is as a predictor of party choice, and does not take onto account directional or intensity models discussed above.

7

The geography of Liberal Democrat support

Introduction

The recent success of the Liberal Democrats has been established on a distinctive geography of support, based on contemporary developments and historical patterns of voting. As discussed in Chapter 1, the rise of the Labour Party in the 1920s and 1930s as the new party of the working class forced the Liberal Party back into the nonconformist and remote 'Celtic fringe', where regional identity and religion, rather than class, remained the main determinants of voting behaviour (see Cox, 1970; Tregidga, 2000). As Figures 7.1a and 7.1b shows, the Liberals were unable to break out of those 'heartland' areas for the next sixty years; the geography of Liberal-held seats in 1929 being similar to the geography of seats held in 1992 (indeed, further ground was lost to the nationalist parties in Scotland and Wales and Liberal representation was wiped out from eastern England). However, in the 1997 and 2001 General Elections the Liberal Democrats were more successful in transforming votes into seats, winning 46 and 52 constituencies in those two elections respectively (their best results since 1929). Although the Liberal Democrats retained their strength in the south west of England and in Scotland, the party won a significant number of seats in areas of traditional weakness, such as the south east and London.

While historical voting patterns and other local historical factors, such as the level of nonconformity, can explain why the party continued to win their heartland seats, we must turn to contemporary reasons for why the party was so successful in capturing additional seats in the 1997 General Election. Perhaps most significantly, the Liberals have long suffered from a problem of credibility. As we saw in the previous chapter, the party may be popular with large sections of the electorate, but voters are generally unwilling to support a party they see as having little chance of winning in their constituency or of achieving nationwide success (Fieldhouse and Russell, 2001). This is often recognised in the form of the 'wasted vote syndrome'. The problem of credibility is least apparent in areas where the Liberal Democrats are able to draw on a tradition of Liberal voting (the Liberal heartlands). Outside these areas,

Figure 7.1a **Liberal seats, 1929**

Figure 7.1b **Liberal seats, 1992**

Table 7.1 **Regional strength of Liberal Party, 1886–1910**

Rank	*Area*	*% of seats won*
1	Forth Valley	87
2	North-east Scotland	86
	Rural Wales	86
4	Industrial Wales	77
5	North-east England	74
6	West Riding (Yorkshire)	71
7	Scottish Highlands	67
8	East Midlands	62
9	Clyde Valley	58
10	Southern Scotland	57
	South-West Peninsula	57
12	East Anglia	50
13	Eastern Lancashire	46
14	Lincolnshire	43
15	Severn	38
16	North & East Ridings (Yorkshire)	36
	Cumbria	36
18	Inner London	33
19	Western Midlands	29
20	Wessex	20
	Thames Valley	20
22	Outer London	17
23	Western Marches	14
24	Western Lancastria	11
25	South-east England	7

Source: Searle (1992).

local election and by-election success can be a route to achieving credibility by demonstrating the capacity to win in the locality.

Historical patterns of support: the traditional heartlands

Even at the height of the party's electoral fortunes towards the end of the nineteenth century and the beginning of the twentieth, the distribution of Liberal seats was geographically patchy. As Table 7.1 shows, in the seven elections held between 1886 and December 1910 the Liberals performed particularly strongly in Scotland and Wales (for example, the party won 86 per cent of seats in staunchly nonconformist rural Wales between these dates). In England the party's strength lay particularly in the north east, the east Midlands and the south west, while they fared particularly poorly in large cities (Edinburgh, Leeds and Bradford being the main exceptions – and even here the party's victories were typically restricted to slum areas). The party also under-performed in relatively middle-class areas, winning just 6.5 per cent of seats in south east England, for example.

Lipset and Rokkan (1967), writing on the formation and consolidation of core political cleavages, concluded that by the 1920s voters at the regional level throughout western Europe were subject to conflicting influences. In Britain, the process of industrialisation saw liberalism squeezed out by the rise of capitalism on one side and of organised labour on the other. The decline in liberalism was further affected by the weakening of regional identity as Britain became a much more homogeneous country. For instance, Pelling (1967) has pointed to the effects that the influx of English miners into the coalfields of industrial south Wales and of English labourers into the shipbuilding yards of the Clyde had on spreading socialism and diminishing the Celtic consciousness of these traditional Liberal strongholds.

Although the rise of socialism encouraged a polarisation of opinion based on class and ideology, Lipset and Rokkan (1967) argued that traditional issues could still play an important role in regions remote from central government. They identified three additional cleavages that could help protect the traditional regional patterns of voting from the onslaught of class politics: centre–periphery; state–church; and rural–urban. In theory at least, this meant that the Liberals were in a better position to resist the rise of Conservative and Labour class-based politics in the more rural and remote areas with a combination of strong local identities and Protestant nonconformity. This was particularly the case in the south west of England and in parts of rural Wales and Scotland. The 1851 religious census, for example, suggested that no fewer than 71.8 per cent of those people attending a place of worship in Cornwall were nonconformists and although comparable figures for later years are rare, Kinnear's estimates of the distribution of nonconformists in 1922 suggested that the relative strength of nonconformist in both the south west and Wales had survived (Kinnear, 1968: 125–37).

The distribution of the Liberal vote in the four elections between 1922 and 1929 (Table 7.2) clearly shows the effect the growth of the Labour Party had on Liberal representation. The party was all but wiped out in industrial South Wales, the Clyde valley and the Midlands. In the Scottish Highlands and in rural Wales, however, Liberals were still able to win over three-quarters of the seats in the elections held between 1922 and 1929, while in the south west the figure was nearly 50 per cent. In short, the Liberals retained their strength only in rural areas with high levels of religious nonconformity, areas that had resisted the rise of socialism and the Labour Party. Cox (1970) and Agnew (1987) have shown that once embedded in a local political culture, traditions of voting can survive external influences. Through their own momentum such local traditions are reinforced and provide a solid basis of support. This in part helps to explain why the Liberals were able to retain pockets of support even when the very existence of the party was in doubt. As we will show below, these heartland areas of support remain crucial to the modern party.

Table 7.2 **Regional strength of Liberal Party, 1922–29**

Rank	*Area*	*% of seats won*
1	Rural Wales	79
2	Scottish Highlands	75
3	Western Peninsula	46
4	North-east Scotland	36
5	Forth Valley	23
6	East Anglia	22
	Southern Scotland	22
8	Severn	20
9	Lincolnshire	19
	East Lancastria	19
11	East Midlands	16
12	North-east England	14
13	West Riding (Yorkshire)	13
14	South-central England	12
	Wessex	12
	West Lancastria	12
17	Rest of Yorkshire	12
18	North-west Midlands	11
19	Inner London	10
20	South-west Midlands	8
21	Clyde Valley	7
22	Salop	5
23	Cumbria	4
24	Outer London	3
	South-east England	3
	Industrial Wales	3

Source: Searle (1992).

Contemporary patterns of support: the emerging heartlands

As discussed in Chapter 1, the Liberals survived the nadir of the party's fortunes in the late 1940s and 1950s and were able to begin a slow road to recovery from the 1960s onwards. As we showed in Chapter 1, this was very much based round the idea of community or 'pavement' politics, with local government representation seen as a mechanism from which to build up the party's organisation. Although the 1980s saw the Liberal–SDP Alliance) achieve impressive shares of the vote, they were unable to make electoral progress in terms of seats won.

The 1997 General Election, however, marked a significant breakthrough for the Liberal Democrats. Although their share of the vote fell to below 17 percent, the 46 seats they won represented the party's best performance for nearly seventy years. Significantly, as Table 7.3 shows, the party won a substantial number of seats outside their traditional heartlands. The party captured seven seats in the outer south east and a further five in outer London – areas of particular historic weakness. The success in these new areas was derived not from historical success but from recent electoral achievements, including creditable (second place) performances in the 1992 election, success in local government elections, and in some cases in parliamentary by-elections. Consequently, these seats can be considered an 'emerging heartland' of Liberal Democrat support. No matter what mechanism was used, the key to winning these seats was bridging the 'credibility gap'.

Table 7.3 **The geography of the Liberal Democrat vote, 1997**

Rank	*Area*	*% seats won*	*Number of seats won*	*% vote*
1	South-west	44	7/16	35
2	Rural Scotland	39	9/23	22
3	Wessex	20	7/35	29
4	Outer south east	13	7/54	23
5	Rural Wales	12	2/17	15
6	Outer London	11	5/47	15
7	Rural north	7	2/28	20
	South Yorkshire	7	1/15	16
9	Merseyside	6	1/16	14
	East-central Scotland	6	1/18	10
11	Greater Manchester	4	1/25	16
	Inner London	4	1/27	13
13	Rest of west Midlands	3	1/29	16
14	Outer metropolitan	2	1/63	20
15	East Anglia	0	0/22	18
	East Midlands	0	0/43	14
	West Yorkshire	0	0/23	13
	Rest of north west	0	0/28	12
	West Midlands conurbation	0	0/29	11
	Industrial north east	0	0/27	11
	South Wales	0	0/23	11
	Strathclyde	0	0/31	7

The credibility gap

At the beginning of the book we introduced the credibility gap hypothesis. That is, the party has difficulty converting latent support because voters in many areas do not believe the party can win, either nationally or locally. In order to overcome the wasted vote syndrome, the party must convince voters it has a chance of wining, at least in the constituency where the voter resides. This can be achieved in a number of ways but is easiest if the party has a tradition of winning in the constituency. In the heartland constituencies, such as Montgomeryshire and Devon North, electoral credibility already exists. However, if no such traditions exist, local campaigners must argue they are the best placed challenger to the incumbent MP or point to success in local elections. Typically, Liberal Democrat election leaflets will include local opinion polls or local election results in order to demonstrate the party's winning credentials. As a parliamentary candidate in the 1997 General Election noted: 'Every piece of literature we put out between '92 and '97 had a bar-chart saying we were 929 votes short. I mean . . . people like the idea that they're participating in a contest where their vote will make a difference. And the traditional inhibition against voting for us is that "Well, you're not going to win, are you?"'

Local elections as a platform

As noted above, one of the main mechanisms for bridging the credibility gap is success in local elections. A strong local government base can be used as a stepping-stone to success in Westminster elections (although local representation is also particularly important for the organisational strength of the Liberal Democrats). Breakthroughs in local elections are easier for the party as wards are much smaller than constituencies and therefore the electoral system is less of a handicap. A cursory glance at local election results in the 1990s confirms this point. As Rallings and Thrasher (2000) note, it is difficult to translate local election results into estimates of national support as local elections take place in different parts of the country each year and never encompass the whole of Great Britain. However, they have estimated 'the national equivalent vote' at local government elections from 1979 onwards. Their figures show clearly that the Liberal Democrats consistently perform better in local elections, polling in the mid-20s throughout most of the 1990s and peaking at 27 per cent in 1994. In terms of number of councillors elected, between 1995 and 1997 the Liberal Democrats actually overtook the Conservatives as the second largest party across the country as a whole (see Chapter 2).

Once the party is well represented on the council it is in a better position to convince the electorate it is a credible electoral force in the constituency.

As one agent suggested: 'If you're perceived as a party who can win at one level, then the electorate then sees you as a player at a different level and they're prepared to admit you into the game, which you'll be normally precluded from because the game is between the two major parties.'

Table 7.4 **Council representation as a basis for Westminster success**

	Largest party on council, 1997	*% seats held on council, 1997*	*% of council seats won, 1994–97*	*% of vote in council seats, 1994–97*	*% in General Election, 1997*
'Heartland' seats (18)	6/18	32.6	45.4	33.1	44.0
'Emerging heartlands' (30)	24/30	55.2	62.3	42.3	43.3
Other seats (593)	84/593	17.8	17.1	19.2	14.4

Table 7.4 clearly shows just how crucial a strong council representation has been in the 'emerging heartlands'. In no less than 24 of the 30 constituencies the party captured from the Conservatives in 1997 the Liberal Democrats were the majority party on the local council.[1] Indeed, in these 30 constituencies the Liberal Democrats won 62 per cent of the council seats contested between 1994 and 1997, on a share of the vote of 42.3 per cent. In only two seats (Brecon and Radnorshire and Edinburgh West) the party held under 30 per cent of the local council seats at the time of the 1997 election. Although the party also performed relatively well in the heartlands seats, the local election base was nowhere near as evident (the Liberal Democrats were the majority party on the local council in only six seats and won a considerably lower proportion of the vote).

The ability of the Liberal Democrats to transform strong local representation into Westminster seats is not lost on the other parties. One Liberal Democrat MP noted a conversation between two Conservative agents at a Conservative Party Conference: 'Divert all your resources into stamping them [the Liberal Democrats] out even if it means losing some seats to Labour because Liberals are like cancer cells, once they take root you know they'll be invading and spreading all over your borough. For God's sake it would almost be worth losing the council just to keep it a Liberal free zone.' It is clear, then, that local elections provide the Liberal Democrats with a good opportunity to build a strong base from which to fight constituency contests.

BY-ELECTIONS

A further and more immediate way of bridging the credibility gap is through by-election success (see Chapter 1). The Liberals have been particularly impressive at not only winning by-elections but also in retaining the seat at subsequent General Elections. The party has won 17 by-elections since 1983 and of the four seats they captured from the Conservatives after the 1992 election they retained two (Eastleigh and Newbury) at the 1997 election. The party were slightly unlucky in respect to where by-elections arose in the 1997–2001 parliament – mostly being in solid Labour areas or where Labour were the main challengers to the Tories. However, following a legal challenge by the Conservatives to the 1997 General Election result in Winchester (which the Liberal Democrats had won by 2 votes) the courts ordered a re-run. In these unusual circumstances, the Liberal Democrats achieved a massive swing of almost 20 per cent to retain the seat. More significantly, in 2000 the Liberal Democrats pulled off one of their most spectacular by-election wins to date in capturing the Hampshire constituency of Romsey, which had been a safe Conservative seat (it is interesting to note that Labour's vote collapsed to such an extent that the party lost their deposit, suggesting considerable tactical voting among Labour supporters). Against most expectations, Liberal Democrat MP Sandra Gidley retained the seat in the 2001 General Election.

Simon Hughes' seat of Southwark North and Bermondsey is perhaps the best example of how the Liberals are able to win a seemingly hopeless seat at a by-election and build it into a relatively safe seat at subsequent elections. One MP summed up the importance of by-elections to the party: 'I think it's one lesson I really learnt from Paddy Ashdown, you could have positions and policies and strategies and so on but politics is all about momentum, and by-elections give you momentum.' In short, by-elections present smaller parties with a unique opportunity as they give the chance for the voter to cast a protest vote (without having to worry about the overall outcome of a General Election) and allow limited resources to be concentrated in one constituency. With finite resources but a reputation for fighting intense and highly organised local campaigns, by-elections are particularly important to the Liberal Democrats in achieving the initial electoral breakthrough.

Creeping Liberalism?

Research by Dorling *et al.* (1998) into the success of the Liberal Democrats in local elections has shown that compared to the vote for the Conservative and Labour parties, support for the Liberal Democrats is not easily explained using ward level socio-economic data (although the party performed relatively well in very rural wards). In addition, models of uniform swing are not effective in projecting Liberal Democrat seat gains/losses as the party performed consistently better than forecast. For example, using figures from Market and Opinion Research International (MORI) Dorling *et al.* (1998)

estimated that the Liberal Democrats won 21 per cent of the vote in the 1991 local elections, which represented a fall of 6 per cent from 1987. They predicted this drop in the vote should have seen the party lose approximately 200 seats. In fact the party made huge gains, winning an additional 500 seats.

They turned to geography for a possible explanation for why the Liberal Democrats perform better than expected. By analysing voting trends according to whether or not a ward neighboured another already controlled by the party they were able to show that there appears to be a spatial pattern in Liberal Democrat voting. Put simply, the party was more successful in areas in which they already had council representation. This led Dorling *et al.* to conclude that, for the Liberal Democrats, spatial proximity may be more important than social proximity.

One reason for this effect comes back to the importance of credibility. The Liberal Democrats perform better where they are seen as having a chance of winning. Voters in wards neighbouring Liberal held seats are more likely to vote for the party because they are seen as a credible local force. At the constituency level there also appears to be a similar spatial pattern in the seats won by the party at the 1997 and 2001 General Elections. One MP noted that:

> There is undoubtedly a cross-over effect from one constituency to another to some extent from one region to another and we have seen the sort of spread of the yellow virus, I shouldn't call it a virus, but there we are, up from the South West, comes across my sort of area just beginning to edge into the further areas in the South East as well . . . its history, its credibility. We are capable of winning absolutely everywhere if we have the credibility to do it.

Figure 7.2 seems to confirm this assertion. In some areas, notably the south west of England, Liberal Democrats successes in 1997 merely reinforced the traditional strength of the party in these regions. However, in other areas the party was able to win new groups of constituencies, most notably in 'Wessex' and the south west of London. The party was some way off winning any seats in south west London in 1992 but captured a block of five contiguous seats at the 1997 election (holding them all – with increased majorities – in 2001). The strength of the party in local government clearly was a major factor, as may have been the synergy brought about from campaigning strongly in five contiguous seats. In fact there are now very few Liberal Democrat parliamentary seats that are not contiguous or at least geographically close to other seats held by the party (as we will show below, these patterns cannot be accounted for by demographics alone). It is also interesting to look at where the party finished second in 1997. As Figure 7.2 shows, the majority of the party's 104 second places finishes occurred in the south of England. Indeed, over one-third were in the south east while a

Figure 7.2 **Map of Liberal Democrat seats, 1997, and second place finishes**

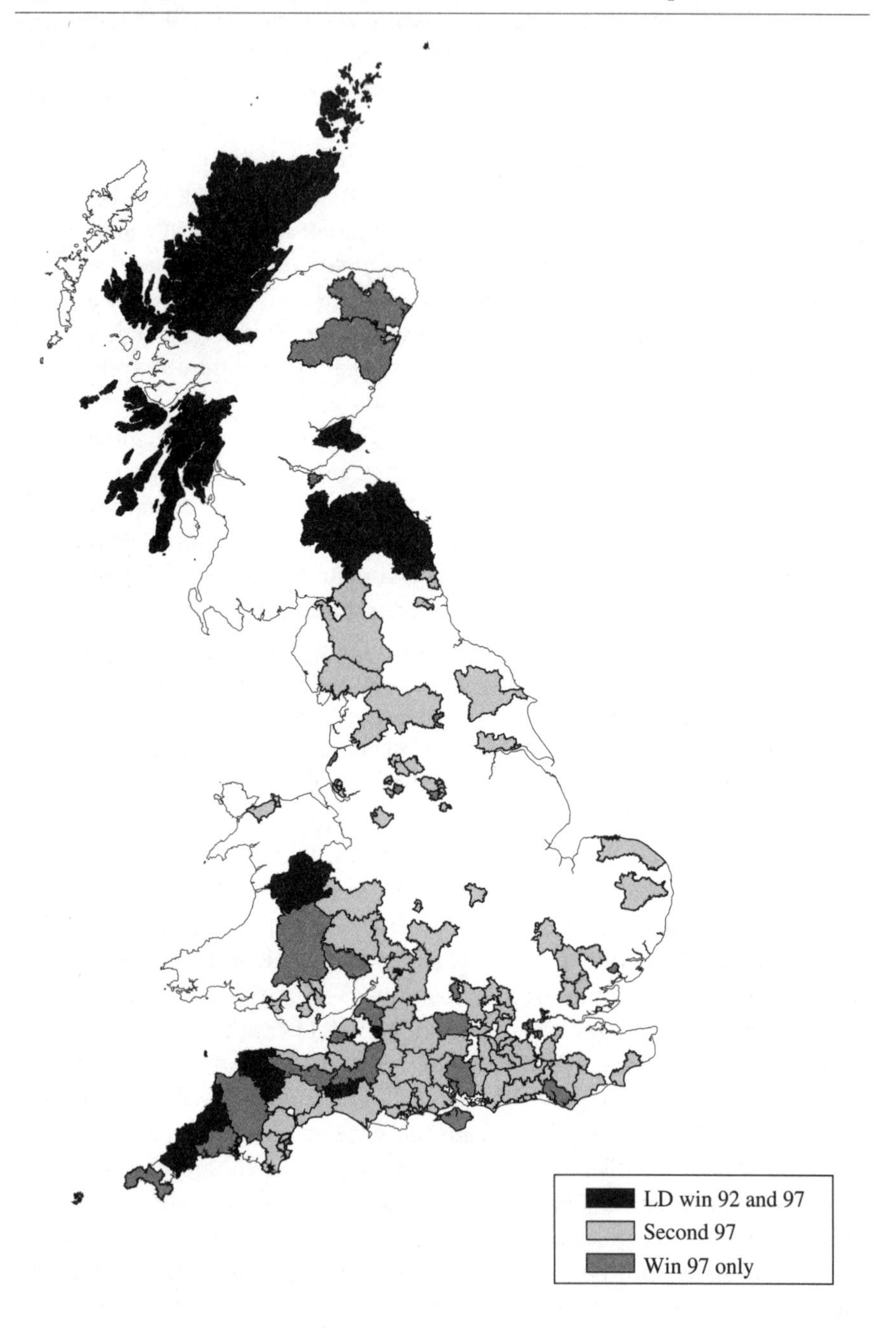

further 16 were in Wessex (out of a total of 35 seats in that region). This would seem to confirm that there are opportunities for the party to develop as a real political force in these emerging heartland areas.

Understanding the geography of Liberal Democrat voting: modelling the 1997 General Election

After the 1997 General Election, Liberal Democrat seats could be said to fall in to one of two categories; traditional heartland seats and emerging heartlands. Although the *source* of electoral credibility was different for these two categories, it was paramount in accounting for success in both. Under SMSP it is essential to be seen as either the dominant electoral force or the main challenger. In traditional heartland areas the Liberal Democrats meet this requirement. In the emerging heartlands they can achieve such credibility in other ways, for example through local election performances and by-elections. Thus by combining historical and contemporary factors, we should be able to account for the geography of Liberal Democrat support (and success) in the 1997 and 2001 General Elections.

To assess the relative importance of the factors discussed above on the Liberal Democrat vote at the 1997 General Election a dual modelling strategy was employed. We have chosen to model the 1997 General Election for a number of reasons. Firstly, the data on council representation by constituency has only been produced for the 1997 election and, as we will see below, it is a very important factor in explaining the Liberal Democrat's recent electoral success. Secondly, at the time of writing the 2001 census had not yet been published. Finally, 1997 represented an electoral breakthrough for the party and, as we will show, the further successes in 2001 were based on exactly the same foundations. It is for those reasons that 1997 is the most appropriate date from which to explore the reasons for recent Liberal Democrats successes.

The first part of the modelling strategy was to model the geography of Liberal Democrat voting by using a series of constituency level linear regression models of the percentage share of the vote won by the party. The second was to model whether or not the Liberal Democrats won each constituency using the appropriate logistic regression approach for binary response data. It is important to note that these are constituency level models, not individual or voter level, and are designed to explain where the party does well, rather than simply who votes for the party (we discuss an extended individual level support for the Liberal Democrats below).

For both sets of models a five-stage approach was adopted (see below). The sequencing of stages is approximately chronological and is meant to reflect causal processes. For example the demographic profile is considered causally prior to the tactical context. Local election success is entered last as in one sense it is another way of expressing the popularity of the party. However, as noted above, it may also be an important factor persuading people to vote Liberal Democrat at a General Election. For clarity we report the models both before and after entry of each set of variables.

All the variables included reflect important dimensions of Liberal Democrat support discussed above and which have been shown to be important elsewhere (e.g. Russell *et al.*, 2002; Johnston *et al.*, 1998) or have emerged through the qualitative stage of the research. The variables included were as follows:

Historical factors

As noted, only in areas where the Liberals survived the rise of the Labour Party following World War I did the party remain a credible force. Therefore variables detailing the number of times the Labour and Liberal parties won a constituency in the seven elections between 1918 and 1935 were included. The two variables in this category were derived from work done by Danny Dorling. He has estimated notional constituency results based on the 1997 boundaries for each seat in each General Election dating back to the nineteenth century.

Demographics

Five census variables were selected from the 1991 Census of Population reflecting important dimensions of Liberal Democrat support (see Dorling *et al.*, 1998, for a discussion of identifying constituency profiles from census variables). These were the percentage employed in agriculture; the percentage employed in manufacturing; the percentage of the population of pensionable age; the percentage holding a degree; and the percentage of households with two or more cars.

Local context

As electoral credibility appears crucial for the Liberals, the following five variables were entered into the model:

- *Majority on council*: One way in which the party gains visibility and can be seen as a real alternative to the other major parties is through a strong local government base. A dummy variable indicating whether the Liberal Democrats were the majority party (or equal biggest party) on the local council was included.
- *Liberal by-election wins*: A more immediate mechanism for bridging the credibility gap is through a by-election win. A variable indicating

whether the party has won a by-election in the seat since 1983 was entered.

- *Contiguous seats*: As spatial proximity appears to play an important role in Liberal Democrat success, a dummy variable was used to indicate whether a constituency was contiguous to a seat already held by the party.
- *Campaign spending*: The Liberal Democrats are a party dependent on strong local campaigning (Denver *et al.* 1998; Johnston *et al.* 1998; Whiteley and Seyd, 1999). To examine campaign intensity the amount spent by the Liberal Democrats in each seat as a percentage of the legal maximum was included.
- *Target seats*: A dummy variable was used to indicate whether the seat was a Liberal Democrat target seat, which attracted additional campaign resources.

Tactical situation

A five-category variable indicating the tactical situation in the constituency was used. The categories were: Liberal Democrat incumbent; Conservative–Liberal Democrat marginal; Conservative–Labour marginal, Labour–Conservative marginal (marginal was defined as a majority of under 12,000); and other tactical contexts. If tactical voting between Labour and Liberal Democrat supporters occurred we would expect to see a large increase in Liberal Democrat support in Conservative–Liberal Democrat seats and a fall in their share of the vote in seats where Labour were challenging the incumbent Conservative. Due to the limited numbers of cases a more detailed variable for the tactical context was not possible.

Local council success

Success in local elections is crucial to the Liberal Democrats and so the percentage of seats won by the party on the local council between 1994 and 1997 is included in the final stage of the model.

Explaining the Liberal Democrat share of the vote

The results of the five-stage linear regression model are shown in Table 7.5. The models show that historical voting patterns had a clear impact on Liberal Democrat vote share in 1997. While the number of times the Liberals won a constituency in the seven elections held between 1918 and 1935 did not enter the model, the number of times Labour won was significant in all five models. In models one and two the numbers of times the Labour Party won a constituency is strongly negatively related to Liberal Democrat support in 1997. In model one, for example, for every additional time Labour won a constituency in the period between 1918–35 the Liberal Democrat vote in 1997 was around 1.8 per cent lower. This is what would be expected; as noted above, the rise of the Labour Party came at the expense of the Liberals with Labour all but replacing the Liberals as the main opposition to the Conservatives in large parts of the country. Historical factors alone explained 13 per cent of the variance in Liberal Democrat support in 1997. However, after the local context was entered into the model the relationship between historical voting patterns for the Labour Party and Liberal Democrat support in 1997 was reversed – support for the Labour Party between 1918 and 1935 was positively associated with Liberal Democrat voting. This is because the variable is related to several of the variables entered at this stage. Given that the Liberal Democrats performed well in 1997 in areas where they have been historically weak, such as the south east, it is perhaps not surprising that support for the Liberals in the period between 1918 and 1935 is not significantly related to Liberal Democrat vote share in 1997.

The demographic characteristics of constituencies also play an important role in predicting Liberal Democrat support. The older and more middle class the profile of a constituency the better the party performed. Even when the local political context is controlled for, the party's vote increased by a quarter of a per cent for every additional 1 per cent of the population of pensionable age. The percentage holding a degree is also significant in the final model, with the party doing significantly better in constituencies with a high proportion of degree holders. Combining historical voting patterns and the demographic profile of constituencies explained one-third of the variation in Liberal Democrat support in 1997.

As suggested above, the local political context has an important influence on the ability of the Liberal Democrat to transform voter sympathy into actual votes, a key mechanism for bridging this credibility gap being a strong local government base. Indeed, being the majority party (or equal largest party) on the dominant local council had a very positive effect on Liberal Democrat vote share. In model three, for example, in constituencies where the Liberal Democrats were at least the equal largest force on the local council the party won an extra 5.6 per cent of the vote in model three (although this advantage diminished as the tactical context and recent council success were entered into the model). As we would expect, whether a seat had been won at a by-election (since 1983) was significant across all models. The party performed between 2 and 4 per cent better in such seats. Perhaps surprisingly, being contiguous to a seat already held by the party was not significant. It is important to note that whilst most Liberal gains tend to be contiguous or proximate to other Liberal seats (see Figure 7.2) the corollary is not necessarily true: neighbouring a Liberal Democrat seat does not have a statistically

Table 7.5 **Linear regression model of Liberal Democrat support, 1997**

	Model 1 *coeff.*	*Model 2* *coeff.*	*Model 3* *coeff.*	*Model 4* *coeff.*	*Model 5* *coeff.*
Historical					
Liberal wins 1918–35	–	–	–	–	–
Labour wins 1918–35	−1.79**	−0.53**	0.19*	–	–
Demographics					
Agriculture		0.65**	–	−0.16**	–
Manufacturing		–	–	–	–
Pensioners		0.80**	0.23**	0.25**	0.25**
Degrees		0.41**	–	–	0.06*
Two cars		0.30**	0.10**	0.18**	0.14**
Local context					
Majority on council (base: no majority)			5.60**	3.95**	–
Lib by-elect wins (base: not won since 1983)			3.38**	2.83**	2.53**
Contiguous seats (base: not contiguous seat)			–	–	–
Campaign spending			0.21**	0.14**	0.09**
Target seats (base: not a target seat)			7.57**	4.58**	4.69**
Tactical situation					
(Base: other tactical situation)					
Con–LD marginal				7.36**	6.20**
LD win 1992				18.53**	16.92**
Con–Lab marginal				−3.43**	−2.96**
Lab–Con marginal				–	–
Council success					
% Council seats won 1994–97					0.15**
R^2	0.13	0.33	0.77	0.85	0.88

Notes: ** = significant at 5% level; * = significant at 10% level; – = not significant. Due to missing cases seven constituencies are omitted from the analysis.

significant impact on Liberal Democrat support. This can be explained by the sheer number of constituencies neighbouring Liberal Democrat seats: for example the Liberal Democrat seat of Lewes neighbours seven other constituencies, none of which are Liberal Democrat held.

Turning to the two campaign related variables – campaign spending and target seats – both had a very significant influence on Liberal Democrat voting in 1997 (for a discussion of campaign effort see Denver and Hands, 1997;

Whiteley and Seyd, 1999; Denver *et al.*, 2002). Put simply, the party performed better in seats where they spent more. In model three, for example, for every additional 10 per cent spent the party's share of the vote increased by 2 per cent. Although when the tactical context and local council success were entered the impact of campaign spending is reduced, an extra 10 per cent spent only being translated into an increase in the vote of 1 per cent. Whether a seat was one of the party's designated target seats had a clear impact. The party performed consistently better in these seats, the advantage being between 4 and 8 per cent over the three models. This is hardly surprising given the increased resources these constituencies received to fight the campaign. However, it does reinforce the notion that local campaigning is crucial to Liberal Democrat success. Adding local context to the historical and demographic models explained over three-quarters of the variance in Liberal Democrat support.

Tactical context also had a very significant effect on vote share. In Conservative-Liberal Democrat marginal seats the party gained an extra 6 to 8 per cent compared to seats where they were not a close second to the Conservatives. In Conservative-Labour marginals the Liberal Democrat vote share fell by around 3 per cent (all other factors held constant). Together, these figures would seem to indicate considerable tactical voting among the supporters of the two main opposition parties, both parties clearly benefiting from an anti-Conservative alliance in marginal Conservative-held seats. As expected, the party performed considerably better in constituencies they notionally held in 1992.[2] In those seats they party's support was 18.5 per cent higher than in seats they did not hold. Although this figure decreased somewhat when recent council success was entered the effect of incumbency was clear. Adding the tactical context to the model meant that no less than 85 per cent of the variance was explained.

Finally, the percentage of council seats won in each constituency in the run-up to the 1997 election was entered into the model. As indicated above, this is not simply tautological. Although the variable could be related to vote share in 1997 it is not inevitably so. There are many places where the party performed well in local elections between 1994 and 1997, but this was not translated into an increased vote share at the national level, and vice versa. For example, the party won all the local council seats in the Birmingham Yardley constituency between 1994 and 1997 but were still some way off defeating the incumbent Labour MP. Nevertheless, success in local elections has a positive impact on Liberal Democrat support in 1997, for every additional 10 per cent of council seats won between 1994 and 1997 the Liberal Democrat's vote share increased by 1.5 per cent (after controlling for all other factors). Including this final variable increased the predictive power of the model to 88 per cent.

Modelling Liberal Democrat success

By using data on historical voting patterns, the demographic profile of constituencies and the local political context the great majority of the variance in Liberal Democrat support at the 1997 General Election can be explained. The next task is to examine whether the same model can also predict which constituencies the party won. The dependent variable in this model was Liberal Democrat wins in 1997 against all other seats (Table 7.6).

In the logistic model the number of times the Liberal Party won a constituency in the seven elections held between the 1918 and 1935 was significant in predicting where the Liberal Democrats won in 1997 (in both models one and two). In model one, for example, for every additional time the party won a constituency in this period the likelihood that the party also won the seat in 1997 increased by 35 per cent. Given the success of the party in 1997 in areas outside their traditional heartlands, a similar model for seats won at the 1992 election would have shown historical voting patterns to be even more significant in that election. Once again the success of the Labour Party over the same period is negatively related to Liberal Democrat victories in 1997. However, although the relationship between historical and current patterns of support is clear these variables alone were not successful in predicting any of the Liberal Democrat wins in 1997 (i.e. no constituency had an estimated probability of being Liberal Democrat of greater than 0.5).

Turning to demographic data, the percentage employed in agriculture was significant in all four models (given the geographical profile of Liberal Democrat held seats – see Figure 7.2 – this is perhaps not surprising) The proportion of the electorate holding degrees was also significant in models two and five. The party performed better in rural constituencies and those with high levels of educated voters, although the effect of education was less pronounced in later models than the level of agriculture. Combining the historical data with the demographic profile of the constituencies did not improve the predictive ability of the model to any great degree, with only one Liberal Democrat seat correctly predicted.

The inclusion of the variables detailing the local political context had a major impact on the model, with no fewer than 31 of the 45 Liberal Democrat held seats being correctly classified. A strong local council base was crucial, the party was over four and a half times more likely to win a constituency if they were at least the equal largest party on the council (although once the tactical context and the level of recent council success were entered the impact of this variable was greatly reduced). It is hardly surprising that the two campaign-related variables were significant in all the models. Clearly, the more the party spent in a constituency the greater the chance they won the seat,

Table 7.6 **Logistic regression model of Liberal Democrat success, 1997**

	Model 1 *exp. (B)*	*Model 2* *exp. (B)*	*Model 3* *exp. (B)*	*Model 4* *exp. (B)*	*Model 5* *exp. (B)*
Historical					
Liberal wins 1918–35	1.35**	1.24**	–	–	–
Labour wins 1918–35	0.44**	0.57**	–	–	–
Demographics					
Agriculture		1.20**	1.28**	1.28**	1.72**
Manufacturing		–	–	–	–
Pensioners		–	–	–	–
Degrees		1.09**	–	–	1.15*
Two cars		–	–	–	–
Local context					
Majority on council (base: no majority)			4.54**	3.59*	–
Lib by-elect wins (base: not won since 1983)			–	–	–
Contiguous seats (base: not contiguous seat)			–	–	–
Campaign spending			1.19**	1.14**	1.17**
Target seats (base: not a target seat)			4.63**	6.07**	7.56**
Tactical Situation					
(base: Other tactical situation)					
Con–LD marginal				18.44**	17.98**
LD win 1992				855.41**	823.84**
Con–Lab marginal				–	–
Lab–Con marginal				–	–
Council Success					
% Council seats won, 1994–97					1.07**
−2 log likelihood	282.6	265.7	102.7	70.9	58.8
LD seats correctly classified	0/45	1/45	31/45	39/45	40/45
% Overall correctly classified	92.9	92.5	96.5	97.8	98.4

Notes: ** = significant at 5% level; * = significant at 10% level; – = not significant. Due to missing cases seven constituencies are omitted from the analysis, one of which is the Liberal Democrat held seat of Orkney and Shetland. There are therefore 45 Liberal Democrat held seats in the model.

even controlling for target seat status. Being assigned as a target seat had obvious benefits and this was even more critical once the tactical context and local election success were taken into account. In model five, for instance, the party was over seven and a half times more likely to win a target seat than one that was not given this status. By-election success and being contiguous to a seat already held by the Liberal Democrats were not significant.

As in the linear model, the tactical context was entered into the equation at the penultimate stage. The very large coefficients shows that either being a close second to the Conservatives or holding the seat in 1992 had a very significant impact on the Liberal Democrat's ability to win seats in 1997. The size of the coefficients may appear odd, this is due to the small number of cases in certain categories. Being in third place (or worse) in Conservative–Labour or Labour–Conservative marginals had no significant effect on the probability of the Liberal Democrats winning the seat, all other variables held constant. Including the tactical context increased the number of Liberal Democrat seats correctly classified to 39.

Finally, the percentage of seats won in local council elections in the three-year period prior to the General Election was also significant. Controlling for other variables, the probability that the Liberal Democrats would win a constituency was increased by 7 per cent for every additional 1 per cent increase in the number of seats won at the local level. As noted above, this is not a circular argument – there were many cases where the Liberal Democrats performed well in local elections but did not win the constituency at the General Election. However, in only 6 of the 30 *new* seats captured in 1997 had the party failed to win at least half of the council seats contested over the period 1994 to 1997. A strong local government performance, therefore, does not guarantee that the Liberal Democrats will win the seat but in most cases it is one of the factors that needs to be present if the party are going to capture seats in areas outside their traditional heartlands. This final model correctly predicted an impressive 40 of the 45 Liberal Democrat held seats. It is tempting to conclude that a strong local government performance is almost a necessary but insufficient condition for Liberal Democrat success at the parliamentary level.

The continuing importance of nonconformity

We have argued that Liberal strength has been historically linked with religious nonconformity. Certainly, many of the Liberal heartland seats coincide with areas traditionally associated with high levels of nonconformism (e.g. rural Scotland, south west England). Furthermore, although the absolute numbers belonging to a nonconformist denomination may have fallen (as has the numbers belonging to all major religions) our research suggests it is still an important factor in predicting Liberal Democrat strength.

To explore the continuing effect of nonconformity on the Liberal Democrat vote figures from the 1979 Census of Churches were analysed. Figure 7.3 shows a close relationship between Liberal Democrat success in 1992 (when the party was still largely restricted to its heartlands) and the percentage in each county belonging to nonconformist Christian churches. The census, undertaken by the Nationwide Initiative in Evangelism, examined the religious denomination of churches and the size of their congregations by counties in England (NIE, Vol. 2, 1980). The distribution of nonconformists is similar to Kinnear's 1922 estimates, suggesting that although the absolute numbers may have altered their geographical concentration has not (1968, 125–9).

In order to investigate the statistical significance of nonconformism on the geography of Liberal Democrat voting and success the linear and logistic regression models were re-fitted for England including these county level data. The level of nonconformity was entered at the first stage of the regression model with the other historical factors. All other variables were entered as above. It should be noted that including the level of nonconformity did not

Figure 7.3 **Liberal Democrat vote, 1992, by % nonconformist, by county**

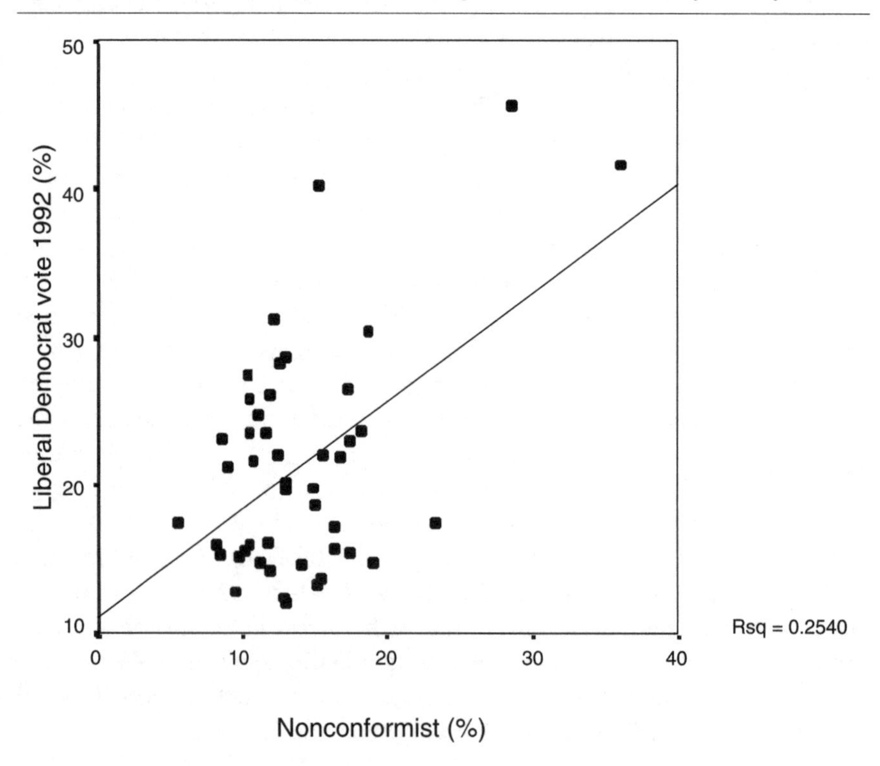

considerably alter the other model parameters, and the same variables were significant (it is for this reason that the full regression tables have not been reproduced). Table 7.7 shows that the level of nonconformity was significant in explaining both the level of Liberal Democrat support in 1997 and predicting where the party won. In the linear model nonconformity is significant in all five models. Even when the demographic profile of the constituency and the local political context are controlled for the percentage belonging to a nonconformist denomination is still positively related to Liberal Democrat vote share. In model 5, for instance, for every 1 per cent increase in the level of nonconformity the Liberal Democrat share of the vote increased by 0.18 per cent. The level of nonconformity by county is also significant in the first three logistic regression models. Including the nonconformist variable resulted in model one correctly predicting 4 of the 34 seats the party won in England at the 1997 election (historical voting patterns alone were unable to predict any of the Liberal Democrat victories). Even when local context was controlled for a 1 per cent increase in the per cent belonging to a nonconformist denomination increased the probability that the Liberal Democrats would win the seat by 9 per cent.

Table 7.7 **Effect of nonconformity (England only)**

	Linear		*Logistic*	
Model	*Coefficient*	*R^2*	*Coefficient*	*Correct*
1	0.63**	0.18	1.13**	4/34
2	0.50**	0.41	1.14**	4/34
3	0.20**	0.79	1.09*	26/34
4	0.11**	0.87	–	
5	0.18**	0.88	–	

Notes: ** = significant at 5% level; * = significant at 10% level; – = not significant.

It should be remembered that this an area level relationship and although there is some evidence of this relationship at the individual level (see Chapter 6) the area level effect is likely to be bound up with other contextual factors. More specifically, the historical link of Liberalism with nonconformism means that in some areas where nonconformism was widespread in the nineteenth century (and remains so today) the Liberals were traditionally strong and that this strength has survived through its own momentum (for example through the electoral credibility gained from being a significant local political force and the strength of the grassroots in the area). Whether the relationship is individual and direct or contextual, there is little doubt that nonconformity is still an important factor in understanding the geography of Liberal Democrat support.

Departures from the model

Any model is a simplification of reality. Perhaps the most interesting aspect of modelling is to see which constituencies do not behave as one might expect. Table 7.8 lists the ten constituencies not captured by the party in 1997 that have the highest predicted values (using the fifth stage logistic model for Great Britain without nonconformity data). In many ways these examples show that although many of the mechanisms providing the Liberal Democrats with electoral credibility can be present in certain constituencies, this is not always enough to guarantee success. The party must keep 'knocking at the door' as it were.

Table 7.8 **Seats not won in 1997, by highest predicted values**

Constituency	*Predicted value*[a]
Inverness, Nairn & Lochaber	0.96
Wells	0.90
Rochdale	0.76
Dorset Mid & North Poole	0.70
Dorset North	0.55
Oldham East & Saddleworth	0.45
Salisbury	0.45
Hastings & Rye	0.45
Southend West	0.40
Tiverton & Honiton	0.37

Note: Predicted value of more than 0.5 means that the model predicted a Liberal Democrat win.

It is not surprising that Inverness, Nairn and Lochaber and Rochdale have very high values, as these were the two seats held by the party in 1992 but lost to Labour at the 1997 election. Sir Russell Johnston's decision to stand down from Inverness, Nairn and Lochaber may have robbed the party of a strong personal vote and Liz Lynne in Rochdale seemed to fighting a rear-guard action since she took over from Cyril Smith. Wells was one of the party's target seats and with a strong base on Mendip Council they would have expected to win the seat from the Conservatives. A number of the seats rank high due to a strong local government performance (e.g. Dorset Mid and North Poole, Dorset North and Oldham East and Saddleworth) that was not matched in the General Election. In the two Dorset seats the party won 89 per cent and 65 per cent respectively of the local council seats, while in Oldham East and Saddleworth the Liberal Democrats captured 25 of the 27 seats contested in the constituency over this period. Of the remaining seats with high predicted values, some were targets seats while most had a relatively strong local government base. Interestingly, many are in the south west of England even though no regional variable was included. This reflects the Liberal Democrats' strong base in this area.

It is also interesting to look at the five seats won by the Liberal Democrats in 1997 but which the model failed to predict (Table 7.9). While the logistic model very nearly predicted Lewes, Portsmouth South and Southport (predicted values of over 0.45) both Kingston and Surbiton and the seat of current Liberal Democrat leader Charles Kennedy, Ross, Skye and Inverness West, had low predicted values. In Kingston and Surbiton the Liberal Democrats trailed the Conservatives by over 15,000 votes and perhaps did not expect to win the seat. However, Edward Davey captured for the Liberal Democrats from the Conservatives with a majority of just 56 votes. One reason for this could be that the seat is amongst a group of five captured by the Liberal Democrats in the south west of London. With the party concentrating resources in neighbouring target seats some sort of spillover effect could have occurred. Electors may have been more aware of the Liberal Democrats' campaign effort than would have been the case elsewhere. Moreover, the south west of Greater London was (and still is) an area with a strong Liberal Democrat local government base. For instance, they were the majority party in the Richmond-upon-Thames, Kingston-upon-Thames and Sutton Councils in the run up to the 1997 election. This provided the party with the sort of visibility and credibility that is so essential if a breakthrough

Table 7.9 **Liberal Democrat seats won but not predicted**

Constituency	*Predicted value*[a]
Lewes	0.49
Portsmouth South	0.46
Southport	0.46
Ross, Skye & Inverness West	0.14
Kingston & Surbiton	0.02

Note: [a]Predicted value of more than 0.5 means that the model predicted a Liberal Democrat win.

at the national level is to be achieved.

The case of Ross, Skye and Inverness West is also intriguing. There are several possible reasons why this relatively safe Liberal Democrat seat was not predicted. Firstly, there is an almost complete lack of partisan local government in the Highlands (the Liberal Democrats failed to capture any seats on the Highland Council in the period from 1994 to 1997) and this was reflected in the low predicted value. Secondly, as the constituency was perhaps as safe as a Liberal Democrat seat can be, the campaign effort that went into defending it was perhaps not as great as in more marginal seats, such as the neighbouring seat of Inverness, Nairn and Lochaber. This was reflected in the fact the seat was not a designated target seat and that only four-fifths of the legal maximum was spent on the campaign. Finally, there may have been a significant personal vote for Kennedy in the constituency that is not incorporated in the model. Of all the major parties, the Liberal Democrats perhaps rely most strongly on well-known local personalities.

Local context and individual behaviour

So far in this chapter we have examined the relationship between various geographical characteristics and the Liberal Democrat vote (and success). However, aggregate level relationships can persist for a number of reasons which may not always be causal. This is sometimes referred to as an ecological fallacy (Robinson, 1950). Thus it is also helpful to examine whether or not these relationships exist at the level of the individual voter. Thus below we extend the survey based models of Liberal Democrat voting introduced in Chapters 5 and 6 to include key contextual variables.

Crucially, the mechanism of vicious or virtuous electoral circles seems to be tactical voting (see also Chapter 9 below). This is the essence of the credibility gap hypothesis: traditionally, the Liberals, as the third party, suffered most from tactical voting. Many potential supporters in areas where the party had little hope of victory voted tactically in favour of one of the other parties. However, in contrast, voters in areas where the Liberal Democrats stood a 'credible' chance of winning (where the party has previously been in first or second place), were more inclined to support the party. Such seats were more common in 1997 than in previous elections, as the Liberal Democrats had started to build localised heartlands of support, particularly in the south west. The relationship between the local context of party competition and Liberal Democrat performance in the 1997 General Election is shown in Figure 7.4 (see Chapter 9 for a similar discussion of the 2001 election). A typology of seats was adopted, similar to that presented in Chapter 5. This differentiates seats according to the type of electoral competition in each of the mainland British constituencies. After the boundary changes following the 1992 election, the Liberal Democrats notionally held 19 seats and had also gained 4 seats via by-elections. The Liberal Democrats typically performed best where they were already in first place and the biggest improvement in their fortunes (from the notional 1992 results) came in the by-election seats (Figure 7.4). This is consistent with the argument that, having established they were capable of winning a seat, the party closed the 'credibility gap' and could more effectively mobilise voters.

Figure 7.4 **The change in Liberal Democrat share of the vote, 1997, by constituency outcome, in 1992**

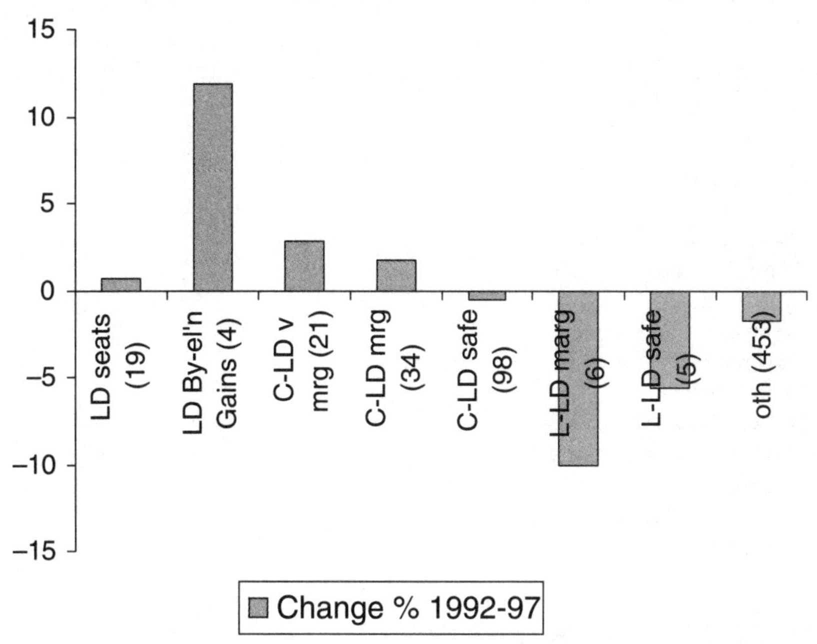

Next the marginality of non-Liberal Democrat seats was taken into account. Seats held with a majority of less than 7,000 votes over the Liberal Democrats were classified as 'very marginal'. Majorities over the Liberal Democrats of between 7,001 and 12,000 votes were classed as 'marginal'. Majorities over 12,001 were categorized as 'safe'. In general, the Liberal Democrats performed better where they faced a Conservative incumbent than a Labour or Nationalist one (as the Conservatives lost support). The rise in Liberal Democrat voting was greatest in very marginal Conservative-Liberal Democrat seats and second greatest in marginal ones. In contrast, in the 98 safe Conservative-Liberal Democrat seats the Liberal Democrat vote actually fell. It fell more in seats where the incumbent MP belonged to Labour or the nationalist parties and in constituencies where the Liberal Democrats were in neither first nor second place. In short, electoral context influenced Liberal Democrat voting.

An important consequence of the credibility factor that arises form the working of the electoral system is that, in order to maximize votes the party has to concentrate on target seats and 'target voters in target seats' (see Chapter 9). All hitherto evidence suggests that any attempt to predict who might vote Liberal Democrat, ought to take account of the tactical situation

Table 7.10 **Determinants of Liberal Democrat voting. Logistic regression model stage III: social and demographic characteristics, attitudes and feelings towards party and leadership, and political context**

Variable	*Model III* *Exp. (B)*
Region (vs. Scotland)	
South east	–
East Anglia	–
Greater London	–
South west	–
West Midlands	–
East Midlands	–
Yorkshire-Humberside	–
North west	2.3*
North Wales	–
Class (vs. manual work)	–
Professional/managerial	1.4*
Intermediate	–
Religion (vs. Anglican/Church of Scotland)	
Nonconformist	–
Roman Catholic	–
None	1.4*
Education (vs. no qualifications)	
Degree / higher education	1.6*
Proximity EU integration (vs. nearer others/none)	
Nearest LDs	1.9*
Nearest LDs and other(s)	–
Proximity inflation vs. unemployment (vs. nearer oths/none)	
Nearest LDs	1.9*
Nearest LDs and other(s)	–
Proximity Nationalisation (vs. nearer others/none)	
Nearest LDs	2.0*
Nearest LDs and other(s)	–
Proximity redistribution (vs. nearer others/none)	
Nearest LDs	1.8*
Nearest LDs and other(s)	1.3
Proximity tax and spend (vs. nearer others/none)	
Nearest LDs	1.8*
Nearest LDs and other(s)	1.7*
Proportional representation (against PR)	
In favour	2.8*
Neutral/neither	2.3*
Ashdown as PM (vs. no good)	
Very good	9.4*
Quite good	3.4*

Table 7.10 **(continued)**

Variable	*Model III* *Exp. (B)*
Neutral/don't know	1.9
Context of seat (vs. LDs not second or first)	
LD held seat from 1992	10.4*
Con–LD seat:very marginal (>7k votes)	7.3*
Con–LD seat marginal (>12k votes)	12.0*
Con–LD seat: safe (< 12k votes)	2.7*
Lab–LD seat: safe (< 12k votes)	–
% Liberal Democrats correctly predicted	32.6
% Total correctly predicted	85.6
Cox and Snell R^2	.21
−2 * Log likelihood	1867

Source: 1997 *British Election Survey* cross section.
Note: * = 0.01 significance level (else = 0.05), — denotes insignificant at 0.05.

in each seat. This is explored in Table 7.10 (Model III), which extends the logistic regression model from the previous chapter to include the local context of party competition. The same typology of marginality was employed.[3]

Model III reveals that, although a wide range of variables were included, predicting Liberal Democrat voters proved difficult, precisely because of their amorphous nature. Overall, 21 per cent of the variance in Liberal Democrat voting is explained, and 33 per cent of Liberal Democrat voters are correctly predicted by Model III. However, this constitutes a significant improvement on Models I and II.

Once constituency context was added, individuals in the north west were marginally more likely to vote Liberal Democrat than Scottish voters. In contrast the large effect for the south west becomes insignificant. Anglicans were still less Liberal Democrat than the non-religious and degree holders still more likely than those without educational qualifications to vote Liberal Democrat. Individuals' proximity to party positions and attitudes to PR and the leader all remained significant and the relationships were consistent with the expected patterns.

Constituency context, then, was important to the incidence of Liberal Democrat voting in 1997 at the individual level. Voters represented by a Liberal Democrat MP were – *ceteris paribus* – 10.4 times more likely to vote Liberal Democrat than those from a constituency where the Liberal Democrats were neither first nor second. Voters in Conservative–Liberal

Democrat marginals were 12 times more likely to vote Liberal Democrat than those from a constituency where the Liberal Democrats were neither first nor second. In contrast being second to Labour did nothing to improve the prospects of Liberal Democrat candidates, indicating that the Liberal Democrat vote in 1997 was essentially an anti-Conservative vote.

Overall, the results of the logistic regression model support the argument that it is political context – or the chance of success – that most influences Liberal Democrat voting rather than social characteristics or attitudes alone. Just as the Liberal Democrats do not have a distinct social heartland, they also appear to lack a reliable or solid attitudinal heartland that can withstand the independent effects of constituency context.

Building on the Base: 2001

As Figure 7.5 shows, after the 2001 election the Liberal Democrats remained a party with a distinct heartland, the spread of their first and second places – although more extensive than in 1997 – is still geographically specific. Liberal Democrat success is still largely confined to the traditional Liberal heartlands on the Celtic periphery and increasingly along the south coast of England.

As shown above, in 1997 the party was able to build a wider basis of support – based on electoral credibility derived from local election and by-election success and historical tradition, along with the careful targeting of resources. Table 7.11 divides seats into three categories: the first group comprises those seats that had a heritage of Liberal voting – the heartland seats, the second those that the Liberal Democrats won for the first time in 1997 – the emerging heartlands. Those seats not held by the Liberal Democrats make up the third category. Examining the change in vote shares between 1997 and 2001 for the three main parties reveals some interesting patterns.

Table 7.11 **Percentage change in vote share, 1997–2001, by seat type**

	Con 97–01	*Lab 97–01*	*Lib–Dem 97–01*
Lib–Dem Heartland	1.2	−1.7	0.9
Lib–Dem New	−0.9	−1.5	3.5
Non-Lib–Dem	0.8	−2.0	1.4

Labour support fell slightly in all three categories of seats while Conservative support rose slightly in non-Liberal Democrat seats and in the traditional heartlands. In fact, Conservative support recovered best, and Liberal Democrat levels of support improved least in those seats where there was a tradition of Liberal voting. Three reasons for this can be suggested.

Figure 7.5 **Liberal Democrat representation by constituency, 2001**

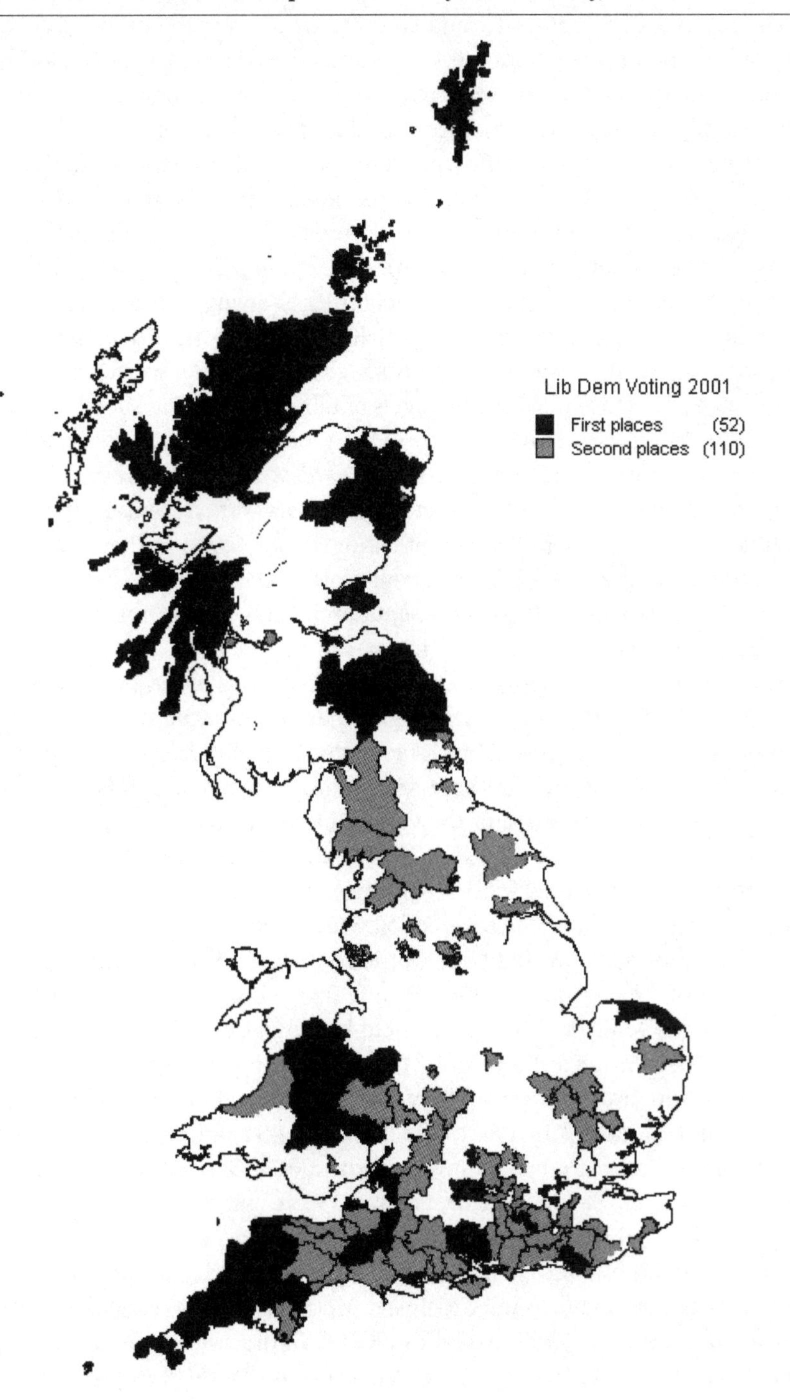

Firstly, it could be that the level of Liberal Democrat support in these seats was already near its full potential, and so there was less scope to 'squeeze' extra Liberal Democrat votes from these constituencies. Second, traditional liberal voters in the rural heartland seats may have baulked at a 'new' liberal agenda. Perhaps the ending of equidistance and the repositioning of Liberal Democrat policy put distance between the traditional base of liberal voters and the party. Thirdly, a number of Liberal heartland seats had been badly affected by the 2001 Foot and Mouth Disease (FMD) outbreak. It was generally felt that the Conservatives benefited electorally from the epidemic and this could, in part, explain the Liberal Democrats' relatively poor showing in those areas.

Liberal Democrat support typically increased the most in constituencies where they had first made a breakthrough in 1997. As we have seen, the single biggest factor in explaining levels of Liberal Democrat success is electoral credibility. Voters are more likely to vote for the Liberal Democrats if they feel that they can win in that constituency and winning the previous election constituted firm proof that the Liberal Democrats were a credible option. The incumbency effect Liberal Democrat candidates enjoyed in these 'new' seats saw their vote increase by 3.5 per cent from 1997 (compared to a boost of 0.9 per cent in Liberal heartland seats and 1.4 per cent for other Liberal Democrat candidates). Critics of the party may suggest that the increases merely reflected continued anti-Conservatives tactical voting by Labour supporters and did not necessarily signify an endorsement of the Liberal Democrat MP. However, as Table 7.11 shows, the relatively small decrease in Labour's share of the vote in these seats would suggest that this was not the case (indeed Labour's share of the vote fell least in such constituencies).

Turning to the seats captured in the 2001 General Election, a similar pattern to that discovered in 1997 emerges. In Romsey, the source of electoral credibility is obvious: the by-election win in 2000. In Chesterfield, perhaps one of the more unexpected wins (although not within the party itself), the retirement of the popular Labour MP Tony Benn coupled with the gains made by the Liberal Democrats on Chesterfield Borough Council (the party won 19 of the 47 seats in the 1999 election) provided the Liberal Democrats with a solid platform from which to fight the General Election. A similar story emerges in Guildford (the party held 19 out of 45 seats and were the largest party on the local council going into the 2001 General Election), North Norfolk (where the Liberal Democrats were in competition with the Conservatives to be the largest party in 1999), Ludlow (the party had a strong presence on South Shropshire District Council) and Cheadle (where the Liberal Democrats controlled Stockport Metropolitan Borough Council). As we noted above, the 1997 model of Liberal Democrat success actually predicted that the party would win Mid Dorset and Poole North and with the party less than one thousand votes behind the Conservatives and remaining strong locally, it is perhaps not surprising that the party captured the seat in 2001. Teignbridge was also almost won from the Conservatives in 1997 and is in the Liberal Democrat's stronghold of the south west, being contiguous with the Liberal Democrat-held seats of Devon & West Torridge and Torbay. Given the party's strength on Teignbridge District Council, many of the important factors for Liberal Democrat success identified above were present and paved the way for victory for the Liberal Democrats' Richard Younger-Ross in 2001.

The 2001 General Election was not a complete success story for the Liberal Democrats, however, and shows that if the party loses even some of their electoral credibility with voters it is liable to lose seats. The Isle of Wight is a good case in point. Few outside the party had considered the Isle of Wight at risk, the Liberal Democrats held the constituency with a majority of almost 9 per cent – in percentage terms it was only the twenty-first most vulnerable seat. In the end, however, the Conservatives captured the seat with a swing of 6.6 per cent. On closer inspection though, the warning signs were there as the party had lost control of Isle of Wight Council in 1998 for the first time since 1981. It is exactly this loss of credibility that the Liberal Democrats cannot afford. The second seat lost in 2001 – Taunton – may have had peculiar local factors. Sitting Liberal Democrat MP Jackie Ballard – a leadership contender in 1999 – strongly supported government plans to ban fox hunting. This would seem to have been at odds with a large section of her rural constituency and – along with FMD and the poor relationship between local Liberal Democrats and the Labour party, may contributed to this loss.

The party also failed to capture a number of key target seats in 2001, which, given the electoral circumstances, we may have expected them to win. The reasons for these failures are varied, and often reflect very local issues, but it is worth noting that the Liberal Democrats were losing ground to the Conservatives in council elections in a number of localities approaching the 2001 General Election. Indeed, on election day itself the party lost control of both Somerset and Devon County Councils (which encompassed a number of the party's key targets) and this seems to have been symptomatic of what was happening on the ground in those areas in the lead up to 2001 General Election (although, of course, Teignbridge stands out as an exception).

Conclusion

We have argued that the first-past-the-post electoral system means that the Liberal Democrats, as the third largest party in a predominately two-party system, face a problem of credibility. Voters are dissuaded from voting for the party unless they are perceived as having some chance of success, either locally or nationally. The notion of a 'credibility gap' is not only consistent with the empirical patterns of Liberal Democrat support but was widely recognised by party activists, strategists and MPs. In order to bridge the credibility gap the party must demonstrate to the electorate they are a serious electoral force in any given locality. Until 1997 such credibility was derived primarily form local traditions of Liberalism in the 'heartland' areas of the south west of England, rural Scotland and isolated pockets in areas such as Montgomeryshire in mid-Wales. These heartland areas are typically rural with high levels of affiliation with nonconformist churches and fall outside the areas where trade unionism and the Labour Party became most influential in the early twentieth century. These are the areas where, in Lipset and Rokkan's terms, the old state versus church, centre–periphery and rural–urban cleavages survived the emergence of the dominant class cleavage. However, in 1997 the Liberal Democrats broke out of their heartland areas and emerged as a credible force in a number of areas of previous weakness. Whilst many of these constituencies were contiguous or geographically proximate to heartland seats, perhaps more significantly many were in areas where the party had made incremental and sustained progress in local elections and had begun to be seen as the main challenger to the Conservatives during the previous decade. Others were gained in by-elections and subsequently held in the General Election. Once the initial credibility gap had been overcome the party was in a much stronger position to persuade voters that a vote for the Liberal Democrats was no longer a wasted vote, and thus new heartlands began to emerge. In the 2001 General Election, the party built on the 1997 base, retaining all but two of the 1997 wins and capturing an additional eight seats, primarily in areas where they had strengthened their local base since 1997. It seems apparent, therefore, that future Liberal Democrat success will continue to be built incrementally on a foundation of electoral credibility based on a combination of historical tradition and local activity.

Notes

1 This variable is derived from work done by Ron Johnston and colleagues at the University of Bristol. They calculated the political composition of councils by parliamentary constituency prior to the 1997 General Election. Where a constituency crossed more than one council boundary we have used figures for the majority council.

2 The parliamentary constituency boundaries were redrawn after the 1992 election. Rallings and Thrasher have estimated the notional 1992 results using the new 1997 constituency boundaries. They calculate that two Liberal Democrat held seats – Gordon and Liverpool Mossley Hill – were notionally won by other parties (the Conservatives and Labour respectively) in 1992.

3 However, none of the 4 Liberal Democrat by-election seats were included in the sample.

Part III

Party strategy

This part considers the electoral strategy of the Liberal Democrats, in the run-up to the 2001 General Election. We look first at how the party aimed to maximise its number of votes, and then examine how they attempted to convert this into the maximum number of parliamentary seats. In Chapter 8 we show that contrary to classical models of party behavior, the Liberal Democrats responded to a shift to the right of the Labour Party by ending the policy of equidistance, and identifying themselves as an anti-Conservative Party. In doing so they attempted to build a distinctive and radical identity, outside of the confines of the traditional left–right spectrum. This enabled the party to win an increasing number of seats at the expense of an unpopular Conservative party. This increase in representation was facilitated by the strategy of targeting which has helped the Liberal Democrats to begin to overcome the wasted vote syndrome (Chapter 9). The strategy for maximising votes and seats however, did not play out equally everywhere. As we argued in the previous section the Liberal Democrats are faced with a number of micro-contests, in some of which their main opponent is Labour whereas in others it is the Conservatives. In Chapter 10 we draw on the case studies to illustrate the variety of problems and opportunities faced by the party in different locations around the country, and the different strategic responses they arrived at.

8

Neither left nor right but forward? The electoral strategy of the Liberal Democrats, 1997–2001

Everyone knows that a vote for the Liberal Democrats is a vote to remove this Conservative Government. (Letter to Liberal Democrat party members from Paddy Ashdown, Leader of the Liberal Democrats, May 1995)

Introduction

In 1992 the British Liberal Democrats fought their first General Election campaign from the same position as their predecessors in the Liberal–SDP Alliance; that is, as a party of the centre. This was enshrined in the party's policy of 'equidistance' between the Conservative and Labour parties. However, the failure of the Labour Party in the 1992 General Election and the succession of Tony Blair as Labour Party leader in 1994 altered the landscape of British politics and had important strategic implications for the Liberal Democrats.

Labour's response to defeat in 1992 was to speed up its reforming programme. Labour's subsequent shift towards the centre ground, under the leadership of Neil Kinnock, John Smith and especially Tony Blair, presented the Liberal Democrats with a number of strategic problems. The abandonment of Clause IV, a defining symbol for the Labour Party, showed just how far towards the centre Blair was willing to take the party. The Liberal Democrats were faced with the choice of either moving to the right in order maintain equidistance between the two major parties or to accept that the party was now closer to Labour. The latter option had drawbacks as the party risked being seen as a Trojan horse for Labour.

The move to abandon equidistance was signalled shortly after the 1992 election. Leader Paddy Ashdown's speech at Chard (9 May 1992), called for an attempt to realign British politics 'to assemble the ideas around which a non-socialist alternative to the Conservatives can be constructed'. It may not have been universally welcomed in the party but Chard was a clear first step towards closer ties with Labour. Ashdown's diaries suggest that he and Blair had been discussing ways of realigning the centre-left even before Blair's election to the leadership (Ashdown, 2000). Early in his leadership, Blair called for a 'dialogue of ideas' and expressed his party's willingness to work with the Liberal Democrats in the event of a hung parliament.

The alternative response might have been a Liberal Democrat move to the right in order to maintain equal space between themselves and the two major parties. This would have been consistent with a standard interpretation of Downsian approaches to the spatial placement of parties (Downs, 1957). Instead, the Liberal Democrats positioned themselves in close proximity to the Labour Party and set out to develop a set of radical and distinct policies, which served not only to abandon 'equidistance' but also blurred the position of the Liberal Democrats on a traditional left–right axis. An orthodox Downsian model of party placement would regard the increasing closeness between Labour and the Liberal Democrats resulting from the abandonment of equidistance as detrimental to the smaller party. Yet in the 1997 General Election, Liberal Democrat representation more than doubled to 46 seats in the House of Commons – the best performance by a third party in Britain since 1929. In 2001, Liberal Democrat representation increased again to 52 seats.[1] However, as noted in the previous chapter, modifications of spatial theory also considers other issues-based factors such as the direction between a party and a voter (Reynolds, 1974; Mathews, 1979) and the intensity with which attitude positions are held (Rabinowitz and Macdonald, 1989), both of which have implications for how vote-maximising parties will operate.

In this chapter we explore the utility of spatial models and also a political strategic marketing analysis framework (see Butler and Collins, 1996) in understanding the Liberal Democrats' strategic decision-making. We also argue that by manipulating the ideological dimensions around which the party competes with its rivals, and by adopting local strategies for different electoral contexts, the party aims to escape the centre party squeeze. We argue that in order to maintain support, the Liberal Democrats attempted to define a clear identity (or market niche) on the progressive edge of British party politics and to break out of the traditional left–right dimension. In doing so they aligned themselves, at least temporarily, as an anti-Conservative party. Rohrschneider (2002) suggests that to arrive at a better understanding of how parties attempt to target voters in election campaigns, it is essential to investigate how parties reach their campaign decisions both in relation to motivations and behaviour.

Electoral strategy and spatial models of elections

Downsian modelling of public preferences tends to assume that third parties are destined to fight for a limited political space around the 'centre' of political opinion (see Downs 1957). In short, Downs argued that voters act to 'maximise expected utility' and would vote for whichever party most closely matches their ideological positions, leading to convergence around the median voter (Black, 1958). However, in a multi-party system this will not necessarily mean the parties cluster around the centre or that parties closest to the median voter will necessarily be successful (Eaton and Lipsey, 1975; Merrill, 1988). Indeed a simple proximity model suggests that for a three-party system no equilibrium exists: parties will converge on the centre, but eventually the centre party will leapfrog either of the more extreme parties and the process repeats itself *ad infinitum* (Merrill and Grofman, 1999).

Under different assumptions of voter behaviour, equilibrium may exist, but how rational parties respond to the movement of their competitors will depend on those assumptions of the model. For example, under the Mathews directional model the centre party might gain nothing by moving so long as their own position stays stable with reference to the 'neutral point' (Mathews, 1979). In other words it predicts stability. In contrast, the directional model with an intensity component (see Chapter 6) proposed by Rabinowitz and Macdonald suggests that parties taking more extreme positions are advantaged as voters want *more* of what they like (Rabinowitz and Macdonald, 1989). Similarly, a mixed model taking direction, intensity and proximity into account suggests that rational parties will often be more extreme than voters (Iverson, 1994; Merrill and Grofman, 1999). Furthermore, in a multi-candidate election, the existence of substantial non-issues/non-policy or partisan voting (as found traditionally in Britain) may cause a non-centrist equilibrium, or in other words may promote divergence rather than convergence (Merrill and Grofman, 1999).

The situation is further complicated by multiple issue dimensions under which proximity models become unstable. This is of particular importance to the Liberal Democrats for whom, as we will show, escaping the constraints of the left–right dimension is central to their electoral strategy. We demonstrated in Chapter 5 that for the Liberal Democrats to occupy the position of the 'average' voter did not necessarily equate to being the most popular party (see also Russell and Fieldhouse, 2001). Whilst a routine application of spatial proximity theory would suggest that a party moving away from the political centre would fail to maximise its recruiting potential, Dunleavy (1991) argued that the aggregate distribution of preferences may be twin peaked rather than unimodal – and thus that the number of voters at the midpoint may not equate to any 'maximum'. Others have argued that it is not possible to represent the complexity of political ideology on a single left–right dimension, making the whole concept of equidistance problematic (e.g. Inglehart, 1971).

The logic of the proximity model does suggest, however, that if parties of the left and right converge towards the centre, any centre parties would have their vote squeezed. In keeping with this, it has been noted that (empirically) the Liberal Democrat's predecessors, and centre parties elsewhere, have indeed performed relatively poorly in periods of consensus, though whether it is major party polarisation or centre party strength which is the cause (and which is effect), is open to debate (see Hazan, 1996; Nagel 2001). It has also been noted that any centre-party squeeze would be particularly apparent where the parties are competing in a majoritarian system. As Duverger (1954, 215) asserted 'the centre does not exist in politics' and a first-past-the-post-system will tend to produce a two-party a system (although see Daadler, 1984, and Hazan, 1996). In short, voters in a first-past-the-post-system are faced with the reality that, should they vote for a third or minor party, their vote may be wasted. Smaller parties therefore can only make progress where they are perceived to have a chance of winning (see also Fieldhouse and Russell, 2001). Duverger's law would imply therefore that the Liberal Democrats should wither away. However, it is also apparent that local organisational strength may have insulated the party (see Gudgin and Taylor, 1978; Cox, 1997; MacAllister *et al*, 2002). As Duverger (1954) described, there are different electoral dynamics under different party and electoral systems, which may explain why the Liberal Democrats have survived and prospered (see also Taagpeera and Shugart, 1989; Cox, 1990). Cox (1997) shows how the median voter theorem (Black, 1958) rests on certain assumptions, notably the existence of a single issue dimension and 'voter sincerity'. The validity of both these assumptions are questionable, and we find that through the encouragement of tactical voting, geographical targeting and through the promotion of alternative issue agenda, the party aims to escape from the centre party squeeze.

Rational parties?

Rational choice approaches provide a framework that covers parties as well as voters. Assuming that parties seek to maximise votes, just as voters seek to maximise their 'utility income', it is possible to construct a model of party competition. For Sartori 'ideological distance' plays a pivotal role in the creation of space from which a centre party can emerge. The space between parties tends to be elastic.

> A short space does not allow, or does not facilitate, the perception of a centre. It has, so to speak, no room for it. A short space is defined by its ends – left and right. A third point of reference – the centre – becomes meaningful only as the space extends, and particularly when the ends of the space are perceived as being two poles apart. (Sartori, 1976, 347)

Thus voters' policy preferences provide a 'space' within which parties manoeuvre for position. Parties will tend to move to areas where public opinion is strongest, assuming they can move into regions of the policy space which have been traditionally occupied by other parties. The conundrum for students of the British Liberal Democrats is that they failed (in Klingemann *et al.*'s phrase) to 'wander about in the middle' (1994, 254) but sought to redefine themselves politically at the radical edge of British politics. In one sense this is no real great surprise. As indicated above, different spatial models have different implications for the behaviour of vote-maximising (rational) parties. It could be argued that they have been forced to place more ideological distance between themselves and the two main parties partly, at least, due to the increasing centrism of the Labour and Conservative parties in the post-Thatcherite era.

As indicated above, simple proximity models would suggests that the shift to the right of the Labour Party might result in a reactive shift in the Liberal Democrats' position to maintain equidistance, but the reality was quite different. The narrow reading of Downs, encouraged by his 'fundamental hypothesis' of the motivation for party action, that 'parties formulate policies in order to win elections, rather than win elections in order to formulate policies' (1957, 28) relegates the role of ideology and core political principles, and would struggle to explain the abandonment of equidistance by the Liberal Democrats. A wider interpretation of public preference shaping and political policies would be open to the possibility that parties are not completely ideologically flexible and preference accommodating (see Dunleavy and Ward, 1981; Dunleavy, 1991). Consequently, a move towards the centre may not be the most effective way of increasing potential support. The key point here, however, is that the reactive movement of political parties in order to adjust to movement of other parties might be unpalatable to existing party members and supporters. Political parties may stand for some principles that are non-negotiable and therefore do not fit into an economic model of party behaviour. A useful critique of the narrow interpretation of party motivation and policy-making is offered by Rose and McAllister (1986): 'A theory of unprincipled electoral competition implies that parties will alter policies and personalities in a continuing effort to catch the votes of an electorate open to the most ephemeral and transitory campaign influences' (1986, 116).

Rather, they contend that durable political principles informs voter choice at election time. If policy changes were unpalatable to existing voters' underlying principles, a party could be punished for not remaining true to its core beliefs. As we have seen, Merrill and Grofman (1999) and others have argued that Downsian modelling needs to be extended from its emphasis on proximity to consider direction and intensity and not simply proximity. As inheritors of a long-standing tradition of liberalism in Britain, the Liberal Democrats might be particularly vulnerable to haemorrhaging support if a reactive move to the relative centre was perceived as an opportunistic shift to the right or away from the ideological core of liberalism. In answer to one of Rohrschneider's (2002) key questions that arises from spatial models, the Liberal Democrats clearly see longer-term benefits of retaining their integrity on key issues, even if this may not optimise the vote in the short run.

Being anchored to a set of ideological issues may be particularly important for those that support a party unlikely to gain office. If existing supporters were clustered around an identity of the Liberal Democrats as 'liberal' it might go some way to explain the determination of the Liberal Democrats not to react to Labour's move to the centre by realigning themselves. As Webb found an individual's libertarian disposition has a positive effect on the likelihood of that individual voting Liberal Democrat, an observation that is supported by our findings presented in Chapter 6 (see also Fisher 2000). A senior politician argued that it was a set of core beliefs that actually defined politics in general, and the Liberal Democrats in particular: 'You stand and die politically on certain things. Sometimes it is actually better to lose, because the issue is important.'

If, as it seems, the Liberal Democrats were tied to particular ideological positions, then the party's decision to drop equidistance was largely academic. In fact, the dominant view in the party was that, it was not the Liberal Democrats who moved, but the other parties. This is also endorsed by voters as shown by data from the BES (see above). In particular the Labour Party's move to the right opened up more space for the Liberal Democrats on the left of centre. A senior strategist pointed out: 'I wouldn't say we abandoned equidistance as much as Labour shifted . . . People are trying to suggest we've become a more left wing party, because New Labour shifted to the right. Well no, we haven't; we've decided to stay basically where we always were.'

Indeed it was widely believed within the party elite that a modern professional party should not be defined by the position of its opponents, but should have a clear identity of its own. Either way, going into the 1997 election, the Liberal Democrats found themselves closer to Labour than to the Conservatives, and after eighteen years of Conservative rule, it seemed unthinkable that they might enter into coalition with the outgoing Conservative government. Thus it seems clear that the advantages of maintaining equidistance were affected not only by the ideological space left by the major parties, but also by the popularity of the major parties themselves. The Conservative Party were clearly regarded as unpopular, and the Liberal Democrats saw the advantages of backing the winning side.

Despite their limitations, spatial models appear to provide a useful starting point for exploring the strategy of a centre party in a first past-the-post-system. Indeed, a great many of our interviewees referred to the notion of the third party squeeze, and overcoming this was a key issue in Liberal Democrat strategy. However, we now turn to political marketing concepts to investigate whether there are not more promising interpretations of the Party's abandonment of equidistance.

A niche party?

Butler and Collins (1996) argue the case for utilising marketing concepts in order to understand the strategic positioning of parties. The analogy of political parties as companies and voters as consumers certainly has some prima facie attraction. There are clear parallels between the company's search for markets, with the political strategists attempt to maximise electoral returns, and Butler and Collins illustrate how a widely accepted typology of companies (for example, Porter, 1980) can be applied to political parties. This typology identifies four types of competitive market positioning; (1) market leader, (2) challenger, (3) follower and (4) nicher. Butler and Collins identify examples of each form in various democracies around the world. Here we focus on the fourth category (the market nicher), though we also consider the second (the challenger) and third (the follower) as these have the most potential for improving our understanding of the Liberal Democrats electoral strategy.

The challenger party seeks to overthrow the market leader (the 'natural party of government') by an aggressive strategy of either attacking the market leader or eliminating smaller rivals. The parallels in political systems are obvious. The market nicher (or niche party) is defined by its ability to carefully define and successfully target a market segment where it specialises in serving the needs of those customers (Butler and Collins, 1996, 39). The normal method by which parties achieve this is through appeal to specific or sectional interests (such as special issue parties such as environmentalists or regional parties). The Liberal Democrats do not fit neatly into either of these categories as they attempt to appeal to the electorate across the full range of issues and compete in almost all geographical areas. This largely reflects their aspirations to be more than a niche party – to be the challenger to the market leader, which requires them to demonstrate competence and vision across all the issues of the day. The third category, the follower, imitates and adapts elements of the leaders appeal. Follower parties can be differentiated from niche parties by their preference for national campaigns and tend to address the full range of issues rather than specialising. Whilst some market followers use 'direct cloning', others prefer to retain some 'product' differentiation or adaptation to alternative markets or market segments. This fits the description of the Liberal Democrats more closely, if we assume that Labour can be described as the 'leader'. The adaptive strategy appears especially promising as the Liberal Democrats tend to be stronger in geographical areas and social groups where Labour are relatively weak (as shown in Chapters 5 and 7 respectively).

Thus the Liberal Democrats might also be considered a follower party using market niching in order to consolidate their 'market share'. We will see how they seek to do this through the development of a distinctive policy position and locally specific strategies. However, we also argue that there are clear limitations of this approach as the utility derived from voting (unlike product purchase) is potentially dependent on the behaviour of others. In other words, because of the nature of electoral systems, in particular the simple plurality system used in British General Elections, voters may waste their votes. As we identified above, this is a particular problem for smaller parties. We suggest that whilst market niching and adaptive-follower strategies are aimed at combating the centre party squeeze and maximising the national share of the vote, centre parties in a simple plurality system also require a solution to the wasted vote syndrome. This leads to an associated electoral 'tactic' of targeting (which is discussed in Chapter 9).

Challenging left–right analysis: 'neither left nor right but forward'

One of the key assumptions underpinning Downsian spatial proximity theory of elections is that parties can be located on a single ideological (usually left–right) dimension. Indeed, the very notion of equidistance implies a single dimension upon which all parties can be located. Thus traditionally the Liberal Democrats and their predecessors have been regarded as a party of the centre (and evidence in chapter 6 supports this). There are a number of examples of left–right scales used by political analysts (see for example Castles and Mair's (1984) 11–point scale and the scales used by Laver and Hunt (1992) and Janda (1979)) but there is also an everyday notion of left–right that has a resonance in British politics. However, many commentators have noted that there are other dimensions of political ideology not captured on the left–right scale such as the authoritarian–liberal dimension (e.g. Heath *et al.*, 1991) and post-materialism (Inglehart 1971) and multiple dimensions have been incorporated into spatial models (e.g. Merrill and Grofman, 1999). For the Liberal Democrats, the left–right scale has long been perceived as problematic. The long-term political strategy of the third party from the leadership of Grimond to that of Ashdown has been described as the 'realignment of the left' (MacIver, 1996, 174) but elements of Liberal (and Liberal Democrat) support often fall outside left–right classifications (for example, environmental and libertarian concerns). Below we explore other potential issue dimensions using data from the 1997 BES.

Identifying attitude structures

Voters hold divergent views on a wide range of issues regarding political issues of the day. However, it is well observed that rather than holding randomly assorted attitudes towards these issues, voters tend to structure their attitudes around common ideological themes (see Scarbrough 1984, Heath and Evans, 1988; Fieldhouse, 1995). Packages of attitudes measuring ideological positions or policy dimensions tend to be more robust than single issues alone. It should be borne in mind that parties rarely compete for votes around single issues (the Referendum Party in 1997 being a notable exception) but tend to mobilise support across broader ideological issues (see Robertson, 1984; Scarbrough, 1984). Hence a methodological approach – such as principal components analysis – that facilitates the study of these broader attitudinal packages or policy dimensions ought to be better placed to capture the 'system of beliefs' that inform an ideological choice of party (Scarbrough, 1984, Fieldhouse, 1995).

The questions included in the following analyses all relate to voters position on policy issues, rather than general attitudes at the 1997 General Election. More specifically, the selected variables measure attitudes to policies including taxation and government spending, inflation and unemployment, privatisation and nationalisation, income redistribution, and European integration (all of which were measured by the BES on an eleven point scale). Further attitudinal questions using metric data values on Likert scales and also relating to policy issues, but with fewer than eleven data points, were also included in the analysis. Comparable data for 2001 is not available.

The selected variables were used to identify attitudinal structures in the electorate as a whole (and then also among the supporters of the three main political parties in Britain). This identification process was conducted using principal component analysis. The extracted components are composite hidden (or latent) variables or issue dimensions which are highly correlated with as many of the original variables as possible and unrelated to all the other new variables (see Tabachnick and Fidell, 1989). A number of variables were eliminated after preliminary analyses revealed insignificant correlations with other variables. These eliminated variables measured attitudes to defence cuts, autonomy in the workplace, the reforming function of prisons and the desirability of proportional representation in Britain. This does not necessarily mean (for example) that the desire for proportional representation was irrelevant to the British electorate in 1997 only that PR was not part of a structured coherent package of beliefs held by voters.

Parallel analyses for the voters of each of the three political parties were conducted but confirmed that the attitudinal structures of Conservative, Labour and Liberal Democrat voters were insufficiently different to be regarded as significant. In other words, people supporting different parties may hold different views but they structure their views in a very similar way.

The principal components analysis for these attitudinal policy issues suggested a six component solution which explained 56.4% of the variance in public attitudes. Table 8.1 demonstrates the existence of distinct dimensions of import in the structure of public attitudes. For ease of reading, those scores for each variable relating to the component that the variable best fits with are presented here in italic type. These six dimensions can be said to represent 'law and order', 'government spending', 'internationalism', 'economic choices', 'egalitarianism' and 'environmentalism'. The law and order component is dominated by attitudes to crime and punishment; government spending by attitudes to spending on education, the NHS, and the elimination of poverty; the internationalism component is dominated by attitudes to Britain and the world; economic choices measures attitudes to trade-offs between unemployment and inflation, taxation and spending, and private and public sector industrial production; egalitarianism captures public attitudes to issues such as private health care and education; environmentalism is dominated by attitudes to the use of private transport and roads policy.

Overall, the views of voters seem to be reasonably coherent but not highly structured, with each component representing a set of logical issue dimensions about which the political parties hold distinctive positions. These coherent policy dimensions would tend to support the claim that there is not a simple left–right/liberal–authoritarian agenda as often assumed, but issue positions are structured around a number of different policy areas, with new agenda such as the environment and internationalism becoming increasingly hard to ignore. This is a view very much reflected in the perceptions of the party and in the party strategy, as we shall see below. Rather than simply plumping for the middle position on these policy dimensions, the Liberal Democrats may benefit from a more radical stance on certain agenda, that distinguishes them from the Conservative and Labour parties. This would appear to open up potential new heartlands of support for Liberal Democrats.

Attitudes and votes

Table 8.2 gives the mean (standardised) component scores for supporters of the major parties. As might be expected, the position held by Liberal Democrat voters appears to occupy the middle ground in three of the six dimensions. Nevertheless, in a further two policy dimensions the Liberal

Table 8.1 **Principal components analysis component loadings**

	Comp. 1	*Comp. 2*	*Comp. 3*	*Comp. 4*	*Comp. 5*	*Comp. 6*
Law and Order						
Stiffer sentences	*0.742*	0.079	−0.200	0.050	0.013	0.048
Life should mean life	*0.693*	0.108	−0.226	0.007	0.089	0.116
Death penalty	*0.659*	−0.091	−0.296	0.018	0.040	0.116
TU laws	*0.584*	−0.054	0.100	−0.062	−0.321	0.005
Govt spending						
Govt sp. education	−0.046	*0.832*	0.064	0.085	−0.046	0.034
Govt sp. NHS	0.074	*0.790*	−0.017	0.160	0.108	0.012
Elim. poverty	0.028	*0.586*	0.106	0.130	0.249	−0.086
Internationalism						
Nat. co-op.	−0.163	−0.019	*0.749*	−0.046	0.055	−0.068
EU integrate	−0.205	0.018	*0.692*	0.144	0.123	0.027
Govt aid	−0.163	0.201	*0.578*	0.028	−0.032	−0.234
Economic choices						
Infl./Unemp.	−0.030	0.075	0.025	*0.800*	−0.029	0.013
Tax/sp.	−0.035	0.298	−0.029	*0.661*	0.021	−0.109
Priv./Nat.	0.071	0.026	0.103	*0.529*	0.362	0.030
Egalitarianism						
Priv. educ.	0.059	0.116	0.223	0.042	*0.711*	0.030
Priv. med.	0.215	−0.045	0.152	−0.018	*−0.701*	0.044
Inc. equality	0.167	0.254	0.173	0.378	*0.466*	0.014
Environmentalism						
Car allow.	0.124	−0.055	0.015	0.019	−0.087	*0.812*
Car tax	−0.076	−0.035	0.226	0.073	−0.085	*0.753*

Source: *British Election Study* 1997.
Notes: Variance explained = 56.4%. Extraction method: principal components analysis. Rotation method: varimax with Kaiser normalisation. Kaiser-Meyer-Olkin Measure of Sampling Adequacy = 0.785.

Democrat voter group take up a more extreme position than their counterparts who reported voting for the Conservative and Labour parties in 1997. This would tend to suggest that the Liberal Democrats have had significant success in marketing themselves as a party of the radical edge of British politics on certain issues. Liberal Democrat voters tended to be the most liberal of all respondents on the policy dimensions dominated by law and order and environmentalism (factors 1 and 6). Furthermore, even where the Liberal Democrat position does occupy the middle ground it fails to do so in a strictly mathematical sense. Indeed on the remaining dimensions the Liberal Democrats were either identical (on internationalism) or closer to Labour than to the Conservatives. In other words the notion of equidistance on these more detailed issue dimensions looks to have been firmly rejected by Liberal

Table 8.2 **Policy dimensions and attitudes, by reported vote**

	L&O factor	*G.sp. factor*	*Intern. factor*	*Ec.ch. factor*	*Egal. factor*	*Enviro. factor*
Con Mean	−0.17	0.45	0.25	0.33	0.67	−0.04
Lab Mean	0.03	−0.20	−0.11	−0.24	−0.31	0.02
Lib-Dem Mean	0.27	−0.14	−0.11	−0.01	0.01	0.17
No.	846	2846	2846	2846	846	2846

Source: *British Election Study* 1997.

Democrat voters in the 1997 General Election.

In view of these findings, and because of their position in the vulnerable centre of the left–right continuum, perhaps it is not surprising that the third party has often been reluctant to identify itself in terms of left and right, particularly as such terminology defines the party in relation to its main opponents rather than in its own terms. Interview evidence suggests that with the abandonment of equidistance the party sought to offer a distinct and radical alternative that would be seen as *'neither left nor right, but forward'.* Indeed many in the Liberal Democrats reject the notion of the simplistic left–right continuum of politics. Others tried to identify other political dimensions, independent of left and right, typically describing some version of Inglehart's 'post-materialist' agenda (Inglehart 1971). As one MP put it: 'Too many people see politics in terms of a one-dimensional structure, the traditional left-right economic structure . . . We have a different view of what I call the "tolerance axis".'

Despite openly rejecting the left–right terminology many in the party accepted that the Party might be perceived as left of Labour. For example, one MP placed them 'left of Labour and more egalitarian than the Tories' and also indicated this is how it is perceived by the electorate (see Chapter 6 for survey evidence of this). This perception was certainly shared by the broadsheet press in the run-up to the 2001 General Election. However, while many commentators placed the party to the left of Labour, senior strategists and MPs appreciated the danger of such a label – that it could cost the party votes from disaffected Conservatives. Despite this, in private many in the party agreed with the political commentators that the party was to the left of Labour (notwithstanding their dislike of such a classification). In public the party seemed to enjoy the description 'radical' but shied away from being labelled 'left-wing'. This was very clearly reflected in the official line 'neither left nor right but forward' and was summed up by one MP.

> We're not allowed to say that we're to the left of Labour, of course, you know that! We are allowed to say we're more radical and that we're ahead of Labour I believe

> is the right thing. But, I mean, one of the problems there is that everybody thinks that we're talking about a two-dimensional political axis and you have to be somewhere on the two-dimensional axis.

It is this rejection of the left–right placement which party strategists hoped would circumvent the problems the spatial models predicted (the third party squeeze) whilst allowing them to retain their political integrity with respect to their core values. In the following section we explore how they attempted to identify and occupy a niche in the 'radical centre'.

Developing distinctiveness

It has been widely argued that the electorate in many western democracies are becoming more sophisticated, and in particular more volatile and instrumental (Sarlvik and Crewe, 1983; Crewe and Denver, 1985). Thus it is crucial for any party, not least a third party, to develop a distinctive image, not dissimilar to the notion of a niche market. Whilst being the party of the centre meant defining itself in relation to others, rejection of this position meant the party had to carve out a new niche in which they would be readily identifiable. This problem is particularly acute for a third party in a predominantly two party system.

This search for distinctiveness is not new. In 1988 the Liberal Democrats' ruling federal executive expressed its desire for crisp and simple themes that would create a clear and distinct image for the new party. Very few people actually knew what the party stood for, as one MP noted: '[The party's focus groups] had no concept of what we were all about. It wasn't that they thought we weren't very good, or that we were wearing open-toed sandals or anything, they were blank, they didn't know.'

To counter the problem of a lack of image, and to lift the party's profile in the media and the electorate a paper entitled *Our Different Vision* was produced. The themes developed in the paper provided the basis for the preparations for the 1992 election campaign; the manifesto – *Changing Britain for Good* – concentrated on a few selected issues that would create a distinct policy position easily recognisable to the electorate. This marked a change from the 1987 manifesto, which was characterised by what one strategist referred to as an 'excessive blandness'. The issues the party chose to focus on became known as the five 'Es' – Enterprise Economy, Education, Environment, Europe and Electoral Reform. It was hoped that focusing on such a small number of issues would allow the party to establish their 'ownership' of these issues (these were discussed in more detail in Chapter 6).

Perhaps more important than the policy content was the style of politics adopted by the party. In 2001 the party highlighted the issue of honesty and responsibility. The Liberal Democrats, accepting they were unlikely to form a government, found greater scope for candour than their opponents. This gelled well with a perceived image of the party of the individual citizen. The most important area for this policy of honesty (or 'telling it as it is') was in the field of taxation. The policy of openness and honesty on taxation reflected the well-established Liberal Democrat policy of hypothecated taxation. A minor line in an Ashdown speech in 1990 about the necessity to raise some taxes had been developed by 1992 into a policy nostrum. Leading figures within the party saw this as a good opportunity to develop a policy that would be radical and distinct so that by 2001, it was a defining characteristic of the party. As one of its major architects stated: 'The penny on income tax – you were either in favour of it or you were against it, you can't just shrug your shoulders and say 'yes, everybody says that' . . . we had no idea that it would be as popular as it was, but it was absolutely crucial to try and make the party have some definition.'

Labour's anxiety to be seen as financially prudent after 1992 gave the Liberal Democrats more space to re-run the penny on income tax in 1997 and again in 2001. While Labour ran 'Education, education, education!' the Liberal Democrats felt able to counter with 'Resources, resources, resources!' (Holme and Holmes, 1998). This gave the party the opportunity to differentiate themselves from Labour, claiming that they were being honest about what things cost and being responsible in the pursuit of their policies (in contrast to the major parties' promises of improved services and reduced taxation). As one senior strategist noted: 'It gave that sort of edge on Labour, which was crucially important, that we're not just an echo of Labour, we're the guys that tell it as it is. And honesty and taxation became the sort of underlying theme that overlaid policy issues.'

However public perception of ideological closeness to Labour was fuelled by the close political ties between the parties, especially under the leadership of Paddy Ashdown (for example Liberal Democrat representation was granted on the Joint Consultative Committee of the Labour cabinet; Lord Jenkins was asked to oversee the commission into reform of the electoral system; the Liberal Democrats entered coalitions with Labour in the Scottish Parliament and a partnership agreement with Labour in the National Assembly for Wales). Although it was recognised that there was political credibility derived from involvement in government, the need to be seen as both independent and distinctive was central to the party's strategy for 2001. According to a senior figure: 'The first main challenge for us will be to get clearly in to the public's mind that we are an independent party, that we are, we have our own distinctive agenda and that we can differentiate ourselves from the Labour Party.'

Fighting the Conservatives, competing with Labour

In short, in search of distinctiveness, the party embarked on a course of programmatic renewal that sat uncomfortably with spatial models of party behaviour (e.g. Downs, 1957, Panebianco, 1988). The party chose to 'brand itself' using issues, such as education and taxation, which resulted in the party's image becoming increasingly radical and distinctive rather than centrist and non-controversial. The 2001 campaign strategy continued to attack the Conservatives more vehemently than Labour. One MP revealed that, despite the fact that Labour were now in office, the Liberal Democrats were gearing up to re-run the 1997 campaign.

> The difference is, one competes with Labour but fights the Tories. We can have a nice competition, respectful and even quite friendly between Labour and Liberal Democrats . . . there is still in political circles, a very bitter aftertaste to Conservative government and what is common between Labour and Liberal Democrats is a fierce desire to prevent a Conservative government returning.

The electorate seemed to share the view that the Liberal Democrats rather than being a centre party were primarily an anti-Conservative party. In Chapter 5 we showed that voters of all parties shifted dramatically in their perception of the position of the Liberal Democrats. Figure 8.1 shows the steady decline (particularly since 1987) amongst voters of all parties who see the Liberal Democrats closer to the Conservatives than to Labour (the reverse being true for Labour). Furthermore, a majority identified Labour as their second preference (see Chapter 5). Both these statistics mark a reversal of public perceptions at the 1992 General Election. Although comparable information is not available for 2001, the flow of the vote does show that voters did switch from the Liberal Democrats to and from both the major parties, but are more likely to have switched between Labour and Liberal Democrat. For example, according to the 2001 British Election Survey 31% of Liberal Democrat voters claimed to have voted Labour at the previous General Election (1997) compared to 15% who had voted Conservative (and 44% Liberal Democrat). Voters were also more likely to switch from the Liberal Democrats to Labour than to the Conservatives.

This anti-Conservative sentiment was overwhelming within the party elite. They were clear about who the 'real enemy' were in 2001, despite their weak position in the opinion polls. Thus the party clearly branded itself as an anti-Conservative Party in both 1997 and 2001. Many in the party argue that there is a straightforward choice (in the words of a Liberal Democrat MEP) between 'the forces of progress and reform and the forces of reaction'. However, being an anti-Conservative party did not mean abandoning the appeal to disaffected Tories. The importance of cross-party appeal remained

Figure 8.1 **% of voters believing Liberals closer to the Conservatives**

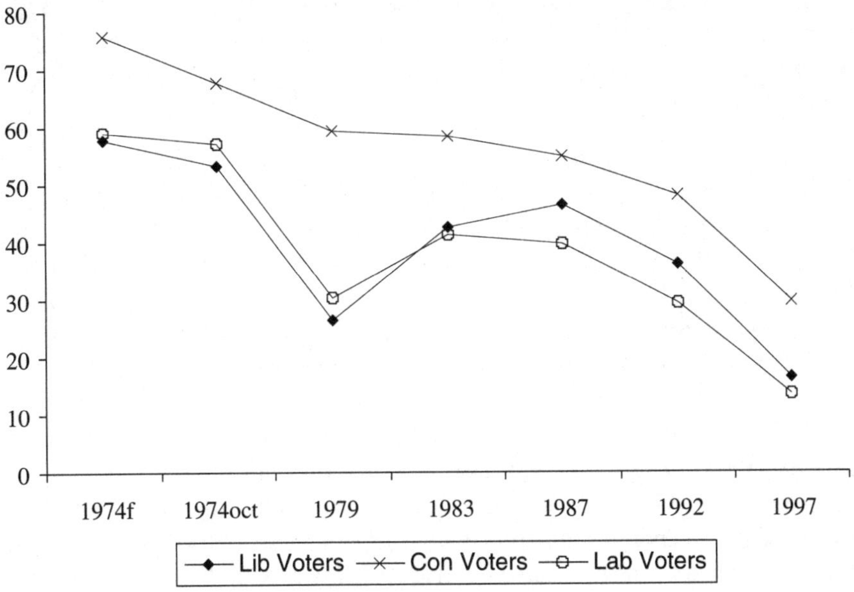

80
70
60
50
40
30
20
10
0

1974f 1974oct 1979 1983 1987 1992 1997

Lib Voters Con Voters Lab Voters

Source: *British Election Study* surveys 1974–97.

(and remains) paramount; especially as in many areas the main opponents are Labour and not the Conservatives (see below). Thus although the Liberal Democrats were positioned as an anti-Conservative party, it still was faced with a battle on two fronts. Many were acutely aware of this dilemma:

> I realise to gain power you have to win people from both sides including traditionally the majority who were Tory. Interestingly, the paradox now is that we need to win more Tory seats to make progress and yet most of the seats in the country aren't Tory. So we've got to be careful we don't distort our appeal to win what is only potentially a minority and ignore what is actually the majority of the vote.

Electoral necessity

The anti-Conservative stance not only suited the party's ideological principles, but also made electoral sense in 1997 and in 2001. In both elections, the party found itself fighting the Conservatives in the majority of its existing and target seats. It became clear that the party's strategy in the run-up to the 2001 election would be a refinement of the 1997 strategy. One MP claimed:

> The fact is most of the seats which the Liberal Democrats either hold or potentially can win, can be gained at the expense of the Conservatives. Therefore you're trying to squeeze the Labour party and you're seeking tactical votes from Labour supporters and therefore you want to be seen as close in terms of values if not in terms of style.

In 1997 Liberal Democrat victories came largely at the expense of the Conservatives, but they found it harder to compete against the Labour party. In the run-up to the 2001 election, the Liberal Democrats stood to gain or lose much more in contests with the Conservatives than with Labour. Even a relatively modest uniform swing of 5% from the Conservatives to the Liberal Democrats could have seen the party win 12 extra seats. Similarly if the Conservatives were to achieve a swing away from the Liberal Democrats a large proportion of the seats won in 1997 would have been lost (see Russell *et al.,* 2002b). The Conservatives were second in the nine most vulnerable Liberal Democrat seats. In addition to this, it was shown in Chapter 5 that, as well as the geographical profile, the social profile of Liberal Democrat support is also more similar to the Conservatives than it is to Labour. This means that the Liberal Democrats were competing with the Conservatives for the same constituency of support, thus making this strategy all the more attractive. However it also makes them vulnerable to a Conservative revival. The challenge for the Liberal Democrats was to be sufficiently anti-Conservative to retain their core constituency of support yet not so hostile so as to alienate disaffected Conservative voters in predominantly Conservative areas.

Local strategies

The logic of an anti-Conservative stance did not apply everywhere equally. Analysis of the geography of Liberal Democrat support, and the case study constituencies has shown that the party must tailor its message to suit different local contexts (see Chapter 7). In fact the Liberal Democrats are faced with a series of 'micro-contests' at the constituency level, requiring different strategic approaches. In many key constituencies the party is in close competition with the Conservatives, but in some Labour are the main opponents. One MP told us:

> There are loads of places where we fight Labour tooth and nail and have done for years and will carry on doing so, where the battle is between us and them. And then here are some places at a local level, where we're pretty close to the Labour party because we're both fighting the Tories, or because it happens to be the kind of Labour party that is similar. I mean the Liberal Democrats are not the same party all over the country.

There were different views on the effect of closer co-operation with Labour, depending on the type of seat. Some MPs argued that the anti-Conservative message in 1997 could have been potentially damaging in traditional Conservative areas and wished to play down the anti-Conservative identity: 'I think that at local campaign level we'd like to try to minimize the perception that we are closer to Labour than we are to the Tories.'

On the whole, most acknowledged that the message had to be tailored for the individual constituency. Local strategies are associated with marginality, the scope for tactical voting and the relationship between the local constituency parties. For example, in Liberal Democrat–Conservative marginals the image of an anti-Conservative party could be unproblematic. In contrast, in some key seats the local party was forced to fight an anti-Labour campaign, against a backdrop of the perceived closeness between the parties at the national level. This is reflected in the comments of many interviewees, especially in the north. The local political context was also influenced by Liberal Democrat involvement in government in Scotland and Wales. The party's strategy was clear: to emphasise the contribution the party had made in the Scottish Parliament (for example on student tuition fees) but also to stress their disappointment with the Labour government in Westminster.

The importance of local strategies should not be understated. It is local strength that insulates the party from the third party squeeze, and thus it may be more important to maximise votes in specific locations rather than across the country. This is reflected in the party's emphasis on targeting since 1992, although, in 2001, it was a declared aim of the party to maximise votes, as opposed to seats, in order to build a long-term platform for success (see Chapter 9).

Impact

So did the Liberal Democrat strategy of identifying themselves as an anti-Conservative party, with debatably more radical policies than Labour, pay off at the General Election of 2001? In short, the election was a qualified success for the Liberal Democrats. They increased their level of representation in the House of Commons from 46 to 52 MPs and their share of the vote from 17% to 18%. However, whilst they had won more seats than any third party since 1929, they were no closer to becoming a major force in Parliament, despite the unpopularity of the Conservatives. The changing geographical pattern of Liberal Democrat support was also highly variable in 2001, with pockets of improvement and deterioration across the country. In part this reflected the electorates differential response to this anti-Conservative strategy in the constituencies.

In Chapters 7 and 9 we show how the tactical context of each constituency affected the swing to or from the Liberal Democrats and in Chapter 10 we examine the constituency context in our case studies of campaigning in 2001. In line with anti-Conservative tactical voting, there was an average 5.9% increase in the Liberal Democrat vote share where the Liberal Democrats were defending the seat from the Conservatives in second place in 1997 and the margin was less than 10% (compared to 1.5% nationally). This suggests that the Liberal Democrats were still feeling the benefits of being an anti-Conservative party, attracting tactical votes from potential Labour supporters. In contrast the Liberal Democrat vote fell where Labour was in a close fight with the Conservatives indicating a two-way relationship in the informal anti-Conservative alliance. Generally, the geography of changing Liberal Democrat support suggests that the anti-Conservative stance helped the Liberal Democrats exploit anti-Conservative sentiment in some areas, and pick up a small number of additional seats. However, they also gained some ground where they were in competition with Labour, suggesting that they were still able to recruit anti-Labour voters from the Conservatives.

Analysis of constituency marginality after the 2001 General Election showed that the party was again not in a good position to make serious gains from Labour at the next General Election (Russell *et al.*, 2002b, see also Chapter 9). More pressing was the need to defend itself against a potential revival of Conservative fortunes, or indeed to further marginalise the Tories and establish themselves as the main party of opposition. In keeping with this, following the 2001 General Election there was a number of leadership pronouncements aimed at appealing to disaffected Conservative voters and distancing the party from the Labour government. These were also reinforced by changes in the shadow cabinet (see chapter 5), reflecting Kennedy's discomfort with the Ashdown legacy of closer co-operation with Labour. In an interview with the *Guardian* (21 January 2002) Kennedy categorically signalled the end of the 'project' and hinted at an apparent shift back towards a policy of equidistance. 'This is a new era, clearly the project has served the party well, but it has run its course and we will move on . . . I don't see the future in co-operation with Labour if all we achieve is the perception that we are bit part players in someone else's show.'

Conclusions

Contrary to classical models of party behaviour, the Liberal Democrats responded to a shift to the right of the Labour Party by ending the policy of equidistance, and identifying themselves as part of an anti-Conservative bloc.

This presents a paradox in that that they must win support from disaffected Conservatives, yet their main basis of appeal since the early 1990s has been as an anti-Conservative party. In order to overcome this paradox, the party rejected the left–right notion, combining an appeal to 'progressive' voters mainly from the middle classes in traditional Conservative (and Liberal) areas. Thus they attempted to build a distinctive and radical identity, outside of the confines of the traditional left–right spectrum. This position was recognised by the electorate as well as by key party personnel and, furthermore, reflected electoral necessity. However, the party remained aware that as a basis of appeal, this had to be tailored to the local political context.

In conjunction with a careful policy of targeting, this strategy helped the party to win an increased number of seats at the expense of an unpopular Conservative Party in the 2001 General Election. Although on the face of it the strategy of the Liberal Democrats in 1997 and 2001 seemed to defy classical spatial models of party competition, the subsequent shift back towards equidistance perhaps reinforces the argument that, in the long run, a simple plurality system cannot sustain two parties sharing such close ideological space. Thus in many ways, the classical theories identified above, particularly those of Downs and Duverger, have proved prophetic for the Liberal Democrats. As Downs might have predicted, despite substantial short-term progress, the abandonment of equidistance was apparently not sustainable, and has had to be re-thought. Furthermore, despite a strong election performance in 2001, the Liberal Democrats remained a relatively minor force in British politics, and face a struggle just to maintain that position. This, in turn, is in keeping with Duverger's predictions concerning the first-past-the-post system.

However, such an interpretation might risk over-simplification. In reality any centre party has to weigh up the costs and benefits of treading the centre ground, within the context of the specific electoral system and the nature of party competition in the country and in the electoral constituencies. Spatial theories of elections are based on certain assumptions about the nature of the electoral system and the number of ideological dimensions the parties compete around. Although the British system is sometimes identified as approximating to the stylised assumptions of spatial models (Rohrschneider, 2002) there are inevitable departures from these assumptions. By attempting to manipulate the issue of dimensionality (though identifying alternative ideological dimensions), and circumventing the in-built discriminatory effects of the electoral system (through local strategies and targeting) the party aims to escape the centre party squeeze. An alternative interpretation of Liberal Democrat strategy is provided by the literature on political marketing. We find that rather than simply fighting for the over-competitive market in the centre, the Liberal Democrats sought to develop a political niche that would enable them to expand their 'market share' whilst retaining their political and ideological integrity. However, rather than displaying the typical characteristics of a market nicher, the Liberal Democrats attempted to overcome the vagaries of the electoral system by adopting many of the characteristics of an 'adaptive-follower' in the political marketplace. In other words they identified themselves as aligned to the anti-conservative 'market leader', but occupied a niche outside of the traditional left–right dimension, adapting their appeal to maximise their support in alternative geographical areas and in alternative social groups.

From this perspective we can identify a number of coherent strategic reasons why the Liberal Democrats abandonment of equidistance was both logical and beneficial. First, as we have seen, some ideological positions are not open to negotiation, and the centre ground (or median voter position) can shift. Second, it is local strength that insulates the party from the third party squeeze, and thus it may be more important to maximise votes in specific locations rather than across the country (see Chapter 9 below). Third, and related to this, as we have seen, the Liberal Democrats share a geographical and social profile more similar to that of the Conservatives than that of Labour. This has strategic implications that in turn relate to the relative popularity of both parties and the ideological space they occupy. This will inevitably have an impact on the benefits of maintaining equidistance, and the Conservative unpopularity was a major influence on persuading the Liberal Democrats to back (or follow) the centre-left. Fourth (and finally), the Liberal Democrats have shown that it is not necessary (or desirable) for a political party to place all its eggs in one basket. We found that the Liberal Democrats appreciate there is not one simple ideological dimension with a unimodal distribution of preferences. They can therefore attempt to be seen to be simultaneously both distinctive and yet centrist, exploiting a niche in the market. By attacking Labour on their 'illiberal tendencies' (e.g. in relation to civil liberties, style of government and increasingly Europe) the Party signalled the continuation if perhaps the most fundamental aspect of the strategy we identified in our research: to be a distinct and radical party that is 'neither left nor right, but forward'.

Notes

1 Although Liberal Democrat representation more than doubled at the 1997 election, the Liberal Democrat share of the vote actually fell by 1 per cent. The key to Liberal Democrat success in 1997 was the 'key seats initiative' which channelled party resources into targeting winnable seats rather than increasing national vote share (see Chapter 9).

9

From votes to seats: making votes count

In Chapter 8 we argued that contrary to classical theories of voting behaviour and party competition, the Liberal Democrats responded to a shift towards the centre of the Labour Party, by identifying themselves as an anti-Conservative party. However, although the Liberal Democrats were successful in winning 46 seats in the 1997 General Election, increasing to 52 in 2001, this had more to do with an improved return on their share of the popular vote, than an increase in that vote *per se*. Although the number of Liberal Democrat MPs in the House of Commons more than doubled between 1992 and 1997, the party's share of the vote actually fell by 1 per cent. The key to Liberal Democrat success in winning an increased number of seats was the 'Key Seats Initiative' – which channelled the party's resources into selected constituencies at the expense of obtaining a higher national share of the vote. In 2001 the party again adopted a 'target voters in target seats' strategy.

As was argued in Chapter 7, because of the simple plurality system of voting, a smaller party suffers if its support is geographically spread. Strategically, being a third party in a two-party system presents the Liberal Democrats with significant problems (Duverger, 1954). Under first-past-the-post, the party has failed to match its vote share with representation in Parliament (Table 9.1 below). The party won around a quarter of the votes in the Elections of 1983 and 1987 but failed to gain any other than a handful of seats. In this chapter, we see how, in order to counter this, the party has attempted to increase its number of seats through selective targeting (Denver and Hands, 1997, Denver *et al.* 1998) while increasing its share of the vote nationally.

Do seats matter to a third party?

Downs (1957) assumes that parties are motivated by the prospect of gaining office. How then do we explain the behaviour of the British Liberal Democrats a third party in a two-party system? Clearly they are far away from forming a government (gaining 18 per cent of the popular vote in 2001). Downsian analysis might suppose that such a party is motivated by the prospect of getting closer to office either singularly or jointly. Of course it might be claimed that the third party in British politics might seek other means of extending their influence rather than the straightforward search for votes and Westminster seats. However, the potential for influence was intrinsically linked with the size of the parliamentary party. The *Diaries* of the party's former leader make clear that the Liberal Democrats saw their potential for influencing the government of Britain linked to their capability to hold the balance of power in parliament – or to form part of a new axis of the 'progressive left' (Ashdown, 2000, 2001). As one senior strategist told us:

> Perhaps the lesson for the party in the future is, that we could have even greater power over say a Labour government on a lot of issues, but that power would derive not from the fact that we necessarily have Cabinet ministers ourselves in a coalition agreement, but from the fact that we would have the balance of power or more power than we have at the moment actually in Westminster, in the House of Commons.

In truth, without the benefits of a partisan press, state funding or widespread media exposure, the party came to believe that influence was linked with increasing Liberal Democrat representation in parliament. The influx of new Liberal Democrat MPs in 1997 resulted in a surge in party morale while political developments made a realignment of the centre-left more likely. Labour's landslide in 1997 did not halt the talk of further co-operation between the parties. Furthermore coalitions were secured between the Liberal Democrats and Labour party in the devolved Scottish Parliament and National Assembly for Wales because the Liberal Democrats held the balance of power in those institutions.

Sartori (1976) suggests that the political relevance of a political party is measured by its ability to enter coalition and its blackmail potential. In abandoning equidistance (see Chapters 2 and 8) the Liberal Democrats might have reduced their coalition potential (since they rejected the possibility of entering coalition with the Conservatives), but by halving their possible coalition partners the Liberal Democrats were defining their realistic potential for coalition with Labour. The Liberal Democrat potential for coalition was focused on the ability to deliver a sizeable section of Westminster MPs to the equation. Set within the context of the *electoral strategy* discussed in the previous chapter, here we explore the Liberal Democrat *electoral tactics* of maximising its representation in parliament through careful targeting. However, as we shall see, the 2001 General Election saw the party move away from a straightforward emphasis on maximising representation, towards a longer term emphasis on maximizing voter share nationally.

The third party and the simple plurality system

Duverger's law 'the plurality rule tends to produce a two-party system' (1954) has had distinct strategic repercussions for the Liberal Democrats. There are 'psychological and 'mechanical' effects contributing to this (see Myatt and Fisher, 2002). The mechanical effect arises due to the disproportional relationship between votes and seats (see Johnston *et al.*, 2001). Indeed the share of seats won by the Liberal Democrats and their predecessors have routinely fallen short of their share of the vote (see Table 9.1). Perhaps the main strategic problem for a third party in a simple plurality system is the wasted vote syndrome. Only by establishing electoral credibility (demonstrating the ability to win locally and preferably nationally) can a third party hope increase representation (see Chapters 1 and 7 on the credibility gap hypothesis).

Table 9.1 **'Liberal' voting in British General Elections, 1974–97**

	Vote share (%)	*No. of seats*	*% seats*
Feb. 1974	19.3	14	2.2
Oct. 1974	18.3	13	2.2
1979	13.8	11	1.7
1983	25.4	23	3.5
1987	22.6	22	3.4
1992	17.8	20	3.1
1997	16.8	46	7.0
2001	18.3	52	7.9

The psychological effect arises due to the tactical switching of voters away from trailing parties. The credibility gap thesis suggests the party's best electoral strategy is to continue to build incrementally in areas where they can benefit from tactical votes rather than be penalised (see Chapter 7). The method for doing this is to persuade voters in specific constituencies that the Liberal Democrats have a chance of winning and are the best placed party to overturn the incumbent. Consequently, local campaigns in winnable seats will normally emphasise that the Liberal Democrats are the best-placed party to oust the incumbent, whether that be Labour or Conservative (or nationalist). As noted in Chapters 7 and 10, campaign flyers and *Focus* newsletters therefore attempt to demonstrate this by showing the percentage of votes won by the party in the area (defined to tell the best story) at recent local elections or previous General Elections (again depending which casts the most favourable light). By targeting voters in the most winnable seats, the party can maximise the impact of this strategy.

Tactical voting

By appealing on the basis of the ability to win locally, the effectiveness of targeting is closely linked with tactical voting. This is because it relies on persuading voters in specific constituencies that party A cannot win and if the voter wishes to see party B defeated, the best option is to vote for the Liberal Democrats. Given the anti-Conservative strategy pursued by the Liberal Democrats in the period under question, party A would normally (but not always) be the Labour Party, and party B would be the Conservatives. Thus by identifying potential anti-Conservative voters in seats where the Liberal Democrats are first or second to the Tories, the party would hope to win over these votes for tactical considerations. As we argued in Chapter 5, there was a greater degree of political similarity and switching between Liberal Democrat and Labour voters. Evidence from the 2001 election suggested that tactical voting did take place in Liberal Democrat key seats (see Table 9.2). This had also been the case in 1997 (see Chapter 7)

Table 9.2 **Liberal Democrat vote change, 1997–2001, by tactical situation**

Tactical situation 1997	*Mean*	*Lab-Liberal Democrats swing*	*Con-Liberal Democrats swing*	*No.*
LD–Con marginal	+5.9	+4.4	−0.4	18
LD–Con safe[a]	−0.4	−0.2	+0.9	21
LD–Lab/other	+2.9	+3.0	−1.2	7
Con–Liberal Democrats marginal	+0.8	+1.2	−0.8	20
Con–Liberal Democrats safe	+0.0	+0.1	−1.7	53
Con–Lab/Lab–Con marginal	−1.3	−1.0	+1.2	102
Lab–Liberal Democrat	+1.7	+2.4	+0.9	31
Other	+2.3	+2.6	+0.4	385
All	+1.5	1.7	0.35	637

Notes: [a]Safe = <10%. Missing cases: West Bromwich West (Speaker 1997); Glasgow Springburn (Speaker 2001); Wyre Forest (no LD candidate 01); Tatton (no LD candidate 97).

Table 9.2 shows how the tactical context of each constituency affected the swing to or from the Liberal Democrats. In line with anti-conservative tactical voting, there was a strong swing to incumbent Liberal Democrats in those seats where the Conservatives were a close second – an average increase in the Liberal Democrat vote share of 5.91 per cent. However, whilst there was two-way swing of less than 1 per cent from the Liberal Democrats to the Conservatives in these seats, there was a 4.4 per cent swing from Labour to the Liberal Democrats, indicating likely tactical switching.

Incumbent Liberal Democrats in 'safe' seats (where the second-placed Conservatives trailed by more than 10 per cent of the vote) fared less well – on average their vote fell by 0.4 per cent. There was a very variable swing in the seven seats where Liberal Democrat MPs faced non-Conservative opposition (an average increase of 2.9 per cent, but a standard deviation of 10.2 per cent).

Where Liberal Democrats were in second place after 1997, their electoral performance was again tempered by political context. Liberal Democrats placed second to Labour enjoyed an average boost in support of 1.7 per cent and this was mainly at the expense of Labour. Lying in second place to the Conservatives was not a great bonus for the Liberal Democrats in 2001. In 'safe' Conservative-Liberal Democrat contests, the party's share of the vote was effectively unaltered, while in marginal seats, the Liberal Democrat vote share rose by only three-quarters of 1 per cent, again gained at the expense of Labour. It would appear any benefit from tactical voting was largely cancelled about by the modest improvement in the Conservative performance in these seats compared to 1997.

The majority of seats in Britain in 2001 were two-party contests between Conservative and Labour parties. In such contests, the vote of third parties tends to be squeezed (Duverger, 1954). This appeared to be the case in 2001 as in previous elections. In particular there was a swing from the Liberal Democrats to Labour in marginal Labour–Conservative contests, as compared to a national swing of 1.7 per cent in the opposite direction. The epitome of this was the declining Liberal Democrat vote in Falmouth and Cambourne where the party's share of the vote fell while Labour's (who were already in first place) increased, as a three-way marginal turned into a two-way Labour–Conservative contest. Moreover, a party that encourages tactical voting from supporters of other parties in order to maximise its electoral success, can hardly be surprised to find that its supporters chose to do likewise. All in all, Table 9.2 is consistent with fairly widespread tactical voting, particularly where the contest between two parties was assumed to be close.

In Chapter 5 we saw that the Liberal Democrats were probably the biggest gainers and the biggest losers from tactical voting, insofar as more Liberal Democrat identifiers voted against the party, but large numbers of identifiers of other parties supporting the party. We can measure that more directly using the 2001 British Election Survey, which asked respondents why they voted as they did. All those who explicitly mentioned tactical reasons and those who said the party they really preferred could not win, are considered tactical voters for the purpose of the analysis below. Overall, tactical voters accounted for approximately 12 per cent of the electorate. This is higher than estimated figures from previous elections, though this might reflect definitional difficulties as well as a real increase in the opportunity for and the coordination of tactical voting (see, for example, Johnston and Pattie, 1991; Evans and Heath, 1993).

Table 9.3 **Tactical voting by party**

Party	*% of tactical votes received*	*% of party vote which were tactical voters*	*Preferred party of tactical voters*
Conservative	24	11	23
Labour	31	8	28
Liberal Democrat	38	24	30
Other	7	19	19
Total	12	12	100

Source: *British Election Study* 2001.

Table 9.3 shows the percentage of voters of each party who voted for them for tactical reasons. The Conservatives were the least popular party amongst tactical voters and the Liberal Democrats were the most popular. Nearly one-quarter of all Liberal Democrat voters voted for them for tactical reasons. Looking at this another way, 38 per cent of tactical voters voted for the Liberal Democrats compared to 31 per cent for Labour and 24 per cent for the Conservatives. However the corollary of this was that 30 per cent of tactical voters actually preferred the Liberal Democrats but did not vote for them, compared to 28 per cent of Labour supporters and 23 per cent of Conservative supporters. As the constituency data indicated, therefore, it is clear that the Liberal Democrats were the party most involved in tactical voting, but on the whole the benefits were mostly cancelled out by the losses (see also Kim and Fording, 2001).

Targeting and electoral credibility

Targeting is integral to this process of establishing credibility and building on strength. It proved to be a crucial factor in the Liberal Democrat 1997 campaign, enabling the party to mobilise tactical voting to its advantage. The strategy was repeated successfully in 2001. Targeting allows the party with their limited resources to better concentrate their firepower. Under the first-past–the-post system, targeting is one way of ensuring that votes are distributed more effectively. As a Council Leader asserted: 'The only way which you can punch your weight in the plurality system if you have a national share of the vote which is lower than the other 2 parties, is to target . . . Now one of the reasons why we got more seats with a lower share of the national vote in 97 was for the first time the targeting was ruthless.'

Because each constituency contest in a simple plurality system is independent, minor parties with geographically concentrated support can overcome the disadvantage of the electoral system (Gudgin and Taylor, 1978). The problem for the Liberal Democrats (and their predecessors) in recent years has been the even geographical spread of their support. The electoral strategy of targeting certain seats, has allowed the Liberal Democrats to overcome this problem. Cox (1997, 190–201) suggests that third parties can break through at the constituency level (rather than the national) by establishing strong local networks and organisations. It is possible then for third parties to overcome Duverger's Law, at the local level at least, by concentrating resources on winnable seats and building incrementally.

The local campaign and targeting

Although the problem of wasted votes is particularly acute for the Liberal Democrats, they are not alone in adopting a targeting strategy. Despite an apparent decline in the importance of local campaigning in the 1960s recent General Elections have seen a resurgence in the importance of the local campaign, and these have been particularly rigorous and effective in marginal seats (Denver and Hands, 1997). Furthermore, a number of studies have demonstrated that local campaigns could be effective in boosting the share of the vote of the campaigning party, and suppress that of their opponents (see Pattie *et al.*, 1995; Denver and Hands, 1997; Denver, Hands and Henig, 1998). Following the 2001 General Election, researchers at Lancaster University have shown that stronger campaigns by Labour and the Liberal Democrats generally delivered better results than weaker campaigns (Denver *et al.*, 2002). There was only a small effect for Conservative campaigns. Indeed it was the Liberal Democrats who enjoyed the largest bonus for campaign effort. According to the study, after controlling for other factors, a weak Liberal campaign would increase the parties share of the vote by 1.9 per cent, and a strong campaign by 6.8 per cent (compared to comparable figures of 0.6 per cent and 2.0 per cent for Conservatives and 1.4 per cent and 4.2 per cent for Labour respectively). These effects are certainly large enough to make a difference between winning and losing a marginal target seat. Indeed, in Chapter 7 we saw that campaign spending had a significant positive impact on both Liberal Democrat share of the vote and on the probability of success in 1997. Furthermore, as we will see below, Liberal Democrat campaign intensity was indeed much greater in target seats in both 1997 and 2001.

These findings are consistent with the observations of the majority of our interviewees – that a strong activist base and a strong local campaign is particularly important to the Liberal Democrats. One MP from a marginal seat argued: 'You'll never find Liberal Democrats winning by accident. It doesn't happen – anywhere. I've said it lots of time, but I don't think there's such a thing as a safe seat I don't think, for us. We have to work for it every single time. And work, from my observations, ten times harder than the other two.'

The mechanism for doing this is generally through door to door canvassing and leafleting (in particular the *Focus* newsletter), not just at election time but all year round. This is not simply about getting across a message (although this is important) but it is about local visibility. This serves two functions. First, it can give the impression of strength and hence enhance electoral credibility, and, second, it reinforces the message that it is the Liberal Democrats (rather than the other major parties) which are concerned with local issues and local people: 'I think it's most important that people feel that yes, there's local people fighting for them locally and so on and if you look at our literature you'll see that that what we run on all the time.'

Thus the emphasis on local campaigning reflects both their ideological perspective (with an emphasis on subsidiarity and community politics) and their strategic and financial weakness in relation to the other parties. Taking each of these in turn, their ideological commitment to devolution of power to individuals and to local communities and their associated emphasis on 'pavement politics' is particularly suited to local campaigning. Local activists, those most familiar with local issues, are able to shape the local campaign to suit local circumstances. Furthermore, where the party is most vibrant, and the grassroots of support strongest, the party is best equipped to run a strong local campaign. This links with the second factor – the financial constraints. Due to a lack of money in comparison with the two major parties the Liberal Democrats do not possess the ability to run a national campaign to compete with Labour or the Conservatives. However, local campaigning can to some extent compensate for this. As one interviewee told us: 'It really is the case that you're on the phone, you're round the door, you're shoving bits of paper through the door. It's very, very labour-intensive. But it works. We don't have the alternative; we don't have the money for the big media push.'

This works in three important ways for the party. First, as Denver and Hands (1997) argue, local campaigns play a mobilisation role. This is especially important to the Liberal Democrats as potential supporters may be tempted to not vote or even switch to another party because of the wasted vote syndrome (see Chapter 7). However, they can to a limited extent also play a persuasive role, normally the function of national campaigns. Many interviewees articulated how important local activity is in getting a message across. For example an MP from a marginal seat argued: 'Nobody would know what we believed if we didn't deliver it through the doorsteps ourselves. It's a [David] Penhaligon thing. Get it on a bit of paper and stick it through a letterbox. That's what we do. We do it because that's the only way we can be sure of getting our message across. Whatever that message is.'

A third area in which local activity is important is in fund raising. As well as providing the personnel for the local campaign, a strong activist base is a source of income generation. One MP pointed out: 'We haven't got big financial backing and that's, I think, why we need the local activists and the local grassroots – the people who are still prepared to raise funds for us.'

However human resources are too some extent mobile between seats, and one of the benefits of enjoying target status is the ability to attract activists from other areas (see below). Essentially, because the party is considerably less well off than either of the two major parties, it must concentrate its efforts in a smaller number of winnable seats. Of course these are also the seats where the activist base is relatively strong. More than the other major parties, therefore, the Liberal Democrats rely on targeted local campaigning to maximise the return on their support. It is the strong local campaign that allows the party to attain and/or retain a critical mass of support, which provides a basis for convincing the electorate that a vote for the Liberal Democrats is not wasted.

Liberal Democrat targeting: 1983–2001

In the 1983 General Election, the Alliance received 25 per cent of the popular vote but due to the vagaries of the British electoral system, only 3.5 per cent of the Westminster seats. This provided an impetus for change, as one MP recalled: 'We got a huge number of votes but no seats really. Experiences like that [make] you think: "Bugger this for a lark, we've got to change".' By 1992 the party was promoting the strategy of 'targeting' which they appeared to perfect by 1997. Critically the Liberal Democrats attempted to increase their representation in parliament without necessarily increasing their vote share. They had targeted resources into a 'key seats initiative', which promoted winning seats, even if this was at the expense of national performance. This tactic worked supremely well in 1997 as representation doubled even though vote share fell (see Table 9.1).

The main Liberal Democrat electoral strategy at the 1997 General Election was to target winnable seats. What became apparent after the 1992 General Election was that if the Liberal Democrats were to make significant progress in terms of winning Westminster seats, campaigning in the key seats would have to start earlier and more resources would have to be provided: '"Targeting" became the watchword of the party, and the first strategic decision of the 1997 Election, made almost three years earlier, was that funding in those seats would start immediately' (Holme and Holmes, 1998, 17).

Cowley Street encouraged regions to part-fund target seats, the centre would then match the money and provide guidance. Target seats were required to produce development plans for a minimum of two years, which were intended to detail expenditure and fundraising over the period. These seats would be judged and measured against agreed criteria at regular intervals. In 1994–95, the party also began polling in individual target seats and this was to prove invaluable for the party. From this polling a new program of targeting was introduced, this was known as the 'target voters in target seats' (TVITS) strategy. From this polling the party were able to identify the characteristics of potential voters in certain target seats which helped to develop various messages more specifically.

The 1997 General Election marked an important threshold for the party; 46 seats won, and a significant number of victories outside traditional Liberal heartlands (with particular success in south east England and the outer London suburbs). Hence, in 2001, the Liberal Democrats were defending their best electoral performance for nearly seven decades. Significantly, Liberal Democrat success in these new areas was built on creditable (second place) performances in the 1992 election, success in local government elections, and in some cases in parliamentary by-elections (Chapter 7). In the period between 1997 and 2001, the Liberal Democrats' local electoral base was only slightly diminished, and two spectacular by-election victories had invigorated the party. The 1997 re-run of the contested Winchester election, turned the Liberal Democrat majority from 2 into 22,000, and the 2000 Romsey by-election emphatically overturned an 11,000 Conservative majority. This reinforced the belief that more gains could be made in the 2001 General Election at the expense of the Conservatives. However, in 2001 the Liberal Democrats were defending more seats than ever before, and most of them could be considered marginal and demanding priority status. Thus the party adopted the key seats initiative, in effect a system of layered targeting with less than 60 seats demanding the highest priority, although there was no definitive list of targets as this would imply other seats could be effectively written off (58 seats are classed as target seats for the purpose of the analyses presented below, in line with the definition used by Denver *et al.*, 2002). Lower priority seats were also identified as being promising in the longer term.

The benefits of target status

Due to financial constraints, and the organisation structure of the party, there is little the party can do in target seats other than to provide training and guidance on campaign strategy, and ensuring campaign visits from high profile personnel, not least the party leader. The latter privilege is normally restricted to the top 50–60 target seats or, as a key strategist told us of Ashdown in 1997, 'he was rationed like war-time milk'. This proved highly effective, as virtually all the gains made in 1997 and 2001 had been visited by Ashdown and Kennedy respectively.

In addition, in 2001, as well as receiving assistance from the campaign director's team in Cowley Street, two assistant directors (north and south) provided advice to key seats in their region. In addition all target seats had access to a full-time field officer within their region, who might cover up to a dozen seats. Campaign leaflets were produced locally and delivered by hand and there was no centrally organised canvassing or direct mailing/telephoning to the electorate. However there is evidence, again from the University of Lancaster study, that in 1997 and 2001 much stronger and intensive campaigns were run in target seats. Denver *et al.* (2002) measured the campaign intensity through a survey of election agents, and found that whilst the Liberal Democrats had by far the weakest campaign of the major parties in 1997 and 2001, they were the most effective at concentrating their efforts see Figure 9.1). Figure 9.1 shows average campaign intensity scores for the three main parties for 1997 and 2001. It confirms that all parties run stronger campaigns in target seats. However, generally the Liberal Democrats campaigns in non-target seats are considerably weaker than their rivals, but in target seats they are able to compete. In 1997, in particular, the Liberal Democrats' campaign was much more concentrated than the other parties. The pattern was less pronounced in 2001, but still apparent.

The advantage of target status can be measured in terms of additional

Figure 9.1 **Campaign intensity, by target status**

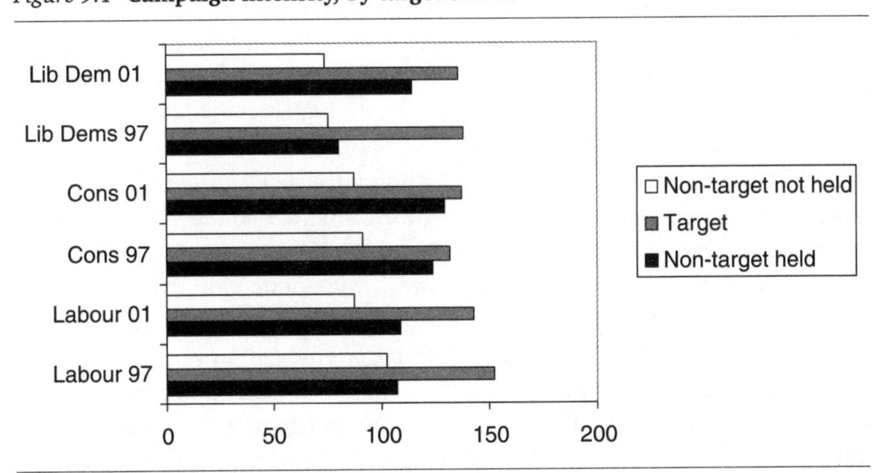

Source: Derived from Denver *et al.*, 2002.

resources, but these are as much knowledge, expertise and manpower as financial. As a successful candidate from a marginal seat told us:

> Well, the obvious advantage is first of all, of resources. In that we attracted resources which Liberal Democrats are constantly short of. And, secondly, it meant that we were taken over by the centre in terms of running our campaign and that brought a new dimension totally . . . The agreement was quite simple. That you either do it our way, or we walk away.

The ability to run strong campaigns in target seats is likely to reflect the health of the grassroots in those areas as much as central planning. However, on a local and regional basis it is likely that human resources were diverted from unwinnable seats to nearby targets. As a candidate neighbouring a target seat explained: 'There is an expectation that people in the surrounding areas are going to spend part of their time at least in that [target] constituency.'

Where target seats were geographically clustered, cumulative advantages could be generated, through two related factors. First, is the availability of strong grassroots in the area, and this ability of individuals to work across more than one constituency. The second is the shared credibility from having a historical and realistic chance of winning seats in the region. The most clear example of this was in the south west of England. This by identifying clusters of target seats additional advantages could be gained. A senior MP told us:

> I also suggested a way of clustering seats which we mainly did in Somerset and Cornwall, elsewhere it didn't work quite as well. Basically providing in effect, paid staff to work with 2 or 3 or 4 seats and get them to work as a team . . . That allowed us to pool resources at a local level in terms of organisation and skills, plus money from the centre, to try and overcome the national problem that we're always squeezed out by the advertising and the overall campaign messages.

How effective is targeting?

In 1997 there were 34 'key seats', and going into the election thirty of these were held by the Conservatives, one by Labour and three by the Liberal Democrats (who were second in 30). In what was a particularly successful election in terms of seat gains, the Liberal Democrats won 24 of these 34 seats, with an average vote share of nearly 40 per cent (compared to 17 per cent nationwide). More significantly the party enjoyed an average increase in support of 4.4 per cent in these seats, compared to a slight decrease in their national share of the popular vote. As we saw in Chapter 7, targeting had a strong independent impact on both the Liberal Democrats share of the vote and probability of success in 1997, after controlling for other factors including campaign spending. This marked a huge success of the targeting strategy, delivering the party the most seats since 1929. Not surprisingly there appeared to be a tactical component to this pattern. As indicated most to these seats were previously held by the Conservatives and the Conservative Party were particularly unpopular going into the 1997 General Election. Analysis of the two-way swing involving the Liberal Democrats (Figure 9.2) we can see that the party was particularly effective at eroding Conservative support in these seats, and there was a reduced tendency of the party to lose support to Labour in these areas. This indicates how the anti-Conservative strategy described in the previous chapter, linked with the tactic of selective targeting to gain seats from the Conservatives.

Of the 58 'target' seats in going in to the 2001 election, 29 were held by the Liberal Democrats, 20 were Conservative held and 9 were Labour. In 1997, of the remaining 28 the Liberal Democrats had been second in 26. The fact that the party already held most of these seats indicates that these are essentially priority seats rather than strictly targets. In the event, 35 of these seats were won in 2001 with the party coming second in 22 of the remaining 23. Perhaps more telling is that they achieved an average increase in vote of 4 per cent in these seats (giving an average vote of 42 per cent) compared to only 1 per cent seats (49 per cent of the popular vote) in the other 17 they held, and 1.2 per cent (18 per cent) in the rest of the country. Figure 9.3 shows that in 2001 the Liberal Democrats were successful in winning over

Figure 9.2 **Two-way swing to Liberal Democrats, by target status, 1992–97**

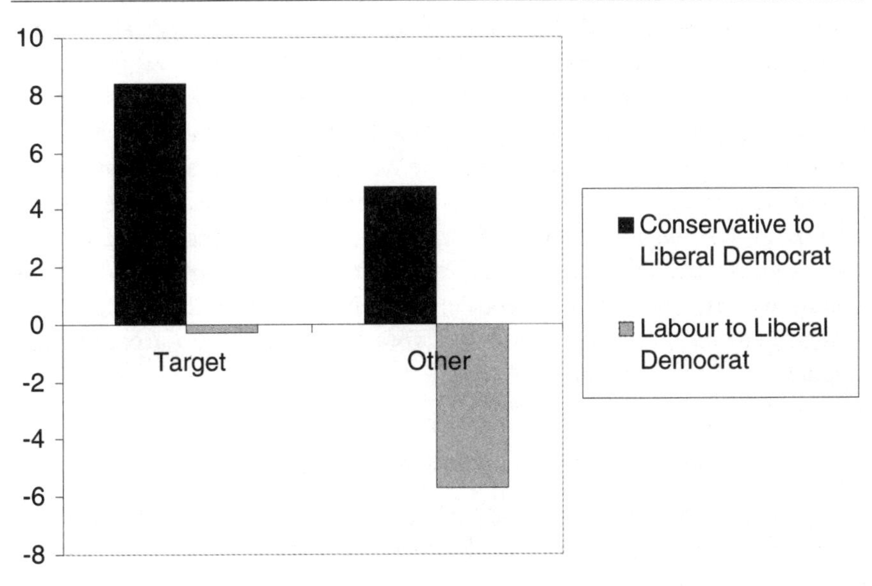

Figure 9.3 **Two-way swing to Liberal Democrats, by target status, 1997–2001**

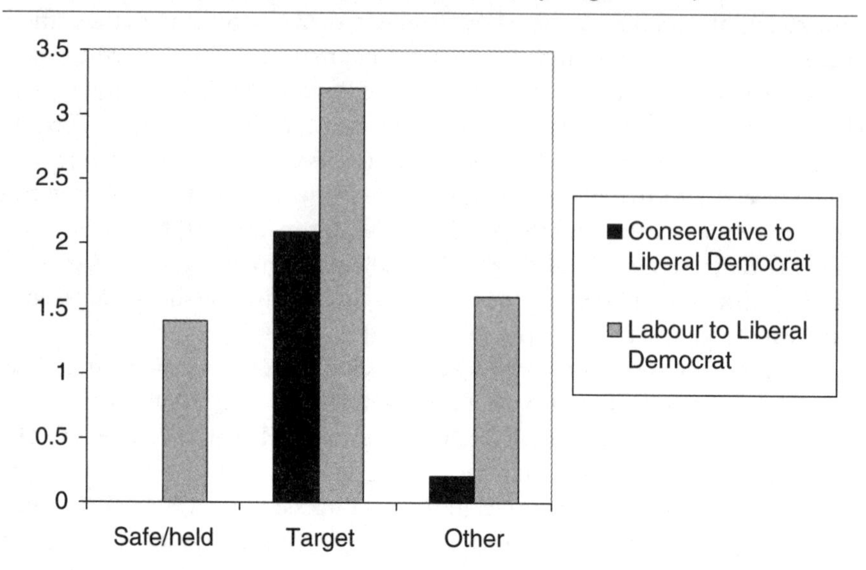

Conservative and Labour voters in greater numbers in target seats compared to other seats.

However, what was notable was the very uneven performance in Liberal Democrat targets. Impressive electoral successes in Cheadle, Guildford and Ludlow was countered by failures to take 'more winnable' seats in Dorset West, Orpington and Surrey South West. In Bridgwater, Tiverton and Honiton, and in Totnes, the Liberal Democrat share of the vote fell, despite the fact that the size of the swing needed was smaller than in five of the party's eight gains. In effect, local factors appeared to override national trends.

However, this indicates a reasonable measure of success for the target voters in target seats initiative. It should also be noted that these seats are more likely to be marginal seats and the party might have benefited regardless of any increase campaign activity. Notwithstanding this, the best explanation of the benefit derived from target status is through increased campaign effort, both through local expenditure and through visits and contributions form the centre. Indeed, model 5 in Table 7.5 showed that target status delivered a 4.7% bonus to the vote after taking into account other factors.

The beginning of the end for targeting?

If the party are to significantly increase their representation in parliament the conditions for winning over tactical voters must exist in a far greater number of seats (for instance, going into the 2001 General Election there were only 13 seats that the Liberal Democrats would win on a 5 per cent swing in their favour. Similarly, going in to the General Election of 2005/6, there are only 17 seats which the Liberal Democrats would win on a 5 per cent swing (16 Conservative and 1 Labour) (see Russell *et al.*, 2002b). Thus in the long run the party must establish itself as creditable challengers in a far greater number of seats. This paradox lay behind a revised strategy in 2001. Despite the success of targeting, interviews conducted in the run-up to the 2001 General Election confirmed that there were limits to targeting as a long-term strategy and that the party may need to reallocate resources in order to build for the future. A senior strategist noted: 'Targeting seats is still very important, but I think we also recognise that we aim to increase our share for next time as well . . . we want to make sure we're in position to gain many more [seats] in say the Election in 2005. So we're not as sharply focused on targeting next time as we were last time.'

While the party increased its number of MPs, its vote share and second placed finishes fell between the 1980s and 1997. To make a substantial breakthrough in the future, it now needed to ensure a strong credible performance in many more seats. The need to capture more voters and more second places was highlighted by a senior party insider: 'One of the reasons Charles [Kennedy] has emphasized vote share is that he is not just looking at the 2001 Elections he is looking a bit further on. And one of the things we want to do next time is get into second place in a few more seats, or get into a more obvious second place or improve on the second place from last time.'

The 2001 results suggest that some progress has been made with this strategy (52 seats from 46, 110 second places from 104). Thus, although targeting was still very important in the 2001 election senior strategists conceded before the election that the strict focus on targeting, which had been so successful in the 1990s (particularly 1997), had its drawbacks and would not be the sole strategic goal in the 2001 election campaign. One activist argued that the party should be increasingly concerned with share of the vote rather than winning more seats. He sees a higher share of the vote as providing the credibility that has been so vital to the party over the years.

> When the difference in your numbers of seats is going to fluctuate between say 25 and 50, does it really make that much difference in terms of your national credibility . . . when most of the electorate wouldn't be able to tell you within 20 seats, I suspect, how many seats we've got. All they perceive is that we are an extremely small third party in parliamentary terms . . . So there's an argument to say that actually what we should be about is increasing our national share of the vote and that that's what gives us the credibility. That would mean a very different campaign strategy, spreading resources much more equally and perhaps

> directing our campaign not to target third party votes in particular constituencies, but to maximise our own voter sympathy vote across the whole country.

Thus targeting and maximising the national share of the vote could be viewed as conflicting strategies. 'The problem with targeting is that it actually limits your ability to roll out your organisation and your operations onto a broader canvas because that is actually counter to the targeting strategy – the targeting strategy is pick 2 or 3 areas, make sure it works there, it's a very, very incremental approach.' Thus in the 2001 campaign increased emphasis was put on maximising the national share of the vote and a broader spread of support. Nevertheless, as we have seen, targeting remained crucial in defending marginal seats and making further gains.

Conclusion

Throughout this book we have argued that in a simple plurality system the issue of credibility is critical, especially to a small party. It is only when the electorate perceives a party has a chance to win that there is any real prospect of success. In this chapter we have shown that by targeting winnable seats, and thus building incrementally from areas of strength, the party can gradually overcome the disadvantages of the electoral system. This works through enhanced local campaigning in target seats, which has been shown to have an impact on the Liberal Democrats vote share. It also relies on the ability to attract tactical voters, especially from the reservoir of potential Labour support in areas where the Liberal Democrats are best placed to beat the Conservatives. The electoral strategy of identifying itself as a distinct but anti-Conservative party was complemented by the electoral tactic of differential campaigning and targeting winnable seats. This has a positive impact on the Liberal Democrat share of the vote and the number of seats won in 1997 and 2001. However, the party recognises that in the medium term, if a big breakthrough is to happen, it is important for the party to maximise its vote nationwide, thus increasing the number of potentially winnable seats in the future.

10

Lib-Dem campaigns in 2001: the case studies

This chapter examines how the Liberal Democrats operated in the run-up to the 2001 election in a variety of the micro-contests that we have identified in previous chapters. For example, we investigate whether local parties function in a similar fashion where their main opposition is Labour and where it is the Conservatives; in marginal and in relatively safe seats; and in areas with strong local networks compared to those with weaker ones. The object of this chapter is to examine the nature of the Liberal Democrats in different locations under different circumstances and to analyse how strategy is adapted to different political contexts.

In the classic study of the 1955 General Election in Bristol North East, Milne and Mackenzie, (1958, 19) dismiss the attempts of the local Liberals to campaign effectively. 'The Liberal candidate was not able to give all his time to the campaign, and was handicapped in the early stages because he had no one to drive him round the constituency. He was not completely mobile until a supporter, able to drive a car, came back from holiday.' Such a vision of chaotic campaigning seems a world away from the contemporary vision of Liberal Democrats at the local level. Even in non-target seats, the pressure would be on for local parties to deliver *Focus* newsletters and specially adapted campaign literature to every door. However, in reality, in many areas local networks are relatively underdeveloped and poorly resourced.

We have argued that dissecting the demographics of the Liberal Democrat vote, and that scrutinising the party's opinion formers and political structure can only tell us so much. For a party whose revival in the 1960s was founded on the principle of community politics, with a formal federal structure and that continues to issue rallying cries to its membership to 'think globally and act locally', we believe that it is imperative to see how the Liberal Democrats function at ground level; in different constituencies, in different regions and within different political environments. This is the party after all that, like G. K. Chesterton, believes that for something to be real, it must be local.

As we have seen in the preceding chapters, a number of key themes have emerged from our research on the Liberal Democrats. Being a third party in an essentially two-party system, the greatest obstacle to Liberal Democrat progress is credibility. In the short term at least, the Liberal Democrats are unlikely to form a government under the first-past-the-post electoral system and as a result may lose many potential voters as a consequence (the wasted vote syndrome). As Chapter 7 showed, the party has endeavoured to breach the 'credibility gap' by building on local traditions of liberal voting in their heartland areas, and on rigorous local activity and local election success outside these areas. Local elections and by-elections can, therefore, be a route to achieving credibility by demonstrating a capacity to win. Similarly, success in contiguous seats can help break down the credibility gap. Together, these factors contribute to apparent creeping Liberalism, as observed in the south west and in areas where an initial breakthrough has been achieved at by-election.

In tactical terms, the Liberal Democrats have aligned themselves as an anti-Conservative party in recent years, despite the fact the class profile of their supporters is similar to that of the Conservatives. The party finds itself competing with the Conservatives for the majority of its existing and target seats. However, if the Liberal Democrats are to make substantial gains in future elections they must also make in-roads in Labour held areas. At local council level the party has been able to make impressive gains at the expense of Labour in a number of large metropolitan councils in the north of England. For example, during the period of this research, the Liberal Democrats gained control of the councils of Liverpool, Sheffield and Stockport. The Liberal Democrats therefore have the difficult task of appealing to different groups in different places. Strategically, this has presented the party with a number of difficulties.

As we discussed in Chapter 4, the Liberal Democrats are a party with a dual identity. They are a party with a tradition of community-based activism, much of their success has been built around this, and many in the party still believe that it is essentially a 'bottom-up' organisation. However, the party has become increasingly professional in recent years, with the successes in 1997 and 2001 contributing greatly to the image of the party as a more efficient and organised electoral machine. For a party with a strong local base, the move towards a more professional identity has not been altogether welcomed.

In order to discover how the themes we have identified manifest themselves on the ground, we studied eight constituencies in depth. Although we are not claiming that the eight constituencies chosen are representative of all constituencies, they did provide us with a good understanding of how the party operates on the ground in different areas and under different electoral conditions in the run-up to the 2001 General Election. All interviews took place during 1999 and were conducted by the authors using semi-structured interviews. In each constituency we interviewed the constituency secretary, chairperson, the 1997 and 2001 General Election agents (if in place), the constituency MP or PPC and the leader of the Liberal Democrat group on the local council (in some cases this was the council leader) and prominent local party members.

The constituencies were selected according to a carefully constructed typology that encapsulated the key characteristics of the micro-contests the party faced in the run-up to 2001. These were Liberal heartland seats, emerging heartland seats, Conservative–Liberal Democrat marginal constituency and Labour–Liberal Democrat marginal seats.

Liberal Democrat seats

Heartland seats

These are traditional Liberal constituencies where the Liberal Democrat candidate was elected in 1997, and the party had some history of success in general and local elections. We selected Devon North and Montgomeryshire as our Liberal Democrat Heartland seats. Both of these seats are part of a long tradition of Liberal support. Devon North was the constituency of former leader Jeremy Thorpe and despite its loss to the Conservatives in 1979 was won back by the Liberal Democrats in 1992. In 1997 the Liberal Democrats held Devon North with an increased majority and a 5% swing from the Conservatives. Montgomeryshire might be seen as the core of Liberal voting since the war, (only being lost once, in 1979). Despite the retirement of the sitting MP in 1997, the Liberal Democrats held the seat comfortably with an increased majority.

The expanding heartland

These are constituencies that were previously target seats and were gained for the first time by the Liberal Democrats in the 1997 General Election. These seats are characterised by proximity to previous Liberal Democrat success at the national or local level (see Chapter 7). We selected Colchester and Sheffield Hallam as our expanding heartland seats for our study of the 2001 campaign. Boundary changes and a candidate steeped in local politics gave the Liberal Democrats hope for victory in Colchester in 1997, despite no real history of electoral success. In the event, the Liberal Democrat victory in Colchester (based on a 6% swing from the Conservatives) showed how effective the campaigns in the Liberal Democrat target seats could be. The famously middle-class Sheffield Hallam was the seat that traditionally kept faith with the Conservatives despite their rejection throughout the rest of South Yorkshire. Local election success since 1992 had given the Liberal

Democrats hope but their victory there in the 1997 General Election was still quite remarkable with a 19% swing from the Conservatives.

Non-Liberal Democrat seats

Conservative–Liberal Democrat marginals

These are seats where the Conservatives held onto power in 1997 and Liberal Democrats were a close second. We selected Bridgwater and Cheadle as our Conservative–Liberal Democrat marginal constituencies. The Conservatives held Bridgwater by a narrow margin, but the story of the 1997 campaign was the 7% swing from the Conservatives to the Liberal Democrats. The announcement that the sitting Conservative MP – Tom King – would not be seeking re-election after thirty years in parliament had given the local Liberal Democrats hope for victory in Bridgwater after 1997 Cheadle remained one of only two Conservative seats in Greater Manchester but the performance of the Liberal Democrats in 1997 was creditable, benefiting from an 11% swing from the Conservatives. Indeed the Liberal Democrats won this seat in 2001.

Labour–Liberal Democrat marginals

These are seats won by Labour in the 1997 General Election, where the Liberal Democrats were placed second, and which might have been considered reasonable target seats for the party in the coming contest. We selected Aberdeen South and Oldham East & Saddleworth as our Labour–Liberal Democrat marginal seats. Both of these seats have a history of Liberal Democrat success at by elections but boundary changes made the Liberal Democrat task harder in 1997. The party's hopes for Oldham East & Saddleworth were high after their victory in the Littleborough & Saddleworth by-election in 1995. However the new seat was a three-way marginal which Labour won with a 3,000 majority over the Liberal Democrats in 1997. Aberdeen South was another bellweather seat that typified the 1997 election, the incumbent Conservative losing to Labour. However perhaps with memories of the 1991 Kincardine & Deeside by-election fresh in their mind, the Liberal Democrats performed well, beating the Conservatives into third place.

Heartlands seats: Devon North

1991 Census data	%
Owner occupiers	74.0
Local authoring housing	10.9
Non-white	0.5
Professional/managerial	33.5
Non-manual	52.3

HISTORY

Devon North, alongside Montgomeryshire, is the exemplar of the Liberal heartland seat. Unlike Montgomeryshire however, the Liberals have not always found it easy to win the seat. In the interwar period, the seat was held by Richard Acland, elected as a Liberal in 1935 (although he reclassified himself as a Common Wealth MP later). Devon North's most enduring relationship with Liberalism however, was that it was the seat of former leader Jeremy Thorpe from 1959 until 1979.

Of course, scandal wrecked Thorpe's leadership of the party, and he was forced to stand down as leader in 1976. He did not however, relinquish his parliamentary seat and attempted to retain it in 1979 – despite being in the middle of the highest of all high-profile trails, on a charge of conspiracy and incitement to murder. The voters of Devon North rejected Thorpe as MP, a matter of days before the jury acquitted him of the criminal charges (see Parris, 1997, for a fuller account).

In truth, the Conservatives' victory in 1979 may have been initiated by the scandal embroiling the old Liberal leader, but it also signalled a long period of Tory rule in the seat. It was 1992 before Nick Harvey won Devon North back for the Liberal Democrats. The retention of the constituency in 1997 with a comfortable majority for Harvey gave rise to talk of another period of Liberal domination but it seems that Harvey enjoys a more tenuous grip on his parliamentary seat than any member of the Conservative or Labour party fortunate enough to represent one of their party's 'safe seats'.

Thus Harvey and the local Liberal Democrats have to work hard to retain links with the local community despite the often-stated grip of Liberalism in the constituency. Nevertheless, as one eminent local politician said to us: 'in Barnstable the Liberal voted isn't counted, it's weighed'. Devon North is a large, mostly rural constituency in the south west corner of England. Tourist and agricultural concerns dominate employment in the area. Industry in the constituency is restricted to the largest town, Barnstaple, which *The Almanac of British Politics* characterises as an 'unexpectedly tough and gritty working class town' (Waller and Criddle, 2002, 298). We saw in Chapter 4 that one of the paradoxes of the Liberal Democrat heartland is that the party manages to be seen as a pro-European party that can pile up the votes of Eurosceptics in rural areas. Devon North fits neatly into this category being a constituent part of the Liberal heartland and yet simultaneously being part of the firm Eurosceptic tradition of British politics. Managing the national image of a Euro-friendly party and the local reality of needing to appeal to a more sceptical audience with farming and fishery concerns anathema to the European integrationist approach is crucial to Liberal Democrat success in Devon North. The intellectual and pragmatic dualism of the party is used to local advantage.

The constituency of Devon North will seemingly be forever linked with former Liberal leader Jeremy Thorpe. Local supporters used to regard him as: 'the uncrowned King of North Devon' (Tregidga, 2000, 214). Thorpe represented the Devon North seat from 1959 to 1979, and casts a long shadow upon the political culture of the region to this day. Countless of our interviewees were quick to talk of the Thorpe era either because they, or their family, were personally involved, or maybe simply because they had heard of the excitement conveyed by the Thorpe years.

Thorpe's leadership of the party and his time as Devon North MP was characterised by a kind of effortless energy, and it is easy to recall photographs of him vaulting barriers and hurdling garden fences when canvassing the area, or sweeping the floors in sub-post offices while the key holder was on holiday. In fact the enigma of the Thorpe era is that it created a notion of North Devon as 'Liberal Country' at a time when Liberal victories were far from guaranteed. Thorpe's victories over the Conservatives were sometimes comfortable (an 11,000 plus vote majority in February 1974) but often marginal (369 votes in 1970, 362 in 1959).

In the 1979 General Election, the Conservative Tony Spellar defeated Thorpe with a majority of 8,473 votes. Of course, the simple tendency is to put Thorpe's defeat in 1979 down to his personal travails but it is worth noting that fellow Liberal John Pardoe was also ousted from the neighbouring seat of Cornwall North. In Devon North itself, Spellar's election was a signal for a further two victories in 1983 and 1987.

The local context

The Liberal Democrat hegemony in the parliamentary seat of Devon North is surely founded in local politics. They dominate the two local councils in the area, North Devon District Council and Devon County Council.

As in Montgomeryshire, there was a tradition of independence rather than party politics in the region. However, in recent times this has been overturned to the benefit of the Liberal Democrats who, as a political group, form a comfortable majority on North Devon District Council (see Table 10.1).

Table 10.1 **North Devon District Council: political affiliation of councillors, 2002**

Liberal Democrats	27
Independents	10
Conservatives	5
Other	2

Table 10.2 **1997 General Election: Devon North**

Candidate	*Party*	*Votes*	*%*
Nick Harvey	Liberal Democrats	27824	50.8
Richard Ashworth	Conservative	21643	39.5
Annie Brenton	Labour	5347	9.8

Notes: Liberal Democrat majority: 6181 (11.3%). Turnout: 77.7%.

In 2001, the outbreak of foot and mouth disease (FMD) had a profound impact on the area and local Liberal Democrats did suffer as a result. By 2002 however, normal service had been resumed and the Liberal Democrats reasserted their dominance.

All in all, it is clear that the Liberal tradition in Devon North is built upon the bedrock of local government. As we explored in Chapter 4, the Liberal Democrats are a party of dual identities. In one respect they are a party dominated by the leadership, and yet at the same time they are characterised by everyday pavement politics. In Devon North, this dualism allows the local party room to manoeuvre, rather than being confined by the strictures of Cowley Street by allowing a Eurosceptic thread to flourish in the local party. In Devon North, the Liberal Democrats have overcome the credibility gap at two levels – firstly by demonstrating that the parliamentary seat is winnable, and, secondly, by plugging into the dominant strand of local politics in the region, a strand that is coloured by Liberalism.

After narrowly winning Devon North in 1992, Nick Harvey consolidated his position in the 1997 General Election (see Table 10.2). Polling just over half of the eligible votes, the Liberal Democrat majority was increased to over 6,000 votes. The 1997 contest is notable for the absence of a potentially problematic opponent in an area characterised by farming, fishing and tourism. The seat was uncontested by the Referendum Party due to Harvey's anti-Maastricht stance, although the United Kingdom Independence Party was to stand against Harvey in 2001.

The election of 2001 was a difficult one for the Liberal Democrats in Devon North (see Table 10.3). Local agriculture had been decimated by the FMD outbreak and the Conservatives had received an unspoken bonus from

Table 10.3 **2001 General Election: Devon North**

Candidate	*Party*	*Votes*	*%*	*Change*
Nick Harvey	Liberal Democrats	21784	44.2	−6.6
Clive Allen	Conservative	18800	38.2	−1.3
Vivian Gale	Labour	4995	10.1	+0.3
Roger Knapman	UKIP	2484	5.0	
Tony Brown	Green	1191	2.4	

Notes: Liberal Democrat majority: 2984 (6.1%). Swing: 2.6% LD to C. Turnout: 68.3%

the mobilisation of the Countryside Alliance and had been seen, nationally at least, as the benefactors of the rural vote.

As noted above, despite his tempered Euroscepticism, Harvey had to fight off the anti-European United Kingdom Independence Party. Moreover the UKIP candidate was well known, Roger Knapman being the former Conservative MP for Stroud no less. All in all, the prognosis for Liberal Democrat victory was less promising than Harvey may have wished for.

In the event, however, Harvey held onto the seat. A small but significant

MP profile: Nick Harvey

Nick Harvey won the Devon North constituency back for the Liberal Democrats in the 1992 General Election with a majority of 794 votes. Harvey is an affable character who seems to have a strong basis of support in Devon North despite his apparent outsider status. He is a genuine free-thinker, and was alone in the Liberal Democrats during the 1992 parliament to vote against the Maastricht Treaty. In the aftermath of Maastricht he had called the party's ideas on Europe 'totally illiberal' and 'utterly shameful', although by 1999 he was praising those countries that had joined the Euro (both cited in Brack and Ingham, 1999, 80). Nevertheless, even if recently diluted, his Euroscepticism makes him unusual, to say the least, in the parliamentary party, although it might offer a hint to his local popularity.

Until the 2003 front-bench reshuffle, Harvey was party spokesperson for Culture, Media and Sports. He had previously held the Liberal Democrat briefs for transport (1992–94), trade and industry (1994–97), the English regions (1997–99) and health (1999–2001). He also spent a long and successful stint at party HQ as chair of campaigns and communications until 1999.

Recapturing the site of former glories, playing a significant role in the campaigning strategy of the party at a time of growth, and standing up for the local over the national and European concerns might have marked Harvey out as future leadership material. In the event, however, Harvey decided not to stand for the leadership of the party in 1999 and threw his weight behind the candidature of Charles Kennedy.

swing from the Liberal Democrats to the Conservatives could not disguise the fact that the Tory vote had fallen too, while Labour's rump 10% of the vote had held firm. Knapman, the UKIP candidate, retained his deposited but probably damaged the Conservative vote as well as that of the incumbent.

After a narrow but decisive victory in 2001, Harvey and the Liberal Democrats seem to have reasserted the Liberal tradition in Devon North. The secret of this was two-fold, appealing to a long standing – if latent – tradition of Liberal support via the building of credibility at the local level, and, secondly, by exploiting the dual identity of the party. The lack of centralised resources, whether by accident or by ideological design, permitted the politics of the Liberal Democrats Devon North to be squarely at odds with the national picture of the party and resist the tide of anti-European and anti-urban sentiment that might in other circumstances have swept away the Liberal Democrats.

Heartlands seats: Montgomeryshire

1991 Census data	*%*
Owner occupiers.	66.1
Local authority housing	18.6
Non-white	0.5
Professional/managerial	34.5
Non-manual	51.7
Welsh speaking	23.3

History

If the Liberal Democrats have a geographic heartland, Montgomeryshire would most certainly be it. The seat of postwar Liberal leader, Clement Davies, the party has only lost Montgomery once in recent times, as Emlyn Hooson was swept aside with the tide of Conservative victory in 1979.

Montgomeryshire lies in the heart of the nonconformist Liberal tradition that has survived any downturn in chapel attendance. Visitors will be struck by the number of chapels in the constituency and the Liberal Democrats still seem to be the beneficiary of the traditional link between nonconformity and politics.

Apart from a slight name change, when Montgomery became Montgomeryshire in the changes effective in the 1997 contest, the constituency has remained relatively unaltered by the electoral engineering of boundary reviews. It is a huge, and mostly rural, seat near the English border with mid-Wales, traditionally seeing a large proportion of its population employed in agriculture. There are two main towns in the constituency boundary, Newtown and Welshpool.

Although Hooson lost Montgomery (as it was then named) to the Conservatives in 1979, normal service was resumed in 1983 when the high flying legal professional Alex Carlile regained the seat for the Liberals. He continued to serve as the area's MP until his elevation to the Lords in 1997 when Lembit Opik won the resultant selection battle for Montgomeryshire.

The local context

Clearly Hooson's 1979 loss to the Conservatives was unexpected and traumatic for the local Liberals, and local activists still refer to the 1979 election the way that some people who have lost close relatives refer to unexpected and sudden demises. Almost to a man and woman, local Liberal Democrats we spoke to referred to the defeat not as a result of a wave of popular Conservatism but because the party had become complacent and neglected the link between elected and local electors. It seems that even in the heart of the Liberal dominion the party must bridge the credibility gap and manage the dual identity of the party – and to do so it has to convince local electors that it has maintained its roots in the local community.

This is a more significant task in Montgomeryshire than outsiders might assume since local politics are not dominated by party labels but by independents. Montgomeryshire lies within the confines of Powys County Council – as does the neighbouring seat (the much more marginal Brecon and Radnorshire). The council has a long-standing tradition of being independent – although some councillors declare their affiliation after election. At the time of our research in Montgomeryshire the political make-up of Powys county council demonstrates the lack of penetration that party politics has in an area that returns two Liberal Democrat MPs (see Table 10.4).

Table 10.4 **Powys County Council: political affiliation of councillors, 2000**

Independents	58
Liberal Democrats	8
Labour	6
Conservatives	1

Of course, the institution of the National Assembly for Wales in 1999 delivered another tier of government in Wales. As a result, the Liberal Democrats have gained another elected representative in Montgomeryshire and further tightened their grip on the constituency's electoral culture. Mick Bates was elected as Assembly Member for Montgomeryshire in the elections of both 1999 and 2003. The representation of the constituency by a Liberal

Democrat MP and a Liberal Democrat AM may go some way to overcoming the obstacle of independence in local politics and amounts to a bridge across the credibility gap for the local party.

The constituency was heavily hit in 2001 by the outbreak of FMD, and Welshpool market was identified as a source of the spread of the disease, 78 of the 118 confirmed cases of FMD in Wales were in Powys, and 15,000 livestock slaughtered. In slightly different circumstances, it might have been expected that the FMD crisis would have caused problems for the incumbent MP. Anecdotally the received wisdom is that the rural Liberal Democrat vote in south west England was cut back due to FMD. Notwithstanding the basis in fact of this argument – and Woods (2002) has cast considerable doubt on it – as sitting MP, Opik must have had more than a weather eye on the electoral impact of the outbreak. Given the potential disruption caused by FMD, the consolidation of the Liberal Democrat vote in Montgomeryshire in 2001 begins to look fairly impressive.

A curious feature of the electoral history of the Montgomery region is that it provides evidence for a particular aspect of electoral geography. Since the 1960s, the population of Newtown has been boosted significantly by sizeable migration from the West Midlands. However, this influx of largely industrial working-class voters from a region with little or no history of third party voting did nothing to dilute the strength of local Liberal hegemony. Rather than transfer their voting patterns into their new circumstances, it seems that once in mid-Wales, the *arrivistes* took on the voting patterns of the existing population; a classic 'neighbourhood effect' (see Miller, 1977) seemingly overpowering the social determinism of class politics. In contrast to Bridgwater (see below) here the credibility gap has been breached and works to the advantage of the incumbent Liberal Democrats (see Table 10.5). As long as the sitting MP continues to work hard on behalf of the local community, it seems the local community is happy to continue its tradition as part of the Liberal heritage.

After establishing himself as the MP for Montgomeryshire, coupled with his high media profile, Opik's position was never really in doubt at the 2001

Table 10.5 **1997 General Election: Montgomeryshire**

Candidate	*Party*	*Votes*	*%*
Lembit Opik	Liberal Democrats	14647	45.9
Glyn Davies	Conservative	8344	26.1
Angharad Davies	Labour	6109	19.1
Helen Mary Jones	Plaid Cymru	1608	5.0
John Bufton	Referendum Party	879	2.8
Sue Walker	Green	338	1.1

Notes: Liberal Democrat majority: 6,303 (19.7%). Turnout: 74.7%.

Table 10.6 **2001 General Election: Montgomeryshire**

Candidate	*Party*	*Votes*	*%*	*Change*
Lembit Opik	Liberal Democrats	14319	49.4	+3.5
David Jones	Conservative	8085	27.9	+1.8
Paul Davies	Labour	3433	11.9	−7.3
David Senior	Plaid Cymru	1969	6.8	+1.8
David Rowlands	UKIP	786	2.7	
Ruth Davies	ProLife Alliance	210	0.7	
Reginald Taylor	Independent	171	0.6	

Notes: Liberal Democrat majority: 6234 (21.5%). Swing: 0.9% C to LD. Turnout: 65.5%.

election. In the event, the Liberal Democrat vote, and the party's majority, increased in percentage terms. The most notable feature of the voting in Montgomeryshire in 2001, however, was the collapse of the Labour vote from 1997 (see Table 10.6). Here the credibility gap seems to exist in reverse, the Liberal Democrats enjoying the benefits of incumbency and Labour, in third place, finding it hard to establish their credentials as a potential winner in

MP profile: Lembit Opik

Opik, the Northern Irish born son of Estonian immigrants, came to the Liberal Democrats through student politics (he was the leader of a non-aligned 'independent' group in the National Union of Students in the mid-1980s), and a career in management, A media favourite, a regular on the television quiz show, *Have I Got News For You* and *Radio 5Live* phone-ins, Opik is probably the most media-conscious of all of the party's MPs and must own the dubious distinction of being the only current Liberal Democrat MP to have made the front pages of the tabloids with details of his heterosexual love life. He has also featured fairly heavily on two occasions when Westminster politics spilled out into the wider national consciousness; he devised the so-called 'middle way' response to the fox-hunting debate, and he will go down in political history as the parliamentary author of Britain's plan to save the earth from imminent destruction by asteroid strike. Probably as a result of this relatively high profile, he is frequently mentioned as a potential future party leader. His appeal is rather bipolar, however, and if he seriously harnesses ambitions to become leader he might want to ensure that he does not become tainted with a 'Kennedy squared' reputation for too much frivolous activity at the edge of 'serious' politics and, like all Liberal Democrat MPs, must work hard to keep connected with the everyday politics of community and constituency.

Opik's victory in 1997 seemingly reaffirmed Liberal Democrat hegemony in Montgomeryshire. With Opik becoming the seat's fourth Liberal representative since the war, the prognosis for a further victory at the next election remains good.

Montgomeryshire. It is noticeable that none of Opik's competitors from 1997 stood again in 2001 – perhaps showing the extent to which the other parties had given up on the seat. However, some of Opik's 2001 opponents did have a reasonably high local profile – for instance, Plaid Cymru's David Senior had fought Montgomeryshire in the 1999 National Assembly Elections.

Opik then, looks more secure after 2001 than he did after 1997. He seems to have overcome any resistance that an outsider to the area might have expected and provided he continues to nurture his constituency activity he ought to retain the seat for the foreseeable future. If he does harbour leadership ambitions, the knowledge that he is likely to be an MP for a good while might not be poor base from which to build.

Emerging heartlands: Colchester

1991 Census data	%
Owner occupiers	69.3
Local authority housing	17.3
Non-white	2.9
Professional/managerial	31.6
Non-manual	55.8

History

Our choice of Colchester as one of the Liberal Democrats' emerging heartlands seats may seen a little odd since there was little tradition of Liberal voting prior to 1992. However, after the 2001 General Election the choice is vindicated as the Liberal Democrats in general, and Bob Russell in particular have come to dominate the parliamentary scene in the constituency.

In a sense, Colchester is the very essence of Liberal Democrat campaigning success. When boundary changes to this part of Essex created a genuine three way marginal constituency in Britain's oldest town, the Liberal Democrats seized the seat through a mixture of old fashioned door-to-door campaigning and a redoubtable belief in the potential of Liberal Democrat victory.

In the 1980s Essex was seen by many to epitomise the domination of Thatcherism. In 1992 the Conservative victory in Basildon became the motif for John Major's unlikely success in the country as a whole while the Conservatives were safely returned to power in the two Colchester seats (Colchester North and Colchester South and Maldon). By 1997 Labour had captured the new seat called Basildon and a string of neighbouring seats in Essex while the Liberal Democrats had captured the new single Colchester seat from the Conservatives.

The redistricting process, which created an extra seat for Essex, made the battle for Colchester an urban war, as some of the more rural wards from the two seats were reallocated to the constituency of Essex North and to Maldon and East Chelmsford. In the single Colchester seat there was hope for all three main parties. The notional results for 1992 – the retrospective estimates of the 1992 votes re-aggregated to the new constituency boundaries – illustrated that there was little to choose between the vote share of the Conservatives (42 percent), the Liberal Democrats (33 percent) and Labour (24 percent).

In the event of the 1997 General Election, the Liberal Democrats emerged only slightly ahead but as we have seen from the Liberal Democrats up and down the country the critical task for the party was to establish their credibility, and this they had done. In Colchester this process was facilitated by a fortuitous redistricting exercise that suddenly made the Liberal Democrats the viable opposition to the Conservatives in the town. Bob Russell, long time Councillor and former Mayor of Colchester became its MP following the narrow Liberal Democrat victory (see Table 10.7).

Table 10.7 **1997 General Election: Colchester**

Candidate	*Party*	*Votes*	*%*
Bob Russell	Liberal Democrats	17886	34.4
Stephan Shakespeare	Conservative	16305	31.4
Rod Green	Labour	15891	30.6
John Hazell	Referendum Party	1776	3.4
Loretta Basker	Natural Law	148	0.3

Notes: Liberal Democrat majority: 1581 (3.0%). Turnout: 69.6%.

The 1997 Colchester result was remarkably close. All three main parties took over 30 per cent of the valid share of the vote – and the nearly 1776 votes secured for the Referendum Party may have been crucial in deciding the fate of the seat. A critical feature of the Colchester seat is the potential for third party squeeze. Liberal Democrats, after 1997, would look to pressurise Labour supporters into voting for them next time around in order to ensure the Conservatives did not return. Yet as many of our Colchester interviewees recognised, local history made this problematic.

> At the last election, I was really sweating. In the last few days, the election couldn't come quick enough because we knew, at the national level it was Conservative or Labour, that's all the papers were full of. There was nothing about the Liberal Democrats in the tabloids or anything; it was all one or the other. And you could feel that unless we got something, got in quick, we were

> just going to erode and the feeling was that perhaps the Labour Party were coming up strong on the rails and we did some good targeting in the last few days in terms of persuading – I know we did persuade Labour voters to vote for us because we stood the best chance of beating the Tories. So you know, you need good targeting in that arena. But as far as the local party's concerned, we agree a lot on policies and we could probably form an administration on a policy only issue, but working together would divide our group and I suspect probably divide the Labour group as well. Part of the difficulty in effecting a squeeze on the Labour vote was personal: 'Bob's a defector from the Labour party. Many years ago but that has influenced the way politics has developed here in Colchester between us and the Labour group. There is enormous antagonism still there. There is a lot of baggage.'

Once established as the MP for Colchester, Russell and his local team would have to work hard to persuade Labour supporters to come across to the Liberal Democrats in order to keep the Tories out, and would have to hope that the personal antagonism between local Labour and Liberal Democrats would not lead to inefficient and counterproductive campaigning techniques.

The local context

Colchester Borough Council consists of 60 councillors, 39 of whom represent wards from Colchester and 21 from North Essex. The Liberal Democrat strength comes from their representation in the Colchester wards. Indeed the Liberal Democrats had made considerable inroads into the local vote in the 1990s, not just leading but dominating the council by the end of the century. Since 2000 the Liberal Democrat local vote has been in decline but local campaign workers were in no doubt about the utility of the local politics platform for national success:

> It clearly won us Colchester in the General Election that we were the dominant party in local government here. So a good solid base meant that Bob had got a good launching pad and you know, we got a candidate who was obviously well known throughout the town – high profile local man etc. you know . . . But the fact that we got a good base and a respected candidate meant that Bob put in a good challenge.

Since 2000 the Liberal Democrats have lost control of the council to the Conservatives. Nevertheless even the distribution of councillors in 2002 reveals that the Liberal Democrats are a credible local force (see Table 10.8). In fact in the run-up to the 2001 General Election, some members of the Colchester campaign team felt that being in charge of the local council was not necessarily a golden opportunity but a slightly poisoned chalice.

> Next year or this year or whatever, it's going to be harder because as a local council we've been going down, and therefore Bob's going to have to launch off that and that may not be easy. He may have to launch off a national level and a personal level in terms of saying what he's done for Colchester as an MP and so on rather than saying, 'You've seen what Liberal Democrats do at local level and I can do the same', because people out there are saying, 'Bloody traffic jams!' Tactically I think the campaign has got to look at it a bit differently to what we did last time.

A curious feature of the 2001 campaign in Colchester is that it did introduce a genuinely different set of local issues – including the preservation of local architectural landmarks – from the localised 'traffic, hospitals and policing' default position seen in many parts of the country. This is not meant to denigerate the impact of such local issues but merely to highlight the uniqueness of Colchester in 2001.

As the above quotation predicted, Russell's campaign literature did emphasise his record as MP for Colchester, and the power of incumbency must have been a powerful string to his bow in 2001. After all there can be no greater proof of the Liberal Democrats' credibility than the fact that they already hold the seat (see Table 10.9).

The Liberal Democrats emerged in 2001 as the dominant force in the electoral politics of Colchester. Russell's share of the vote increased by over 8 percent, and the party managed to gain a positive swing from both the Conservatives and Labour. In effect, this was exactly what the Liberal Democrats had hoped for after 1997. The crucial breakthrough for the Liberal Democrats appeared to be the victory in 1997. This set their credibility and 2001 reaffirmed their electability. This is exactly why Colchester was seen as, and has proved to be, part of the Liberal Democrats' emerging heartland.

Table 10.8 **Colchester Borough Council: political affiliation of councillors, 2002**

Conservatives	24
Liberal Democrats	23
Independents	7
Labour	6

Table 10.9 **2001 General Election: Colchester**

Candidate	*Party*	*Votes*	*%*	*Change*
Bob Russell	Liberal Democrats	18627	42.6	+8.2
Kevin Bentley	Conservative	13074	29.9	−1.5
Chris Fegan	Labour	10925	25.0	−5.6
Roger Lord	UKIP	631	1.4	
Len Overy-Owen	Grey Party	479	1.1	

Notes: Liberal Democrat majority: 5553 (12.7%). Swing: 4.8% C to LD. Turnout: 55.4%.

MP profile: Bob Russell

Bob Russell must be the apotheosis of local campaigning strategies and their ability to break through from the local to the national level. A journalist and university administrator, he was educated in the town and as his profile in *The Almanac of British Politics* has it 'Colchester localness exudes from every pore' (Waller and Criddle, 2002).

A Colchester councillor for over three decades, firstly, as Labour, then SDP and finally as a Liberal Democrat representative, Russell caused a stir in 1997 by deciding to continue serving as a local councillor while also being the area's MP in the House of Commons.

Most Liberal Democrat MPs adhere to the notion of localism but Russell seems to *live* the role of Colchester's cultural ambassador to the Palace of Westminster. This is recognised in the *Ashdown Diaries* where Russell's former leader characterises him as 'one of those MPs who fits his constituency like a glove' (Ashdown, 2001, 66).

In keeping with his sporting brief, Russell has made much of his 'batting average', which shows that he cast the most votes of all opposition MPs in the 1997 parliament. Clearly Russell hoped to demonstrate his commitment to parliament by voting as many times as possible. He has brought a new electoral heartland to the party and through steadfast politicking has ensured that the party's grip on Colchester has tightened since his first victory in 1997.

Emerging heartlands: Sheffield Hallam

1991 Census data	%
Owner occupiers	78.3
Local authority housing	9.5
Non-white	3.1
Professional/managerial	59.3
Non-manual	80.1

History

Sheffield Hallam has to be one of the most unusual constituencies in Britain. When Labour's municipal rearguard action against Thatcherism was at its height in the 1980s, with ultra low bus fares in the nuclear free 'Socialist Republic of South Yorkshire', Hallam stood firm as an island of Conservatism in a sea of Labour strongholds.

In a city typified by industrial decline and attempted urban regeneration, Hallam is decidedly leafy. The wards of Broomhill, Eccleshall and Hunter's Bar in the west of the city display an affluence not typical of the city as a whole, while the wards outside the city centre – for instance Dore and Totley, on the fringes on the Peak District, seem half a world away from the steel and mining communities represented by the film, *The Full Monty*.

Hallam is an educated constituency. According to the 1991 census data, 33 per cent of the population are degree holders – the fifth highest proportion in the entire country and outside London, only Bristol West (36.5 percent) had a higher proportion of graduates. Certainly, the constituency is popular with staff from the city's two universities. As one insider from the campaign team revealed the social structure of the constituency also helps with the organisation of campaigning in Sheffield Hallam – since it is populated with the *kind* of people who are relatively predisposed to becoming active in politics, as leaflet distributors, as petition organisers and as policy and strategy discussion group members.

The local context

Hallam is unusual politically. Sheffield is, of course, a Labour city and Hallam was a Tory stronghold. Indeed the Conservative party whip Sir Irvine Patnick held firm in Hallam even in 1992 when John Major's grasp on power seemed tenuous to say the least. With the financial near disaster that the 1991 World Student Games brought to the city, Labour's grip on municipal politics in Sheffield began to slip – and it was the local Liberal Democrats that made inroads into the hitherto solid Labour wards in Heeley and Hillsborough. Stranger still then that when the Liberal Democrats managed to take a parliamentary seat in Sheffield, their local gains against Labour in the city was not the template for success. Instead the Liberal Democrats – after building a local reputation as the opposition to Labour in Sheffield – took on and defeated the Conservatives in Sheffield Hallam (see Table 10.10). Moreover in order to win Hallam, the Liberal Democrats needed the tactical support of Labour voters in a city where relations between the two non-Conservative parties were poor to say the least.

Despite being the endgame in a particularly drawn out affair, the Liberal Democrat victory in Sheffield Hallam in 1997 was spectacular. Richard Allan romped home with a majority of more than 8,000 votes (21 percent) as Patnick was washed away with the anti-Conservative tide in 1997, while Labour's vote fell by 5 per cent in the year that saw them swept to power nationally.

The context of local politics in Sheffield undoubtedly gave the local Liberal Democrats a fillip in their quest for representation in Hallam. The Liberal Democrats' advance in local politics seemed relentless until they took control of Sheffield City Council in 1999 amid famous scenes of Liberal Democrat rejoicing. They have suffered some slippage since but they remain

Table 10.10 **1997 General Election: Sheffield Hallam**

Candidate	*Party*	*Votes*	*%*
Richard Allan	Liberal Democrats	23345	51.3
Irvine Patnick	Conservative	15074	33.1
Stephen Conquest	Labour	6147	13.5
Ian Davidson	Referendum Party	788	1.7
Philip Booler	Independent	125	0.3

Notes: Liberal Democrat majority: 8271 (18.2%). Turnout: 72.4%.

Table 10.11 **Sheffield City Council: political affiliation of councillors, 2002**

Labour	43
Liberal Democrats	42
Conservatives	2

the effective opposition to Labour in the City politics of Sheffield, and the alternative to the Conservatives in the parliamentary contest in Hallam (see Table 10.11).

One senior player in the constituency told us of the importance for Hallam's Liberal Democrats of the battle for credibility both in the constituency and in the city as a whole:

> We are winning votes from people who have Conservative inclinations, but don't believe the Conservatives are doing a good job any more, and we're winning votes from people who are sort of Labour-inclined, but feel that geographically you're the best bet. And I think, to be realistic, our strongest message is almost – 'We can do it. You should vote for us because we can do it and give us an opportunity, we can inspire you with confidence.' So it's about showing you can deliver in small things and showing you can deliver in a lot of little ways. That's why I think our council base is always very important, we win parliamentary seats when we've got a strong council base. I don't think it's an ideological base at all. There are a lot of people who say 'I'm not really political' and they'll come to us.

In particular, the Liberal Democrats' abandonment of equidistance may have played a significant role in seats such as Sheffield Hallam. Ashdown's refusal to rule out a post-election pact with the Conservatives in 1992 had not gone down well with Labour activists in the constituency where the battle in 1992 had been for second rather than first place.

Having secured the credibility of a comfortable second place in 1992, and a significant presence on the city council, the Liberal Democrats had to look to convert a sizeable section of the constituency's significant Labour support if they were to win Hallam. Their task was made easier by the party's recognition that it was now part of an unofficial anti-Conservative alliance.

If 1997 was a remarkable achievement for the Liberal Democrats, 2001 was another triumph for Richard Allan (see Table 10.12). As the fight for control of local politics in Sheffield remained a bitter contest between Labour and the Liberal Democrats, the highly educated electorate of Sheffield Hallam again voted to ensure the Conservatives did not regain the constituency.

Table 10.12 **2001 General Election: Sheffield Hallam**

Candidate	*Party*	*Votes*	*%*	*Change*
Richard Allan	Liberal Democrats	21203	55.4	+4.1
John Hartman	Conservative	11856	31.0	−2.1
Gillian Harness	Labour	4758	12.4	−1.1
Leslie Arnott	UKIP	429	1.1	

Notes: Liberal Democrat majority: 9347 (24.4%). Swing: 3.1% C to LD. Turnout: 63.4%.

MP profile: Richard Allan

Serving Hallam's educational elite might require an educated MP, and Richard Allan certainly fits this bill. His Archaeology degree from Cambridge was followed by an Information Technology M.Sc. from Bristol Polytechnic. He retains an active interest in technology and governance and was made the party's spokesman for IT in 2002, a post that reflected his personal interests rather than his political ambitions. Allan is one of only two Westminster MPs to date to have their own weblog.

Allan quickly established himself as a fastidious and effective local MP upon entering parliament in 1997. He quickly caught the eye at Westminster, Paddy Ashdown saying of him in his *Diaries* 'One of the best of the new intake: serious, quiet, but a tough and effective politician' (Ashdown, 2001, 59).

After being appointed to the party's Home Affairs team in 1997, Allan might have been seen as a young MP with a long and promising future in London but, in truth, he tended to eschew many of the trappings of life in the Westminster village – often preferring to get on with constituency casework than attend prime minister's questions on Wednesday afternoons. The temptation is to say that in the end he was not sufficiently 'clubbable' to prosper in the atmosphere of Westminster.

In 2003 he announced his desire to stand down at the next General Election. Without the incumbent MP, the Liberal Democrats will find it harder to defend the seat.

Richard Allan's share of the vote in Sheffield Hallam increased by 4 per cent in 2001, while the Conservative and Labour vote share both fell. In the third election since 1992, the Liberal Democrats have emerged from a tight contest for second place to become the dominant party in the constituency with a majority of nearly 25 percent.

It is even possible that Sheffield Hallam may have instituted a bout of creeping liberalism in northern England, although perhaps not in the expected location. While the Liberal Democrats failed to capitalise on promising local performances in other constituencies in Sheffield – they won every council seat in Hillsborough in 2000 but failed to loosen Labour's parliamentary stranglehold in 2001 – the Liberal Democrats did manage to win local seats in the contiguous North East Derbyshire, and won Chesterfield from Labour in the 2001 General Election.

Conservative-held seats: Bridgwater

1991 Census data	%
Owner occupiers	72.5
Local authority housing	16.7
Non-white	0.5
Professional/managerial	28.1
Non-manual	48.5

History

Bridgwater ought to be in the heart of Liberal country. It borders seats with a history of Liberal success Devon North, Taunton, and Somerton and Frome, but like its other contiguous neighbour, Wells, the Liberal Democrats have failed to capitalise on their apparently promising position in Bridgwater.

Bridgwater is a mixed seat. Set among beautiful countryside, the largest urban area Bridgwater itself, is the scene of significant support for the Labour Party. Moreover it is probably the failure of the local Liberal Democrats to convert sufficient Labour support in the town that lies at the heart of the explanation for their non-capture of the seat.

For over thirty years, the MP for Bridgwater was Conservative big-hitter Tom King. The failure of the local Liberal Democrats to emulate local Liberal Democrats elsewhere in Somerset and win the seat was put down by many to the personal vote of the former defence minister. King's last stand in 1997 did appear to give the Liberal Democrats real hope that Bridgwater was eminently winnable with a small Conservative majority looking very precarious once the incumbent had left the scene (see Table 10.13).

Table 10.13 **1997 General Election: Bridgwater**

Candidate	*Party*	*Votes*	*%*
Tom King	Conservative	20174	36.9
Michael Hoban	Liberal Democrat	18378	33.6
Roger Lavers	Labour	13519	24.8
Fran Evens	Referendum Party	2551	4.7

Notes: Conservative majority: 1796 (3.3%). Turnout: 74.4%.

The 1997 candidate, Mike Hoban, had enjoyed considerable freedom, to run his own campaign, and was still held in high regard by many of the local activists we spoke to. However, after an unsuccessful attempt to be selected as Paddy Ashdown's successor in Yeovil, Hoban retreated from active Liberal Democrat politics in general and Bridgwater in particular. As a result the party turned to Ian Thorn a marketing and public affairs consultant who had been on a number of party bodies since he joined the Liberal Democrats at the age of 16.

The local context

Despite the apparently favourable electoral mathematics, two things hampered the cause of the Liberal Democrats in Bridgwater. Firstly, the resilience of the Labour vote in the town of Bridgwater, and, secondly, the lack of a local government platform from which to build.

A key local strategist told us of the urban problem for the Liberal Democrats:

> In my local area I've got a very good relationship with the local Labour Party. But in Bridgwater itself, there are a few members of the Labour party who hate us with a vengeance; they really do hate us. In Minehead, it's the same sort of thing. There are sections of the Labour party in Minehead that have a true hatred for us because they see themselves as the party that ought to be ruling and they don't like it because we are in a position where we have got a better chance of winning the seat than they have.

The second factor is more surprising. Despite their high profile in Somerset the Liberal Democrats are not well represented in either of the two Councils that serve the constituency of Bridgwater. Both Sedgemoor and West Somerset are districts councils that elect their members every four years so the figures presented here are from 1999 the last local elections prior to the 2001 General Election. What is clear is that the Liberal Democrats are fairly moribund at the local level in terms of elected representatives (only 3 Liberal Democrats on Sedgemoor, and a single councillor on West Somerset: see

Table 10.14 **Sedgemoor and West Somerset Councils: political affiliation of councillors, 1999**

Sedgemoor Council	Conservatives	31
	Labour	16
	Liberal Democrats	3
West Somerset Council	Conservatives	20
	Labour	2
	Liberal Democrats	1
	Indep	4
	Other	4

Table 10.14). For a party that thrives on local credibility this was not a good sign.

Another local factor that may have harmed the Liberal Democrats in Bridgwater was the matter of Europe. For those Liberal Democrats who play the national line, this might be problematic. As one councillor told us there were problems with campaigning in Bridgwater: 'The area is generally very xenophobic. If you came from Porlock you might think Europe was on Mars, both from the locals and the incredibly rich. I'm more pro-Europe than I am Liberal – I passionately believe in Europe and all that entails – I keep that under locks.'

As we showed in Chapter 4, the policy area of European integration has developed into a twin track approach in places like Bridgwater. Another insider agreed that the national line of the party could be problematic in this constituency: 'Ah, now there's a thing! I'm very much pro-Europe, but I know that we have some long-term activists who refused to deliver leaflets in the Europe campaign because of the stance of the party as a whole. Governments past and present, have failed because it's been seen as an issue where you lose votes.'

On 9 May 2001, at the start of the campaign, Ian Thorn paid tribute to the retiring Tom King in what seemed a tacit admission that the party was facing an uphill battle. The mobilising of the rural vote, FMD and hostility to Europe may all have played a part, but the fact remains that the Liberal Democrats failed to squeeze the Labour vote sufficiently to threaten the Conservatives and the Liberal Democrats share of the vote fell by about the same amount as the Conservatives' share rose. Ian Liddell-Grainger of the Conservatives may have been expecting a tough fight but he actually increased his party's lead over the Liberal Democrats (see Table 10.15).

If the Liberal Democrats are to improve their standing in Bridgwater it seems axiomatic that they need to close the credibility gap. This could be

Table 10.15 **2001 General Election: Bridgwater**

Candidate	*Party*	*Votes*	*%*	*Change*
Ian Liddell-Grainger	Conservative	19354	40.4	+3.5
Ian Thorn	Liberal Democrat	14367	30.0	−3.6
Bill Monteith	Labour	12803	26.8	+2.0
Vicky Gardner	UKIP	1323	2.8	

Notes: Conservative majority: 4987 (10.4%). Swing: 3.6% LD to C. Turnout: 64.6%.

done at the local level but it is likely to be a laborious process – and still not a guarantee of success, and the party needs to convince Labour sympathisers in the urban parts the seat that the Liberal Democrats are the only show in town for anti-Conservatives.

Conservative-held seats: Cheadle

1991 Census data	*%*
Owner occupiers	87.8
Local authority housing	6.9
Non-white	3.1
Professional/managerial	47.4
Non-manual	75.3

History

In the 1966 General Election, Michael Winstanley won the parliamentary seat called Cheadle for the Liberals. In an era when Liberal breakthroughs at General Elections rather than by-elections were rare this was a significant feat, even though the seat was lost again to the Conservatives by 1970. Although the redistricting process redrew the political constituency boundaries and meant that by 1974 the electoral basis of Winstanley's victory had been located into the neighbouring seat of Hazel Grove (and Winstanley himself won the Hazel Grove seat for the Liberals in 1974). The 1966 victory did give a resonance to the Liberal Democrat challenge in Cheadle.

In 1992 the Liberal Democrat challenge to the Conservatives was strong enough to displace any real threat from Labour, but was still far from a real danger to the incumbent MP Stephen Day.

In an exceedingly poor election for the Conservatives in 1997, Cheadle was one of only two seats in Greater Manchester that they managed to retain (the other being Altrincham and Sale West). Conservative Party whip Stephen Day managed to hold onto the seat despite the travails of the party around him. To the east of Cheadle lies Hazel Grove – which Liberal Democrat Andrew Stunnell won with nearly 55 per cent of the valid vote in 1997. To the south of the constituency is Tatton, scene of the one of the most remarkable contests in twentieth-century British politics where the sitting Conservative MP Neil Hamilton was swept aside by the Independent anti-sleaze candidate Martin Bell. With the Conservatives in crisis in Cheadle's contiguous seats, Day might have been excused an anxious moment or two.

In the event, however, the Liberal Democrat challenge was insufficient to displace the Conservatives in 1997, Patsy Calton trailing Day by six percentage points (see Table 10.16). On the other hand, this performance was one of great promise to the local Liberal Democrats. While not being an official target seat, the sharing of knowledge with Hazel Grove enabled many of the election tactics employed there to be applied in Cheadle also, and with fairly impressive results.

One local party member, closely involved in the 1997 contest, joked about the 1997 General Election and Cheadle's relationship with Hazel Grove:

> Oh yeah. We pinched all their ideas and copied them! No, seriously it wasn't quite like that. Whatever they were doing, we were doing as well but perhaps we weren't doing it as well. Perhaps we didn't have the same level of resourcing that they had, but we kept our eyes and our ears open. And if we heard that something was going down that we thought was a good idea, we did it. We, in a sense, piggy-backed off their ideas. And we were very happy to do that. So, from that point of view it was advantageous, that we were next door, and that we could see a constituency that was working at the level that it was working at. And there are a lot of friendships across the two constituencies as well. That also helps.

Moreover, local determination to acquire target seat status for the next election was strengthened by the 1997 result. Local activists became willing fodder for those who believed in the 'one more heave' school of election success. The gap between the Conservatives and Liberal Democrats, after all, had closed from 16,000 in 1992 to 3,000 votes in 1997, and in a good campaign and with significant support from Cowley Street a 3,000 vote majority might be overturned.

Table 10.16 **1997 General Election: Cheadle**

Candidate	*Party*	*Votes*	*%*
Stephen Day	Conservative	22944	43.7
Patsy Calton	Liberal Democrat	19755	37.7
Paul Diggett	Labour	8253	15.7
Paul Brook	Referendum Party	1511	2.9

Notes: Conservative majority: 3189 (6.1%). Turnout: 77.3%.

The local context

As in so many of the Liberal Democrat successes, the battle for the parliamentary seat in Cheadle had been rehearsed many times at the local level. The Liberal Democrats gained control of Stockport council in 1998 – a move that appeared vital for the local party to breach the credibility gap in Cheadle (see Table 10.17). Calton had been a councillor since 1994, although the Liberal Democrats performance in the wards that comprised the seat of Cheadle was patchy – losing some wards in the affluent areas of Bramhall to the Conservatives in the local elections at the end of the century. In 2000 the Liberal Democrats temporarily lost control of the council, but a defecting Independent handed it back within days.

Table 10.17 **Stockport Council: political affiliation of councillors, 2002**

Liberal Democrats	33
Labour	19
Conservatives	8
Independents	3

We did find evidence, however, to suggest that control of the council was a double-edged sword as far as some local Liberal Democrats were concerned. There was virtual unanimity from those we spoke to that Liberal Democrat control of the council was a good thing, but some did express slight concern that being in charge made the party responsible for the council's failings as much as the successes, and that where the demarcation of responsibility was not clear to the public, the Liberal Democrat council might be blamed for issues that were under the control of central government. In particular, we found strong concern that Stockport council and the local Liberal Democrats were not to be held responsible for Cheadle's notorious traffic congestion problem.

In the run-up to the 2001 campaign, most of the people from the local party we spoke to were certain that with assistance from the central party, the seat could be won, but that the rationale behind success would have to be locally based. As one leading member of the campaign team said of the party's activist base: 'It *is* the party. It's not just a bit of it. It's not an optional extra. The grassroots base is the party.' In the event, the Liberal Democrats were victorious in Cheadle – just! With a majority of 33 votes, Patsy Calton MP for Cheadle finds herself in the most marginal seat in the country (see Table 10.18).

One interesting aspect of the literature sent out by the local party is that much of it targeted the soft Labour vote. 'Only the Liberal Democrats can beat the Tories here' it repeated. A key insider told us of the chords to be struck during the campaign: 'The thing that makes you successful at local level, it seems to me,

MP profile: Patsy Calton

When Patsy Calton entered parliament in June 2001 she became one of only five female Liberal Democrat MPs. A chemistry teacher by profession, Calton became Liberal Democrat spokesperson for Health in 2002, having previously served as Deputy Northern Ireland spokesperson in Westminster. She is well regarded in the party, her experience as Stockport Borough Councillor from 1994 to 2002 (she was Deputy Leader of the Council) giving her a profile in the Liberal Democrats that would not accrue to a similar office holder in the Labour or Conservative parties. She could have a bright future in the party nationally. Given their paucity in numbers the Liberal Democrats are keen to promote their leading female MPs. However, her more immediate concern will be to attempt to hang on to precarious majority. This task may not have been made easier by the reselection of her old adversary Stephen Day as the Conservative PPC for the next election – threatening to undermine Calton's advantage of incumbency, in what is now the Conservatives' number one target seat.

Table 10.18 **2001 General Election: Cheadle**

Candidate	*Party*	*Votes*	*%*	*Change*
Patsy Calton	Liberal Democrats	18477	42.4	+4.7
Stephen Day	Conservative	18444	42.3	−1.4
Howard Dawber	Labour	6086	14.0	−1.7
Vincent Cavanagh	UKIP	599	1.4	

Notes: Liberal Democrat majority: 33 (0.1%). Swing: 3.0% C to LD. Turnout: 63.2%.

is the same thing that makes you successful at national level . . . You don't have to go over the ground twice, because one is national and one is local. You're going over the same ground and you're using the same materials to push the same messages.' So, the national issues of health, crime and education for instance were played out in the 2001 campaign in Cheadle with reference to their impact on local hospitals, local policing and local schools. All of this was packaged with the literature designed to show that the Liberal Democrats were the only credible alternative to the Conservatives in the constituency.

Labour-held seats: Aberdeen South

1991 Census data	*%*
Owner occupiers	61.2
Local authority housing	28.1
Non-white	1.1
Professional/managerial	38.0
Non-manual	61.8

History

The constituency of Aberdeen South comprises land on both sides of the River Dee. Boundary changes meant that in 1997 Aberdeen South was very different from the old seat of that name, bringing in areas from the old Kincardine and Deeside seat. The politics of north east Scotland may seem inscrutable to non-natives. In Aberdeenshire West and Kincardine and in Gordon Liberal Democrats seem firmly in power with the Conservatives a fair distance behind in second place. In Aberdeen North and Aberdeen Central, Labour are able to put considerable daylight between themselves and the challenge from the SNP and then in third place the Liberal Democrats. In Aberdeen South, however, the Liberal Democrats fostered a realistic hope of taking the seat from Labour in 2001.

The local context

Aberdeen South is one of the inheritors of the Kincardine and Deeside constituency (the other being Aberdeenshire West and Kincardine), which was won by the Liberal Democrats in 1991. The victorious Liberal Democrat at the by-election was Nicol Stephen who lost his seat in the ensuing General Election of 1992 as John Major's Conservatives recovered all their by-election losses and clung onto office.

Stephen contested the Aberdeen South seat in 1997, losing fairly comprehensively to Labour's Anne Begg but his performance did establish the Liberal Democrats as second in the locality (see Table 10.19). Moreover Stephen won the Aberdeen South seat in 1999 for the Liberal Democrats at the Scottish General Election in a move that must have increased the local party's credibility.

The rules that prevent MPs and MSPs sitting in both parliaments meant that the Aberdeen South Liberal Democrats had to find another PPC for the upcoming General Election. They chose Ian Yuill a local party man and an Aberdeen councillor since 1995. Yuill had an impressive record of duty on various party bodies, he was convener of the Scottish Liberal Democrats, a

Table 10.19 **1997 General Election: Aberdeen South**

Candidate	*Party*	*Votes*	*%*
Anne Begg	Labour	15541	35.3
Nicol Stephen	Liberal Democrat	12176	27.6
Raymond Robertson	Conservative	11621	26.4
Jim Towers	SNP	4299	9.8
Rick Wharton	Referendum Party	425	1.0

Notes: Labour majority: 3365 (7.6%). Turnout: 72.8%.

vice-president of the UK party and a member of the Scottish party executive. Nevertheless, he was unlikely to have the local impact (or personal vote) that Stephen possessed and it is possible that the Liberal Democrat vote in 2001 suffered as a result.

Aberdeen is a unitary council, meaning that all seats are up for election every four years. The 1999 round again showed that the Liberal Democrats meant business in Aberdeen (see Table 10.20). Although short of power, the Liberal Democrats had done enough in the local elections to deny Labour control of the party. When coupled with Nicol Stephen's victory in Aberdeen South in the Scottish parliamentary election of the same year it is tempting to see the Liberal Democrats as posing a serious threat to Labour's grip on power.

Table 10.20 **Aberdeen Council: political affiliation of councillors, 1999**

Labour	20
Liberal Democrats	14
Conservatives	6
SNP	3

We need at this juncture to say a word or two about the specific context of a General Election in contemporary Scotland. Not only do the Scottish Liberal Democrats receive extra credit or blame for their record of participation in the Scottish coalition, the new constitution has had an effect on the way local Liberal Democrats can campaign. One key actor in Aberdeen South pointed out:

> You're going to start to see some interesting campaigning tactics emerging here because it's very difficult to be able to say in Scotland, 'Well, I'm very sorry, this is now a UK election, which should really be focusing on pensions and foreign policy and defence policy and economic policy and you really shouldn't be discussing health and education because this is now a devolved matter.' Life isn't like that, it isn't going to happen that way. So it's inevitably the sort of issues that are being discussed in the Scottish parliament will have an effect and some of the scandals, some of the crises, some of the issues in the Scottish parliament are bound to have an effect as well.

This is an interesting point for a party whose default campaigning strategy seems to be to rally support around the need to improve or maintain the standards of local hospitals and schools. For some, this might be an inappropriate campaign strategy in a General Election and we even found some activists who were fearful that the electorate in Aberdeen would come to regard the UK parliament contest as a second order election.

In the end, Labour's Anne Begg held onto her seat fairly comfortably. Indeed she even increased her proportion of the valid vote by 4.5 percent.

The Liberal Democrats' performance was disappointing and the result in 2001 represented an 8.5 per cent swing from Liberal Democrats to Labour since the 1999 Scottish election. However, it should not be all doom and gloom for the Liberal Democrats in Aberdeen South, Yuill did manage to increase slightly the Liberal Democrat share of the vote (see Table 10.21). Moreover, with the significant drop in the Conservative vote, there remains a deep reservoir of potential tactical voters if Begg or her successor proves less popular in the future.

Table 10.21 **2001 General Election: Aberdeen South**

Candidate	*Party*	*Votes*	*%*	*Change*
Anne Begg	Labour	14696	39.8	+4.5
Ian Yuill	Liberal Democrat	10308	27.9	+0.3
Moray Macdonald	Conservative	7098	19.2	−7.2
Ian Angus	SNP	4293	11.6	+1.8
David Watt	Scottish Socialist	495	1.3	

Notes: Labour majority: 4388 (11.9%). Swing: 2.1% LD to L. Turnout: 62.6%

One thing is for sure, if the Liberal Democrats are to be successful in Aberdeen South, that success will follow a well-worn path to glory. As a local councillor revealed the local arena remained the key platform for the Liberal Democrats in Aberdeen South: 'At whatever level we operate, it's still starting from pavement politics and still starting from what local people are interested in.'

Labour-held seats: Oldham East and Saddleworth

1991 Census data	*%*
Owner occupiers	70.4
Local authority housing	22.7
Non-white	5.2
Professional/managerial	31.7
Non-manual	53.3

History

In 1995 the death of sitting Conservative MP Geoffrey Dickens caused a by-election in the Pennine constituency of Littleborough and Saddleworth. In a genuinely three-way contest, all the main parties had a chance of winning but in particular there was a dogged fight between Labour and Liberal

Democrats to win the seat. The by-election has gone down in folklore as probably the dirtiest by-election in modern British history. Chris Davies, the triumphant Liberal Democrat found his personal views on the legalisation of cannabis turned into a major campaign issue, and relations between the two local parties were decidedly poor.

With the boundary review effective from 1997, the successor seat to Littleborough and Saddleworth was Oldham East and Saddleworth. The major difference between the two seats was the movement of three solidly Conservative wards to Rochdale and the import of some wards from Oldham. As a consequence the Liberal Democrat–Labour battle first seen in the by-election became institutionalised, as they were the only realistic winners of the new constituency.

In 1997 Labour's Phil Woolas gained revenge on Davies for the by-election as he was elected as part of Labour's landslide with a comfortable, if not convincing, majority (see Table 10.22). The Conservative share fell to less than a fifth of the valid vote. With the end of the 1997 campaign, Davies decided his future lay away from Westminster, and he became Liberal Democrat MEP in the 1999 European Parliament elections. The Oldham East and Saddleworth Liberal Democrats chose Howard Sykes, a local councillor as their PPC for the next General Election.

Table 10.22 **1997 General Election: Oldham East and Saddleworth**

Candidate	*Party*	*Votes*	*%*
Phil Woolas	Labour	22546	41.7
Chris Davies	Liberal Democrat	19157	35.4
John Hudson	Conservative	10666	19.7
Douglas Findlay	Referendum	1116	2.1
John Smith	Socialist Labour	470	0.9
Ian Dalling	Natural Law	146	0.3

Notes: Labour majority: 3389 (6.3%). Turnout: 73.9%.

The local context

In 2000, the Liberal Democrats took control of Oldham council for the first time. By this time Woolas was the parliamentary representative of an area that returned only one Labour councillor and the Liberal Democrats had 25 of the seats 27 Councillors. In terms of bridging the credibility gap the local party were convinced that they had a strong chance of unseating Woolas because they were the local party of governance.

Since the apex of 2000, the Liberal Democrats have lost ground in the local politics of Oldham, losing control of the council in 2002, which was actually regained by Labour in 2003. In fact, it is fair to say that Oldham is the scene of an exceptionally fierce and bitter local rivalry between Labour and the Liberal Democrats (see Table 10.23). Nevertheless, the Liberal Democrats are a credible force at the local level and they would hope to build on this platform for future national level elections. In the spring of 2001, parts of Oldham were the scene of severe rioting that was caused, at least partially, by racial tensions on the city's housing estates. From our interviews with local party personnel, it was clear that this was a simmering issue that had left the Liberal Democrats struggling to address.

Table 10.23 **Oldham Council: political affiliation of councillors, 2002**

Liberal Democrats	30
Labour	27
Conservatives	2
Green	1

One campaign activist told us that local issues like crime and policing were developing a 'racial undertone' that made them hard to play in an orthodox Liberal Democrat sense:

> In Oldham it's a particularly big issue here. There are fewer officers on the beat and local people who we meet on the doorstep (want more). The ward I've been working on the last two years, St Mary's, is three miles away. We're [talking] in one of the 10% richest wards in the entire country I believe, and St Mary's is amongst the 5% poorest. We've got a large ethnic minority community, huge problems of deprivation. Law and order there is a very big issue, with people frightened to go out on the streets and so, little old ladies who won't go out after 9 o'clock at night and gangs of youths, particularly Asian youths, roaming the place. So law and order is an important local issue.

Another local strategist revealed that unlike some neighbouring Liberal Democrats, the party had declined to specifically target the Asian vote:

> There's lots of ways to skin a cat and different places choose to do it in different ways. Just as an example, I know Rochdale in terms of their strategy, are relying very heavily on making inroads into the Asian vote. Their Asian vote is certainly bigger than the Asian vote [for the Liberal Democrats] in Oldham East and Saddleworth. Now we're not going to do that. We are going to do some campaigning targeted directly at Asian voters, but we're not going to invest the time and effort that Rochdale are.

At this point, the British National Party (BNP) entered the fray. Attempting to appeal directly to disaffected white voters they sought to capitalise on the real differences within the constituency and felt sharply by local communities. The Cantle Report (2002) identified some of the differential levels of hardship in the area, but from our interviews it was already clear that local politicians had already noticed. A leading member of the campaign team spoke of their hopes and fears about the constituency:

> Whether it is people's sexual orientation, their colour, their creed, their religion, I generally think we're a lot more comfortable with a multi-religious, multi-cultural country. In other words, solutions should be built around individuals not built about collective groups of individuals. You look at some of the programmes, which are a very collective approach. We've particularly got an issue in Oldham East and Saddleworth that half the wards are priority wards under European funding, so there's a whole raft of stuff if somebody is unemployed on one side of the street they can access, if they live on the other side of the street, they can't access it. Now that's fundamentally wrong.
>
> I mean they've got into real problems because all of their assisted areas stuff kicked back, because they've tried to pull out too many little pockets. There are pockets of acute poverty outside these areas that are not being dealt with and that's fundamentally wrong to me.
>
> There are areas of affluence and that's actually when you then get tensions within the community because you have a real have and have not division.

In the event, of course, these divisions were exploited to an extent and in a fashion that were not foreseen, and the Liberal Democrats found themselves overshadowed by another story, the BNP. Despite coming a clear second to Labour only 6 per cent behind on share of the vote, the Liberal Democrats' performance was overlooked by many in the aftermath of the 2001 General Election.

In 2001, Phil Woolas managed to hold onto Oldham East and Saddleworth for Labour, but the share of the vote for all three main parties fell significantly (see Table 10.24). The BNP – standing here and in neighbouring Oldham West and Royton (where they beat the Liberal Democrats into fourth place) – received 11 per cent of the valid vote, and those 5,000 votes could have been decisive to the electoral outcome of the seat.

It is possible that the BNP were appealing to the disaffected and the disenfranchised, voters who would not have voted for the conventional

Table 10.24 **2001 General Election: Oldham East and Saddleworth**

Candidate	*Party*	*Votes*	*%*	*Change*
Phil Woolas	Labour	17537	38.6	−3.1
Howard Sykes	Liberal Democrat	14811	32.6	−2.8
Craig Heeley	Conservative	7304	16.1	−3.6
Mick Treacy	BNP	5091	11.2	
Barbara Little	UKIP	677	1.5	

Notes: Labour majority: 2726 (6.0%). Swing: 0.1%L to LD. Turnout: 61.0%.

parties at any cost, but it is also possible that the whole dynamic of the electoral choice in the constituency was altered by the BNP. Woolas's second term might reinforce this area as part of New Labour's emerging heartland, and the prognosis for a Liberal revival certainly seems rather more pessimistic than it did in 1999. Nevertheless, the Liberal Democrats remain only 4 per cent behind the Labour vote, with plenty of Conservative votes to squeeze at the next contest. For the Liberal Democrats in Oldham East and Saddleworth there is still hope.

Conclusions

The case studies enable us to investigate the functioning of the Liberal Democrats across a number of different circumstances at a critical time in the electoral cycle. They have provided a valuable insight into how the factors that affect Liberal Democrat performance are played out in these different micro-contests.

In the Labour-held seats of Aberdeen South and Oldham East and Saddleworth the local parties struggled to establish their credentials as the alternative opposition. In both seats they were able to comfortably defeat the Conservatives but they remain short of the final critical breakthrough. In Aberdeen, the Liberal Democrat victory in the Scottish parliamentary seat had established the Liberal Democrats as a viable party, and the control of Oldham council ought to have given hope to the Liberal Democrats in Oldham East and Saddleworth. In each case however, this local credibility appears to have been necessary but insufficient for victory in 2001. In effect they were swimming against the national tide with local hostilities to Labour marring attempts to galvanise the anti-Conservative vote.

In the Conservative-held seats of Bridgwater and Cheadle the party had mixed fortunes. In Bridgwater the lack of a local council platform from which to build appears critical, and the party was unable to convince enough Labour supporters from the urban part of the constituency that they were the best placed party to defeat the Conservatives. On the other hand, the literature produced for the contest in Cheadle that declared 'Only the Liberal Democrats can win here' may have found the type of receptive audience that the Bridgwater campaign material failed to reach. Local Liberal Democrats in Cheadle were also in a position to benefit from the local politics base and the proximity to a previous target seat (Hazel Grove) which interviewees told us was critical in building up the Liberal Democrat vote in 1997 in preparation for 2001. In Cheadle there seemed to be a spillover effect from previous success in a neighbouring seat that did not find expression in Bridgwater, despite the Liberal Democrat successes in Somerset in recent times.

In the traditional Liberal seats, the local parties were able to exploit the distinctiveness of the local political cultures in order to maintain power. In Devon North, the local party's indifference to (rather than independence from) the national line on Europe may have assisted in their continued ability to appeal to the tradition of Liberal voting in the area. In Montgomeryshire, the historical links with nonconformism maintained the connection with Liberal voting despite the reality of declining religiosity. In each case the party was able to exploit a fierce local political culture where the community was connected to a heritage of Liberalism. These cases also show how the credibility gap works in reverse: in seats where there is an unambiguous tradition of Liberal voting, voters are more prepared to back the party.

In the new Liberal Democrat seats of Sheffield Hallam and Colchester, the Liberal Democrats were able to build on a previous victory. Both had a platform from local government, although it is instructive that the Liberal Democrats in Sheffield were used to fighting Labour locally rather than the Conservatives. The party in Colchester had to battle with local Labour for the right to be seen as the anti-Conservative party. Local history may have made this more difficult in Colchester than it might have been, but the critical breakthrough appears to have been 1997, as the Liberal Democrat position in Colchester was strengthened in 2001.

Local issues seemed to be important in all of our case study contests. However, for the most part, national issues seemed to be given a local hue. Europe and farming issues seemed most important in the traditional heartlands where jobs and livelihoods were more likely to be threatened by such matters. Health and crime tended to find articulation in the local realm in most of the other seats – the threatened closure of a local hospital or the number of police in a certain locality.

All in all, the case studies show the importance of credibility. Liberal Democrats tend to prosper where they are seen to be the credible opposition. At the local level this appeared to work best when the Liberal Democrats were in opposition to the Conservatives (persuading local Labour supporters to switch to the Liberal Democrats in a tactical voting alliance); however, as we have seen in Chapter 7 and Chapter 9 the upshot of these local contests could be that the Liberal Democrats are seen as the alternative opposition to Labour at the national level. This remains a difficult trick for the party to pull off since closer relations with one party might repel supporters of the other, and as the third party, the Liberal Democrats need to attract both. The duality of the party is critical since it allows a national focus on one side of the coin and a local emphasis on the other.

Conclusion: the Liberal Democrats and the electorate

We have examined the structure and strategy of the Liberal Democrats in Britain at a very key point in their history. After emerging at the end of the 1980s as a party that sought to displace Labour as the natural opposition to the Conservatives, by the turn of the century they were seemingly part of an anti-Conservative alliance and were talking of replacing the Conservatives as Labour's main opposition. The strategic challenges facing the Liberal Democrats in the period 1995–2002 may never be repeated but they were fascinating in their own right as the Liberal Democrats adopted a set of electoral strategies that did not always seem to fit the conventional patterns of party behaviour as defined in mainstream political science.

The changes within the party itself have been influential in shaping the party's strategic response to the changing political landscape. In 1999 Paddy Ashdown resigned as party leader. In one fell swoop the defining personality of the party had made way for a new leader, and it is no exaggeration to say that the future direction of the Liberal Democrats was genuinely unknown. In the event however, the election of Charles Kennedy signalled a change of pace and style as much as direction for the party.

After the elections to the devolved Scottish parliament, the Liberal Democrats (who after all are the fourth party in Scotland) found themselves the junior partner in coalition with Labour. Moreover, illness and leadership changes in the Scottish Labour party have seen Scottish Liberal Democrat leader, Jim Wallace, act as Scotland's first minister on three separate occasions. The coalition in Scotland was followed by a similar partnership agreement between Labour and the Liberal Democrats in the Welsh Assembly government, although unlike the Scottish variant, the Welsh coalition was not renewed after the second assembly elections in 2003. The importance to the Liberal Democrats of coalition in Scotland and Wales should not be underestimated since they became a party of national government for the first time since the days of Lloyd George. However, the responsibility for government in Scotland and Wales did have implications for the identity of the party (see below).

At the local level, this period of our research has been one of relative success for the Liberal Democrats, with minor setbacks from time to time. During the period of our research the party took control of councils in Liverpool, Sheffield and Oldham (although Sheffield and Oldham subsequently reverted to Labour control) and the party has had to face up to the responsibility of government at the local level. In the 2003 local elections the Liberal Democrats secured more than 30 per cent of the national vote for the first time. For a party that thrives on its activist base, and which relies on its local government performance as a springboard for national election performance, this is absolutely vital.

The run-up to the 2001 election was crucial to the future health of the Liberal Democrats. Having secured many new seats in 1997 they decided not to adopt a defensive position but to aggressively seek to expand their share of votes and seats in parliament. Moreover whilst the party were successful in both aims, they may have hoped for more, and still appear to be a long way from power.

Structurally the party is constrained in its ambition to become the new party of opposition (or even government) by the practicalities of an incremental electoral strategy. Without a significant extension of the franchise there is no precedent for a third party to replace the established two parties, and the weight of history may be against the Liberal Democrats. The close relationship with Labour in Westminster has deteriorated after the shelving of the Jenkins commission's report and the slow death of the JCC. As Ashdown indicated the Liberal Democrats can ill-afford to rely on the poor performance of the Conservatives as their main electoral hope. This strategic dilemma is central to our discussion of the alternative opposition hypothesis to which we now turn. All five of our original hypotheses introduced at the beginning of this account are now revisited in the light of our findings.

Alternative opposition

Ideologically, the Liberal Democrats remain an anti-Conservative party and are therefore best placed to do well where the Labour Party is weakest. This is grounded in historical patterns of support with the Liberal Democrats doing better where the Labour Party never really replaced the Liberals as the main opposition to Conservatism. This is most evident in areas outside the industrial heartland and in the rural parts of England and the celtic fringe. From our case studies we encountered two Liberal regions – Montgomeryshire and Devon North – where the party had become embedded in the local political culture. In Montgomeryshire's case there was a historical connection to nonconformist religiosity. In North Devon Liberalism had never been challenged by the agricultural trade unions and the Labour Party.

The key to expanding from this heartland of Liberal Democrat support is often that the party has built upon success in local government and by-elections, which lends the party electoral credibility (see below). In some areas, predominantly in the north, this capitalised on the unpopularity of Labour in local government. In some cases this has been the platform for further success at the national level (for instance Sheffield), in others it has remained a local government phenomena (such as Liverpool where the parliamentary boundaries do not seem to favour the Liberal Democrats).

The significant feature of the alternative opposition hypothesis is that the Liberal Democrats' status as an anti-Conservative party is largely dependent upon the local political context. In other words, there is a series of micro-contests that the Liberal Democrats are engaged in up and down the country. Liberal Democrats face a war on two fronts and local constituency parties adapt their strategy to the local context accordingly. In rural and south-western England for instance the Liberal Democrats are the party that can challenge the Conservatives, while in some Lancashire and Pennine seats the Liberal Democrats operate within a heritage of anti-Labour sentiment. Furthermore, we have demonstrated that Liberal Democrat voters typically resemble Labour voters in their political outlook and Conservative voters in their social and geographic background. A continuing challenge for the Liberal Democrats as a party is to compete with Labour in Labour held seats but still win over Labour sympathisers in Conservative–Liberal Democrat areas.

Strategically, clashes with the Conservatives remain the vital electoral battleground for the Liberal Democrats in the run-up to the next election. Although the Liberal Democrats are placed second to Labour in 51 seats, and second to the Conservatives in 58, only 4 of the Labour-held seats are not classed as 'safe' (Birmingham Yardley, Bristol West, Cardiff Central, Oldham East and Saddleworth). The paradox faced by a party aiming to be the alternative opposition, is that to replace the Conservatives it must emulate them sufficiently closely in order to appeal to their natural base of support. Whilst socially they are well equipped to do this, politically the basis of their support is very different and any move to the right would be resisted by much of the activist base. Nevertheless, recent changes in policy and personnel have suggested that the Liberal Democrats are beginning to position themselves closer to the typical Conservative voter than they had done during the late 1990s. How the party positions itself with respect to the electorate is the critical strategic dilemma for the Liberal Democrats in contemporary politics.

We have shown in Chapter 8 that the party's move from equidistance allowed the Liberal Democrats – as a centre-left party – to build support incrementally primarily at the expense of the Conservatives. However this strategy is limited because it relies on the continued unpopularity of the Conservative opposition. It is doubtful that the distribution of voter preferences in the British electorate can sustain two successful centre-left parties – at the expense of the centre-right – for a prolonged period of time. Analysis of voter preferences in Chapters 5 and 6 revealed that there is still a strong left–right (Labour and Liberal Democrat vs. Conservative) dimension to voter preferences, and a relatively weak Liberal vs. Labour dimension.

In contrast, whilst a shift to the right might enable the Liberal Democrats to capitalise on a new hostility to the Labour government, it might also antagonise the soft-Labour support in the numerous Conservative–Liberal Democrat marginals and also requires the co-operation of the largely anti-Conservative grass roots of the party. In short, the Liberal Democrats continue to pay the price of fighting a war on two fronts; the pursuit of either strategy runs the risk of alienating voters from one side or the other. However, we find that by adopting different strategies in different areas, the Liberal Democrats are, partially, able to overcome this paradox.

We have shown that a more effective strategy involves moving outside the constraints of the left–right spectrum, circumventing the notion of equidistance altogether and at the same time promoting a set of distinctive policies that can be seen as both centrist and radical. This might even entail – as it seemed to in 2001 – being viewed as to the left of Labour on certain policy issues, whilst being on the centre or right on others. In order to overcome the centre-party 'squeeze', the Liberal Democrats must continue to eschew left or right labels in favour of a multi-faceted set of identities. The other necessary element of this strategy is to overcome the problem of credibility.

Credibility gap

We have argued that credibility is the essence of Liberal Democrat success and failure. This is supported by substantial statistical evidence and also the views and perceptions of the party elite. As a minor party in a system designed for two parties, the Liberal Democrats must overcome their minority status from the outset. To a large extent this has been resolved by allowing the Liberal Democrats to be one of the two parties in a series of two party contests. For the most part the Liberal Democrats find themselves in a battle with the Conservatives but occasionally Labour is the opponent.

One indication that the Liberal Democrats see credibility as the key to their electoral fortunes was provided by the campaign poster the party unveiled in the 2001 General Election (reproduced in the introduction as Figure 0.1). A map of Great Britain, predominantly coloured yellow, is juxtaposed with the phrase, 'If you thought the Lib Dems could win in your area, this is how you'd vote'. The premise is that the people want to vote for the Liberal Democrats but do not wish to waste their vote.

From our case studies we saw how credibility can assist the Liberal Democrats electoral chances and how a perceived lack of credibility can hinder their progress. In Colchester a three-way marginal was transformed into a Liberal Democrat–Conservative contest by the outcome of the 1997 election. Hence the incumbent Liberal Democrats were able to squeeze the significant Labour vote in the urban centre of the seat in order to 'keep the Tories out'. Similarly, the Liberal Democrats in Cheadle used evidence from local election results, and previous General Election results to show that 'Only the Liberal Democrats can beat the Tories here.' The exceedingly narrow victory of the party in Cheadle in 2001 may have been due to a few Labour sympathisers switching votes to the Liberal Democrats as a result of this message.

There are a number of ways of establishing credibility. In heartland areas, credibility has survived historically. Outside these areas, one of the most successful ways in which the Liberal Democrats can establish their credibility is through the platform of local electoral performance. From our interviews we encountered many examples of Liberal Democrats who regarded local performance as the impetus behind their breakthrough. This was demonstrated by Table 7.4, which showed that 24 of the 30 Westminster seats first won by the Liberal Democrats in 1997, also had a majority Liberal Democrat council. As a campaign strategy we were told that the party wants local parties to win wards in parliamentary seats as a sign of their determination to be a target seat. The failure to do so can be damaging. In Bridgwater the lack of a council base from which to spring counted against the local party's chances of winning the parliamentary constituency in 2001. Crucially the geography of the seat meant that the resilient Labour vote in the town of Bridgwater could not be convinced to desert Labour for the Liberal Democrats since they had not established themselves as the credible force in the constituency.

Forming the local council can be a great fillip in the party's search for credibility, although we did encounter some evidence that local parties were occasionally worried that they might be punished rather than rewarded for their record in office. Nevertheless, this is a risk that most Liberal Democrats seemed more than happy to take. After all the coalition agreement with Labour in Scotland has been seen as beneficial to the Liberal Democrats who have seemingly been credited with the coalition's popular policies and not blamed for the unpopular ones.

The other main route to establishing credibility is through local campaign effort and targeting. Strong local campaigns can convince the electorate that the party has a chance and is therefore not a wasted vote. By concentrating limited resources through targeting, we find that the party is able to incrementally expand from its heartland by concentrating these campaign efforts where they will count most. A similar objective is achieved through by-elections since they present an opportunity for a concerted campaign, normally under an intensive media spotlight. In Chapter 9 we saw how local campaigning and targeting were crucial to the increase in the number of Liberal Democrat seats and improving the party's credibility. However, we also found that the party need to increase vote share in a greater number of seats if their Westminster base is to improve dramatically in the future.

Of all our five hypotheses, credibility is perhaps the most potent in explaining Liberal Democrat fortunes. Not only was there significant quantitative evidence to support this, it was also widely recognised by a majority of interviewees. Overcoming the credibility gap constitutes a crucial part of local campaigning and the quest for winning over tactical voters.

Creeping Liberalism

The theory that the success of the Liberal Democrats can spread like a virus throughout regions is an attractive one. Certainly, the map of Liberal Democrat success reveals that the party has moved on from the days of the Alliance – where it had a reputation for coming second everywhere – towards the development of heartland support. The basis for much of the Liberal Democrat heartland is the traditional strength in the periphery of mainland Britain. Hence Liberal strongholds like mid-Wales and Devon are in close proximity to areas where the Liberal Democrats have more recently broken through such as Hereford in 1997 and Ludlow in 2001; or the Somerset seats of Yeovil in 1983, and Somerton & Frome in 1997.

We argue that creeping Liberalism can only function as an aid to Liberal Democrat prospects in neighbouring seats if there is evidence of a spillover effect from Liberal Democrat seats. This may be due to a psychological impact on the electorate or due to the transfer of knowledge and resources between constituency parties. For example Liberal Democrats in Cheadle were adamant that being next to Hazel Grove (the party's chief target in 1997) assisted their 1997 campaign – since they were able to learn from the campaign techniques used there. Moreover, the personal links between the two constituencies meant that there was a shared intelligence that assisted the Cheadle party's fight against the Conservatives in 2001. At the same time it seems plausible that if credibility is an issue, psychologically voters in seats neighbouring Liberal Democrat successes would be more likely to regard the Liberal Democrats as a viable option, especially as constituency boundaries are not visible. However, it would be easy to note areas where the healthy state of the party in one constituency did not transmit to the party in neighbouring areas.

It ought to be remembered however, that creeping Liberalism is based on the credibility of the Liberal Democrat challenge in contiguous areas. Moreover, for every success story there is likely to be a failure. For every Torbay there was a Totnes where the Liberal Democrat challenge failed to materialise. Whilst contiguity to other Liberal Democrat seats may be an advantage, it is certainly no guarantee of success.

Dual identities

The dual identity thesis stipulates that the party benefits from a twin track approach to organisational and ideological politics. On the one hand the party is driven from the top, the leader is granted considerable leeway to influence the party in the way they desire. On the other the party is structurally predisposed to pass power down as well as up. The federal structure of the party gives a voice to ordinary activists and the idea of community politics is enshrined in the party. This is true to such an extent that it is genuinely difficult to characterise the Liberal Democrats as either a top-down or bottom-up organisation.

The party's first leader, Sir Paddy Ashdown seemed to dominate the party from the outset. A senior member of the party described Ashdown as running the party as much as leading it. However this seems to have been a character trait rather than a result of the party structures. Moreover, even Ashdown found himself constricted by the opinion of the party. We argue that the renaming of the party, and the progress of 'the Project' were both checked by the reality of needing to take account of the wishes of the party at large. In the final analysis, Ashdown's stock as leader of the party may have been fatally compromised by the Project and the lack of accommodation from Labour.

The professional elite is a burgeoning part of the Liberal Democrats. We were able to pinpoint a raft of professional party officials who seemed to represent a centralised elite as party organisation literature would suggest. However these officials are, after all, Liberal Democrats, and have to be accommodated within the party structure. Furthermore, the party structure has formalised the power of campaign groups – such as the ALDC – that are separate from the professional wing of the party and play to slightly different audiences, the councillor base rather than the parliamentary party.

We also found evidence of tension between the parliamentary party and the formal constitutional role of the party's organisation. The growth of the party in Westminster and in Edinburgh and Cardiff since 1997 has given the parliamentarians a new source of influence in the party. As one leading MP told us, the FPC has the power to formulate policy constitutionally but the parliamentary party has an unofficial power of veto.

This duality gives the local parties the freedom to emphasise policy as they think best fits the local context. In Liberal heartlands seats, we encountered evidence that the issue of Europe played out locally very differently to the national image of the party. The local campaign can exploit the ideological drive towards duality that characterises the Liberal Democrats.

Earlier we argued that success in Scotland and Wales had ramifications for the dual identity of the Liberal Democrats. Although the party under Kennedy has distanced itself from the (pro-Labour) Project, continued coalition with Labour in Scotland, may have limited their ability to distance themselves from Labour in the eyes of the electorate. We have seen that at the local level, the Liberal Democrats routinely manage to target both Labour and Conservative supporters in different ways depending on local context, but doing so at the national level may prove more difficult.

The dualism we have identified is more than simply the triumph of necessity; it is part of the ideological make-up of the party. Thus the potential tension between grassroots is ideologically and pragmatically resolved. The professional elite in the party exerts a degree of centralised control over campaigning strategy, but lacks the resources and the desire to neutralise the power of the local parties, since they are so often the linchpin for Liberal Democrat success.

Issue based mobilisation

We hypothesised that without the traditional links to trade unions and business communities associated with their main competitors, the Liberal Democrats have to fight for every vote, convincing electors to vote for them on the basis of their policies.

Indeed, the Liberal Democrats seem to be a party with popular leadership and popular policies. Yet they find it difficult to persuade enough people to vote for them. We did find evidence that the Liberal Democrats sought to claim certain issues as their own, to counteract the 'no one knows what they stand for' syndrome. The biggest success appears to be the adoption of the policy of hypothecated taxation and education, which evidence has shown is a policy that the electorate like and associate with the Liberal Democrats.

The adoption of many popular policies, however, has not radically improved the party's share of the vote. In 1997 more voters who agreed with the Liberal Democrat position on education and income tax voted Conservative than voted Liberal Democrat. Furthermore, the position of the 'median voter' may not make sense for the party if the median voter is really a statistical artefact. In other words the middle position is not necessarily a popular position – especially if the centre becomes compressed as the distance between the two larger parties shrinks (as experienced with Labour's move to the right in the 1990s). In order to overcome the problem of being squeezed by both left and right, we found that the party attempted to both adopt distinctive policy positions and also to identify themselves outside of the conventional left–right spectrum: that is 'neither left-nor-right but forward'.

We did encounter the potential for issue-based mobilisation at the local level. For example, in Colchester, the future of local architectural landmarks became an election issue in 2001. In other seats, the national issues of health and crime were played with a local tinge – in campaigns, for instance, to save a hospital, or deliver more police.

Clearly, issue-based mobilisation is not enough for the party; it needs to be combined with enhanced credibility in order to overcome the bias against voting for the Liberal Democrats in order to be effective. We have shown that popular leadership and popular policies have proved to be necessary but insufficient conditions for Liberal Democrat success. In other words it is not lack of popularity of their policies or their leaders, or the effectiveness of their campaign which explains why they continue to be a relatively small third party. Ultimately, this is a reflection of the electoral system and the credibility gap. However, this link is not straightforward: there are negative feedback effects associated with third party status. That is, the Liberal Democrats are relatively under-resourced and their policies and activities are under-reported compared to the major parties and hence their position as the third party is self-perpetuating.

Finally, as we noted earlier, following the 2001 General Election, the Liberal Democrats took a different stance in British politics, and are clearly preparing themselves to fight the subsequent elections with more distance between themselves and Labour than there was before. Coping with the new reality in future parliaments is likely to be the new big challenge for the Liberal Democrats. Our analysis would suggest that rather than the big breakthrough, future Liberal Democrat success will depend on national and local adaptability (or even opportunism), and will continue to be built incrementally on a foundation of electoral credibility based on a combination of historical tradition and local activity.

References

Agnew, J. (1987) Place and Politics: *The Geographic Mediation of State and Society*. Boston, Unwin Hyman.

Ashdown, P. (2000) *The Ashdown Diaries: Volume One 1988–1997*, London, Allen Lane.

Ashdown, P. (2001a) 'Our Party Is in Danger of Being Stranded on the Left of Labour', *Independent*, 13 June.

Ashdown, P. (2001b) *The Ashdown Diaries: Volume Two 1997–1999*. London, Allen Lane.

Babbie, E. (1995) *The Practice of Social Research*. Belmont, Wadsworth.

Bagehot (2001) 'The Trouble with Liberals', *The Economist*, 5 May.

Bartle, J. (1999) 'Improving the Measurement of Party Identification' in J. Fisher, P. Cowley, D. Denver and A. Russell (eds.) *British Elections and Parties Review* Vol. 9, London, Frank Cass.

Bennie, L., Curtice, J. and Rudig, W. (1996) 'Party Members' in D. MacIver (ed.) *The Liberal Democrats*. Hemel Hempstead, Harvester-Wheatsheaf.

Black, D. (1958) *The Theory of Committees and Elections*. New York, Cambridge University Press.

Bogdanor, V. (1983) *Liberal Party Politics*. Oxford, Oxford University Press.

Brack, D. (1996) 'Liberal Democrat Policy' in D. MacIver (ed.) *The Liberal Democrats*. Hemel Hempstead, Harvester-Wheatsheaf.

Brack, D. and Ingham, R. (1999) *Dictionary of Liberal Quotations*. London, Politico's.

Brynin, M. and Sanders, D. (1995) 'Party Identification, Political Preferences and Material Conditions: Evidence from the British Household Panel Study, 1991–2', *Party Politics* 3: 53–77.

Butler, D. (2000) 'Electors and Elected' in A. H. Halsey with J. Webb (eds.) *Twentieth Century British Social Trends*. Basingstoke, Macmillan.

Butler, D. and Butler, G. (2000) *Twentieth Century British Political Facts, 1900–2000*. Basingstoke, Macmillan.

Butler, D. and Stokes, D. (1974) *Political Change in Britain*. Basingstoke, Macmillan.

Butler, P. and Collins, N. (1996) 'Strategic Analysis in Political Markets', *European Journal of Marketing* 30 (10/11): 32–44.

Cantle, T. (2002) *Community Cohesion: A Report of the Independent Review Team*, www.homeoffice.gov.uk/reu/community-cohesion.pdf.

Castles, F. and Mair, P. (1984) 'Left–Right Scales: Some "Expert" Judgements', *European Journal of Political Research* 12: 73–88.

Clarke, H. and Zuk, G. (1989) 'The Dynamics of Third Party Support: The British Liberals, 1951–79', *American Journal of Political Science* 33: 196–221.

Cook, C. (1998) *A Short History of the Liberal Party, 1900–88*. Basingstoke, Macmillan.

Cowley, P. (1997) 'The Conservative Party: Decline and Fall' in A. Geddes and J. Tonge (eds.) *Labour's Landslide: The British General Election 1997*. Manchester, Manchester University Press.

Cowley, P. (2002) *Revolts and Rebellions: Parliamentary Voting Under Blair*. London, Politico's.
Cowley, P., Denver, D., Russell, A. and Harrison, L. (eds.) (2000) *British Elections & Parties Review* Vol. 10. London, Frank Cass.
Cox, G. (1990) 'Centripetal and Centrifugal Incentives in Electoral Systems', *American Journal of Political Science* 34 (4): 903–35.
Cox, G. (1997) *Making Votes Count: Strategic Coordination in the World's Electoral Systems*. Cambridge, Cambridge University Press.
Cox, K. (1970) 'Geography, Social Contexts, and Voting Behaviour in Wales, 1861–1951' in E. Allardt and S. Rokkan (eds.) *Mass Politics*. Cambridge, Mass., MIT Press.
Crewe, I. (1985) 'Great Britain' in I. Crewe and D. Denver (eds.) *Electoral Change in Western Democracies: Patterns and Sources of Electoral Volatility*. London, Croom Helm.
Crewe, I. (1986) 'On the Death and Resurrection of Class Voting: Some Comments on How Britain Votes', *Political Studies* 34: 620–38.
Crewe, I. and Denver, D. (eds.) (1985) *Electoral Change in Western Democracies*. London: Croom Helm.
Crewe, I. and King, A. (1995) *The SDP: The Life and Death of the Social Democratic Party*. Oxford, Oxford University Press.
Crewe, I. and Searing, D. (1988) 'Ideological Change in the British Conservative Party', *American Political Science Review* 82: 361–84.
Crewe, I., Fox, A and Day, N. (1995) *The British Electorate, 1963–1992*. Cambridge, Cambridge University Press.
Crewe, I., Sarlvik, B. and Alt, J. (1977) 'Partisan Dealignment in Britain, 1964–1974', *British Journal of Political Science* 7: 129–90.
Curtice, J. (1996) 'Who Votes for the Centre Now?' in D. MacIver (ed.) *The Liberal Democrats*. Hemel Hempstead, Harvester-Wheatsheaf.
Curtice, J. and Steed, M. (1983) 'The Results Analysed' in D. Butler and D. Kavanagh (eds.) *The British General Election of 1983*. Basingstoke, Macmillan.
Curtice, J. and Steed, M. (1987) 'The Results Analysed' in D. Butler and D. Kavanagh (eds.) *The British General Election of 1987*. Basingstoke, Macmillan.
Cyr, A. (1977) *Liberal Party Politics in Britain*. London, John Calder.
Daadler, H. (1984) 'In Search of the Centre of European Party Systems', *American Political Science Review* 78: 92–109.
Dangerfield, G. (1966) *The Strange Death of Liberal England*. London, Macgibbon and Kee.
Denver, D. (1997) 'The Results: How Britain Voted' in A. Geddes and J. Tonge (eds.) *Labour's Landslide: The British General Election 1997*. Manchester, Manchester University Press.
Denver, D. (2001) 'The Liberal Democrat Campaign' in Pippa Norris (ed.) *Britain Votes 2001*. Oxford, Oxford University Press.
Denver, D. and Hands, G. (1997) *Modern Constituency Electioneering*. London, Frank Cass.
Denver, D., Hands, G. and Henig, S. (1998) 'The Triumph of Targeting? Constituency Campaigning in the 1997 Election' in D. T. Denver, J. Fisher, P. Cowley and C. Pattie (eds.) *British Elections & Parties Review* Vol. 8. London, Frank Cass.
Denver, D., Hands, G., Fisher, J. and MacAllister, I. (2002) 'The Impact of Constituency Campaigning in the 2001 General Election' in L. Bennie, C. Rallings, J. Tonge and P. Webb (eds.) *British Elections and Parties Review, Volume 12: The General Election*. London, Frank Cass.
Dorling, D., Rallings, C. and Thrasher, M. (1998) 'The Epidemiology of the Liberal Democrat Vote', *Political Geography* 17: 45–70.
Downs, A. (1957) *An Economic Theory of Democracy*. New York, Harper & Row.
Dunleavy, P. (1993) 'The Political Parties' in P. Dunleavy, A. Gamble, I. Holliday and G. Peele (eds.) *Developments in British Politics 4*. Basingstoke, Macmillan.

Dunleavy. P. (1991) *Democracy, Bureaucracy and Public Choice*. London, Harvester-Wheatsheaf.
Dunleavy, P. and Ward, H. (1981) 'Exogenous Voter Preferences and Parties with State Power: Some Internal Problems of Economic Models of Party Competition', *British Journal of Political Science* 11: 351–80.
Duverger, M. (1954) *Political Parties: Their Organization and Activity in the Modern State*. New York, Wiley.
Eaton, B. Curtis, and Richard G. Lipsey (1975) 'The Principle of Minimum Differentiation Reconsidered: Some Developments in the Theory of Spatial Competition', *Review of Economic Studies* 42: 27–49.
Electoral Commission (2001) *Election 2001: The Official Results*. London, Politico's.
Evans, G. and Heath, A. (1993) 'A Tactical Error in the Analysis of Tactical Voting: A Response to Niemi, Whitten and Franklin, *British Journal of Political Science* 23: 131–7.
Fieldhouse, E. (1995) 'Thatcherism and the Changing Geography of Political Attitudes, 1964–87', *Political Geography* 14: 3–30.
Fieldhouse, E. and Russell, A. (2001) 'Latent Liberals? Sympathy and Support for the Liberal Democrats in Britain', *Party Politics* 7: 711–38.
Fielding, S. (2003) *The Labour Party: Continuity and Change in the Making of 'New' Labour*. Basingstoke, Palgrave, Macmillan.
Fisher, J. (1997) 'Third and Minor Party Breakthrough?' in A. Geddes and J. Tonge (eds.) *Labour's Landslide: The British General Election 1997*. Manchester, Manchester University Press.
Fisher, S. (2000) 'Party Preference Structure in England, 1987 to 1997' in P. Cowley, D. Denver, A. Russell and L. Harrison (eds.) *British Elections and Parties Review* Vol. 10. London, Frank Cass.
Forslund, M. (1980) 'Patterns of Delinquency Involvement: An Empirical Typology' Western Association of Sociologists and Anthropologists Conference: Alberta.
Franklin, M. N. (1984) *The Decline of Class Voting in Britain*. Oxford, Clarendon.
Fulford, R, (1959) *The Liberal Case*. London, Penguin.
Gallagher, M. (1991) 'Proportionality, Disproportionality and Electoral Systems', *Electoral Studies* 10: 33–51.
Glover, J. (1998) 'Jeremy Thorpe' in D. Brack (ed.) *The Dictionary of Liberal Biography*. London, Politico's.
Greaves, B. (1976) 'Communities and Power' in P. Hain (ed.) *Community Politics*. London, John Calder.
Guardian Editorial (2001) 'The Leaders of the Left', *Guardian*, 16 May.
Gudgin, G. and P. Taylor, P. (1978) *Seats, Votes and the Spatial Organization of Elections*. London, Pion.
Hall, S. (1988) *The Hard Road to Renewal*. London, Verso.
Hazan, R. (1996) 'Does Center Equal Middle?', *Party Politics* 2: 209–28.
Heath, A. and Evans, G. (1988) 'Working-class Conservatives and Middle-class Socialists' in R. Jowell, S. Witherspoon, and L. Brook (eds.) *British Social Attitudes: The 5th Report*. Aldershot, Gower.
Heath, A., Jowell, R. and Curtice, J. (1985) *How Britain Votes*. Oxford, Pergamon.
Heath, A., Jowell, R. and Curtice, J. (1987) 'Trendless Fluctuation: A Reply to Crewe', *Political Studies* 35: 256–77.
Heath A., Jowell, R., Curtice, J., Evans, G., Field, J., and Witherspoon, S. (1991) *Understanding Political Change*. Oxford, Pergamon Press.
Hinich, M. and Munger, M. (1994) *Ideology and the Theory of Political Choice*. Ann Arbor, University of Michigan Press.
Holme, R. and Holmes, A. (1998) 'Sausages or "Policeman?" The Role of the Liberal

Democrats in the 1997 General Election Campaign' in I. Crewe, B. Gosschalk and J. Bartle (eds.) *Political Communications: Why Labour Won the General Election of 1997*. London, Frank Cass.
Huang, D. W. F. (1999) 'Independents, Switchers and Voting for Third Parties in Britain 1979–92' in J. Fisher, P. Cowley, D. Denver and A. Russell (eds.) *British Elections and Parties Review* Vol. 9. London, Frank Cass.
Ingle, S. (1996) 'Party Organisation' in D. MacIver (ed.) *The Liberal Democrats*. Hemel Hempstead, Harvester-Wheatsheaf.
Inglehart, R. (1971) *The Silent Revolution: Changing Values and Political Styles amongst Western Publics*. Princetown NJ, Princetwon University Press.
Iverson, T. (1994) 'Political Leadership and Representation in West European Democracies: A Test of Three Models of Voting', *American Journal of Political Science* 38: 45–74.
Janda, K. (1979) *Political Parties: A Cross-National Survey*. New York, Free Press.
Jenkins, R. (1995) *Gladstone: A Biography* Basingstoke, Macmillan.
Johnston, R. and Pattie, C. (1988) 'Are We All Alliance Nowadays? Discriminating by Discriminant Analysis', *Electoral Studies* 7: 27–32.
Johnston, R. and Pattie, C. (1991) 'Tactical Voting in Great Britain in 1983 and 1987: An Alternative Approach', *British Journal of Political Science* 21: 95–128.
Johnston, R., Pattie, C. and Allsop, J. (1988) *A Nation Dividing? The Electoral Map of Great Britain 1979–1987*. London, Longman.
Johnston, R., Pattie, C., Dorling, D. and Rossiter, D. (2001) *From Votes to Seats: The Operation of the UK Electoral System Since 1945*. Manchester, Manchester University Press.
Johnston, R., Pattie, C., Rossiter, D., Dorling, D., Tunstall, H. and MacAllister, I. (1998) 'New Labour Landslide: Same Old Electoral Geography?' in D. Denver, J. Fisher, P. Cowley and C. Pattie (eds.) *British Elections and Parties Review*, Vol. 8. London, Frank Cass.
Jones, N. (1997) *Campaign 1997: How the General Election Was Won and Lost*. London, Indigo.
Joyce, P. (1999) *Realignment of the Left? A History of the Relationship between the Liberal Democrat and Labour Parties*. Basingstoke, Macmillan.
Katz, R. and Mair, P. (1995) 'Changing Models of Party Organisation and Party Democracy: The Emergence of the Cartel Party', *Party Politics* 1: 5–28.
Katz, R. and Mair, P. (eds.) (1994) *How Parties Organize: Change and Adaptation in Party Organizations in Western Democracies*. London, Sage.
Kennedy, C. (2001) 'We Are the Opposition Now', *Observer*, 10 June.
Kim, H. and Fording, R. (2001) 'Voter Ideology, the Economy and the International Environment in Western Democracies, 1952–1989', *Political Behaviour* 23: 53–73.
Kinnear, M. (1968) *The British Voter*. London, Batsford.
Kirchheimer, O. (1966) 'The Transformation of the Western European Party Systems' in J. LaPalombara and M. Weiner (eds.) *Political Parties and Political Development*. Princeton, Princeton University Press.
Klingemann, H.-D., Hofferbert, R. and Budge, I. (1994) *Parties, Policies and Democracy*. Boulder, Westview.
Koss, S. (1975) *Nonconformity in Modern British Politics*. Batsford, London.
Laver, M. and Hunt, W. (1992) *Policy and Party Competition*. New York, Routledge.
Leaman, A. (1998) 'Ending Equidistance', *Political Quarterly* 69 160–9.
Lijphart, A. (1994) *Electoral Systems and Party Systems: A Study of Twenty-Seven Democracies, 1945–1990*. Oxford, Oxford University Press.
Lipset, S. and Rokkan, S. (1967) 'Cleavage Structures, Party Systems and Voter Alignments: An Introduction' in S. Lipset and S. Rokkan (eds.) *Party Systems and Voter Alignments*. New York, Free Press.

Lishman, G. (1976) 'Framework for Community Politics' in P. Hain (ed.) *Community Politics*. London, John Calder.
Lutz, J. (1991) 'Marginality, Major Third Parties and Turnout in England in the 1970s and 1980s: A Re-Analysis and Extension', *Political Studies* 39: 721–6.
Lynch P. (1998) 'Charles Kennedy' in D. Brack (ed.) *The Dictionary of Liberal Biography*. London, Politico's.
MacAllister, I., Fieldhouse, E. and Russell, A. (2002) 'Yellow Fever? The Political Geography of Liberal Support', *Political Geography* 21: 421–47.
MacIver, D. (1996) 'Introduction' in D. MacIver (eds.) *The Liberal Democrats*. Hemel Hempstead, Harvester-Wheatsheaf.
MacIver, D. (1996) 'Political Strategy' in Don MacIver (ed.) *The Liberal Democrats*. Hemel Hempstead, Harvester Wheatsheaf.
MacIver, D. (ed.) (1996) *The Liberal Democrats*. Hemel Hempstead, Harvester-Wheatsheaf.
Mair, P. (1994) 'Party Organizations: From Civil Society to the State' in R. Katz, and P. Mair, *How Parties Organize: Change and Adaptation in Party Organizations in Western Democracies*. London, Sage.
Mathews, S (1979) 'A Simple Directional Model of Electoral Competition'. *Public Choice* 36, 115–34.
Matthews, H. (1997) *Gladstone: 1809–1898*. Oxford, Oxford University Press.
McKee, V. (1996) 'Factions and Groups' in D. MacIver (ed.) *The Liberal Democrats*. Hemel Hempstead, Harvester-Wheatsheaf.
McManus, M. (2001) *Jo Grimond: Towards the Sound of Gunfire*. Edinburgh, Birlinn.
Meadowcroft, J. (2000) 'Is There a Liberal Alternative? Charles Kennedy and the Liberal Democrats Strategy', *Political Quarterly 71:* 436–42.
Meadowcroft, J. (2001) 'Community Politics, Representation and the Limits of Deliberative Democracy' *Local Government Studies* 27: 25–42.
Merrill, S. (1988) *Making Multi-candidate Elections More Democratic*, Princetown: Princetown University Press.
Merrill III, S. and Grofman, B. (1999) *A Unified Theory of Voting: Directional and Proximity Spatial Models*. Cambridge, Cambridge University Press.
Miller, W. (1977) *Electoral Dynamics*. Basingstoke, Macmillan.
Milne R. and Mackenzie, H. (1958) *Marginal Seat 1955: A Study of Voting Behaviour in the Constituency of Bristol North-East at the General Election of 1955*. London, Hansard Society.
Myatt, D. and Fisher, S. (2002) 'Tactical Coordination in Plurality Electoral Systems', *Oxford Review of Economic Policy* 18: 504–22.
Nagel, J. (2001) 'Centre Party Strength and Major Party Polarization in Britain'. Proceedings of American Political Science Association Annual Conference, San Francisco, August 2001
Nationwide Initiative in Evangelism (NIE) (1980) 'Prospects for the Eighties'. MARC Europe, London.
Norris, P. (1997) *Electoral Change since 1945*. Oxford, Blackwell.
Panebianco, A. (1988) *Political Parties: Organisation and Power*. Cambridge: Cambridge University Press.
Parris, M. (1997) *Great Parliamentary Scandals: Four Centuries of Calumny, Smear and Innuendo*. London, Robson Books.
Parry, J. (1993) *The Rise and Fall of Liberal Government in Victorian Britain*. New Haven, Yale University Press.
Pattie, C., Fieldhouse, E. and Johnston, R. (1995). 'Winning the Local Vote: Effectiveness of Constituency Campaign Spending in Great Britain', *American Political Science Review* 89: 969–83.

Pelling, H. (1967) *Social Geography of British Elections, 1885–1910*. Basingstoke, Macmillan.
Porter, M. E. (1980) *Competetive Strategy: Techniques for Analysing Industries and Competitors*. New York, Free Press.
Pulzer, P. (1967) *Political Representation and Elections in Britain*. London, Allen and Unwin.
Rabinowitz, G. and Macdonald, S. (1989). 'A Directional Theory of Issue Voting', *American Political Science Review* 83: 93–121.
Rae, D. (1971) *The Political Consequences of Electoral Laws*, 2nd edn. New Haven, Yale University Press.
Rallings, C. and Thrasher, M. (1993) *Britain Votes 5: British Parliamentary Election Results 1988–1992*. London, Politico's.
Rallings, C. and Thrasher, M. (1996) 'The Electoral Record' in D. MacIver (ed.) *The Liberal Democrats*. Hemel Hempstead, Harvester-Wheatsheaf.
Rallings, C. and Thrasher, M. (1998) *Britain Votes 6: British Parliamentary Election Results 1997*. Aldershot, Ashgate.
Reynolds, H. (1974) 'Rationality and Attitudes Toward Political Parties and Candidates'. *Journal of Politics* 37: 983–1005.
Riker, W. (1982) *Liberalism Against Populism: A Confrontation Between the Theory of Democracy and the Theory of Social Choice*. San Francisco, Freeman.
Robertson, D. (1984) *Class and the British Electorate*. Oxford, Blackwell.
Robinson, W. (1950) 'Ecological Correlations and the Behaviour of Individuals', *American Sociological Review* 15: 351–7.
Rohrschneider, R. (2002) 'Mobilizing Versus Chasing: How do Parties Target Voters in Election Campaigns?', *Electoral Studies* 21 (3): 367–82.
Rokkan, S. (1970) *Citizens, Elections, Parties: An Approach to the Comparative Study of Political Development*. Oslo, Universitetsforlaget.
Rose, R. and McAllister, I. (1986) *Voters Begin to Choose: From Closed-Class to Open Elections in Britain*. London, Sage.
Rose, R. and McAllister, I. (1990) *The Loyalties of Voters*. London, Sage.
Russell, A. and Fieldhouse, E. (2000) 'Identifying an Attitudinal Heartland of Liberal Democrat Support in the 1997 General Election: An Exploration of Equidistance, Constructive Opposition and Third Party Politics' in P. Cowley, D. Denver, A. Russell and L. Harrison (eds.) *British Elections and Parties Review* Vol. 10. London, Frank Cass.
Russell, A., Fieldhouse, E. and MacAllister, I. (2002a) 'The Anatomy of Liberal Voting, 1974–97', *British Journal of Politics and International Relations* 4: 49–74.
Russell, A., Fieldhouse, E. and MacAllister, I. (2002b) 'Two Steps Forward, One Step Back? The Liberal Democrats 2001 General Election Performance in Perspective', *Representation* 38 (3): 213–27.
Sanders, D., Ward, H. and Marsh, D. (1987) 'Government Popularity and the Falklands War: A Reassessment', *British Journal of Political Science* 17: 281–313.
Sarlvik, B. and Crewe, I. (1983) *Decade of Dealignment*. Cambridge, Cambridge University Press.
Sartori, G. (1976) *Parties and Party Systems: A Framework for Analysis*. Cambridge, Cambridge University Press.
Scarbrough, Elinor (1984) *Political Ideology and Voting: An Exploratory Study*. Oxford, Oxford University Press.
Searle, G. (1992) *The Liberal Party: Triumph and Disintegration, 1886–1929*. Basingstoke, Macmillian.
Seyd, P. and Whiteley, P. (1992) *Labour's Grass Roots: The Dynamics of Party Activism in Britain*. Oxford, Clarendon.
Stevenson, J. (1993) *Third Party Politics Since 1945: Liberals, Alliance and Liberal Democrats*. Oxford, Blackwell.

Stevenson, J. (1996) 'Liberals to Liberal Democrats' in D. MacIver (ed.) *The Liberal Democrats*. Hemel Hempstead, Harvester-Wheatsheaf.

Studlar, D. and I. McAllister, (1987) 'Protest and Survive? Alliance Support in the 1983 British General Election', *Political Studies* 35: 39–60.

Taagepera, R. and Shugart, M. (1989) *Seats and Votes: The Effects and Determinants of Electoral Systems*. New Haven, Yale University Press.

Taagepera, R. and Shugart, M. (1993) 'Predicting the Number of Parties: A Quantitative Model of Duverger's Mechanical Effect', *American Political Science Review* 87: 455–64.

Tabachnik, B. G. and Fidell, L. S. (1989) *Using Multivariate Statistics*, 2nd edn. New York, Harper and Row.

Thorpe, J. (1999) *In My Own Time*. London, Politico's.

Tregidga, G. (2000) *The Liberal Party in South-West Britain since 1918: Political Decline, Dormancy and Rebirth*. Exeter, University of Exeter Press.

Waller, R. and Criddle, B. (2002) *The Almanac of British Politics*, 7th edn. London, Routledge.

Walter, D. (2003) *The Strange Rebirth of Liberal England*. London, Politico's.

Webb, P. (2000) *The Modern British Party System*. London, Sage.

Whitehead, P. (1985) *The Writing on the Wall: Britain in the Seventies*. London, Michael Joseph.

Whiteley, P. and Seyd, P. (1999) 'How to Win a Landslide by Really Trying: The Effects of Local Campaigning on Voting in the British General Election of 1997', paper presented to American Political Science Association, Annual Conference Atlanta.

Whiteley, P., Seyd, P. and Richardson, J. (1994) *True Blues: The Politics of Conservative Party Membership*. Oxford, Clarendon.

Wickham-Jones, M. (1997) 'How the Conservatives Lost the Economic Argument' in A. Geddes and J. Tonge (eds.) *Labour's Landslide: The British General Election 1997*. Manchester, Manchester University Press.

Wilson, D. (1995) 'The Liberal Democrats' in I. Crewe and B. Gosschalk (eds.) *Political Communications: The General Election Campaign of 1992*. Cambridge, Cambridge University Press.

Wilson, T. (1966) *The Downfall of the Liberal Party, 1914–1935*. Ithaca, Cornell University Press.

Woods, M. (1996) 'The Orange Wave: Conservative Decline and Liberal Democrat Success in Somerset', paper presented to the Conference of the Elections, Public Opinion and Parties Specialist Group of the PSA, Sheffield, 1996.

Woods, M. (2002) 'Was There A Rural Rebellion? Labour and the Countryside vote in the 2001 General Election' in L. Bennie, C. Rallings, J. Tonge and P. Webb (eds.) *British Elections & Parties Review 12*. London, Frank Cass.

Young, Hugo (2001) 'Lib Dems Can Be the Opposition: Labour Conservatism and Tory Irrelevance Has Opened up a Gap', *Guardian*, 25 September.

Index